ENGLISH Essentials

What Every College Student Needs to Know about Grammar, Punctuation, and Usage

INSTRUCTOR ANNOTATED EDITION

John Langan

ATLANTIC CAPE COMMUNITY COLLEGE

Beth Johnson

D1294726

Boston   Burr Ridge, IL   Dubuque, IA   Madison, WI   New York   San Francisco   St. Louis
Bangkok   Bogotá   Caracas   Kuala Lumpur   Lisbon   London   Madrid   Mexico City
Milan   Montreal   New Delhi   Santiago   Seoul   Singapore   Sydney   Taipei   Toronto

THE LANGAN SERIES

Essay-Level

College Writing Skills, Sixth Edition
ISBN: 0-07-287186-5 (Copyright © 2005)

College Writing Skills with Readings,
Sixth Edition
ISBN: 0-07-287132-6 (Copyright © 2005)

Paragraph-Level

English Skills, Seventh Edition
ISBN: 0-07-238127-2 (Copyright © 2001)

English Skills with Readings, Fifth Edition
ISBN: 0-07-248003-3 (Copyright © 2002)

Reading

Reading and Study Skills, Seventh Edition
ISBN: 0-07-244599-8 (Copyright © 2002)

Sentence-Level

Sentence Skills: A Workbook for Writers,
Form A, Seventh Edition
ISBN: 0-07-238132-9 (Copyright © 2003)

Sentence Skills: A Workbook for Writers,
Form B, Seventh Edition
ISBN: 0-07-282087-X (Copyright © 2004)

Sentence Skills with Readings,
Third Edition
ISBN: 0-07-301723-X (Copyright © 2005)

Grammar Review

English Brushup, Third Edition
ISBN: 0-07-281890-5 (Copyright © 2003)

The McGraw-Hill Companies

McGraw Hill Higher Education

ENGLISH ESSENTIALS: WHAT EVERY COLLEGE STUDENT NEEDS TO KNOW ABOUT GRAMMAR, PUNCTUATION, AND USAGE
Published by McGraw-Hill, an business unit of The McGraw-Hill Companies, Inc. 1221 Avenue of the Americas, New York, NY 10020. Copyright © 2005, by The McGraw-Hill Companies, Inc. All rights reserved. No part of this publication may be reproduced or distributed in any form or by any means, or stored in a database or retrieval system, without the prior written consent of The McGraw-Hill Companies, Inc., including, but not limited to, in any network or other electronic storage or transmission, or broadcast for distance learning. Some ancillaries, including electronic and print components, may not be available to customers outside the United States.

This book is printed on acid-free paper.

1 2 3 4 5 6 7 8 9 0 VNH/VNH 0 9 8 7 6 5 4

ISBN 0-07-304326-5 (student edition)
ISBN 0-07-304327-3 (annotated instructor's edition)

Publisher: *Lisa Moore*
Senior sponsoring editor: *Alexis Walker*
Editorial assistant: *Jesse J. Hassenger*
Marketing manager: *Lori DeShazo*
Senior media producer: *Todd Vaccaro*
Project manager: *Jean R. Starr*
Production supervisor: *Janean A. Utley*
Media project manager: *Todd Vaccaro*
Cover design: *Photographs by Mark Hertzberg, Beth Johnson, Paul Kowal*
Interior design: *Barbara Solot*
Compositor: *Electronic Publishing Services, Inc., TN*
Typeface: *12/14 Garamond*
Printer: *Von Hoffman Corporation*

www.mhhe.com

Contents

Preface to the Instructor   v

Introduction

About the Book   1

Becoming a Better Writer   3

Writing Assignments   16

PART ONE Fourteen Basic Skills   25

Preview   26

1 Subjects and Verbs   27

2 Irregular Verbs   37

3 Subject-Verb Agreement   47

4 Sentence Types   57

5 Fragments I   67

6 Fragments II   77

7 Run-Ons and Comma Splices I   87

8 Run-Ons and Comma Splices II   97

9 The Comma   107

10 The Apostrophe   117

11 Quotation Marks   127

12 Homonyms   137

13 Capital Letters   147

14 Parallelism   157

PART TWO Extending the Skills   167

Preview   168

15 Preparing a Paper   169

16 Punctuation Marks   171

17 Pronoun Forms   178

18 Pronoun Problems   187

19 Adjectives and Adverbs   197

20 Misplaced and Dangling Modifiers   207

21 Word Choice   214

22 Numbers and Abbreviations   220

23 More about Subjects and Verbs   225

24 More about Subject-Verb Agreement   235

25 More about Verbs   242

26 Even More about Verbs   253

27 More about Run-Ons and Comma Splices   261

28 More about Commas   265

29 More about Apostrophes   271

30 More about Quotation Marks   277

31 More about Homonyms   282

32 More about Capital Letters   289

PART THREE Proofreading   293

Preview   294

33 Basics about Proofreading   295

34 Ten Proofreading Tests   303

PART FOUR Related Matters   313

Preview   314

35 Spelling Improvement   315

36 Parts of Speech   325

37 Dictionary Use   337

Index 343

Preface to the Instructor

"What's the catch?" you might be asking. "What are people's photographs doing in this textbook? And just how will they help me teach *English Essentials: What Everyone Needs to Know about Grammar, Punctuation, and Usage?*"

We think the student-pleasing photographs are just one of a number of features that distinguish this book from other grammar texts on the market:

1   **Personal photos and stories.** All too often, grammar books are dry, dull affairs, about as interesting as a study of rock dust on the planet Mars. As teachers, we sometimes felt we were leading our students on a death march when we moved them through a traditional grammar text. So we have added a strong human dimension to this book by illustrating the grammar skills with photos and stories of interesting people from all walks of life. The stories describe not only their personal lives but also their involvement with reading and writing. Some of these people are pictured on the cover of the book.

2   **Ease of use.** All of the following make the book easy for students to understand and use:

- The essentials are presented in a highly accessible way. Take a look at any of the one-page reviews that open each of the skill chapters in Part One—the first such review is on page 27. Just the basics of each skill are presented on this page, which students can read and understand fairly quickly. Once they have grasped this basic material, they can go on to learn additional information about the skill and practice applying the skill.

    It is better to learn a step at a time than to risk confusion by trying to learn everything at once. For example, dependent-word fragments are the subject of one chapter; other common fragments appear in a second chapter. The most common homonyms are covered in Part One; other homonyms follow in the chapter "More about Homonyms" in Part Two.

- The chapters are self-contained, so that students can work on just those skills they need.

- Explanations are written in simple, familiar language, with a real emphasis on clarity and a minimum of grammatical terminology.

- An inviting two-color design has been used throughout, with headings and other design elements chosen to make the content as clear as possible.

- Finally, the book is written in a friendly and helpful tone of voice—one that never condescends to students, but instead treats them as adults.

3 Abundant practice. The book is based on the assumption that students learn best when clear explanations are followed by abundant practice. For each chapter in Part One, there are three full-page activities and five full-page tests. The last two tests are designed to resemble standardized tests and permit easy grading, including the use of Scantron sheets.

4 Engaging materials. In addition to the photos and true stories, lively and engaging examples and practice materials will help maintain student interest throughout the book.

5 Inclusiveness. The Introduction includes a brief guide to writing and a series of writing assignments to help students practice the grammar, punctuation, and usage skills that appear in the rest of the book. A combined forty years of teaching experience has taught us that applying the skills in actual writing situations helps students truly master them. Part One consists of primary information about fourteen key skills. Part Two presents secondary information about these skills and also covers topics not discussed in Part One. Part Three offers guidance and practice in the crucial skill of proofreading. And Part Four deals with areas that some other grammar texts neglect: spelling improvement, parts of speech, and dictionary use. Within the covers of *English Essentials*, then, are all the basic writing materials that instructors and students are likely to need.

6 Superior supplements. The following supplements are available at no charge to instructors adopting the book:

- An Instructor's Edition that is identical to the student text except that it includes answers to all the practices and tests.

- A combined Instructor's Manual and Test Bank that includes teaching hints, diagnostic and achievement tests, a full answer key, and a bank of additional mastery tests.

- A Student Answer Key consisting of answers for all the activities in Part One and to the practices and tests in the rest of the book. Upon request, a key will be provided for each book that is ordered.

- Software consisting of thirty-four computer mastery tests as well as computerized diagnostic and achievement tests.

- Online exercises for each chapter in Part One. Users of the book can access these exercises by visiting the Townsend Press website.

In short, *English Essentials* is designed as a core worktext that will both engage the interest of today's students and help them truly master the skills they need for writing well.

John Langan   Beth Johnson

● About the Book

"What is this?" you might ask as you page through this book and notice the photographs within it. "Who are these people, and what do they have to do with English essentials? And what are English essentials, anyway?"

The answers to those questions go hand in hand. As you know, "essentials" means things that are basic, necessary, and useful. We've designed *English Essentials* to help you quickly master practical English skills that you need every day. How quickly? Glance at one of the one-page reviews that open each of the chapters in Part One of the book. Chances are that you will be able to read that page in perhaps no more than a minute or two. That page will contain basic information about a particular skill. Once you understand the basics, you can turn to the pages that follow to practice that skill. You can also turn to Part Two to learn anything else you may need to know about the skill.

One advantage of *English Essentials*, then, is that it makes grammar skills easy to master. Basic information is presented in a very clear way on the first page of each chapter; the pages that follow reinforce that information with activities and tests. You will be learning in the best possible way: through doing.

And why the photographs? They provide a second benefit of the book by showing real people—men and women, boys and girls, young and not so young, current and former students—who use essential English skills in their daily lives. Their photographs add a human dimension to a subject that people often find dry and unappealing. At the same time you are learning a given skill, you will share in the real lives of interesting people.

A third advantage of the book is that it provides a full treatment of the essential English skills you need to know. Here is what is covered in the four parts of the book:

INTRODUCTION. This opening overview of the book is followed by a section titled "Becoming a Better Writer," which presents the writing process in a nutshell. Then a section titled "Writing Assignments" provides writing topics you can use to practice the rules of grammar, punctuation, and usage presented in the rest of the book.

PART ONE: Fourteen Basic Skills. Look at the table of contents on page iii for a list of the fourteen basic grammar and punctuation skills presented in Part One. Then turn to the first page of the first skill, "Subjects and Verbs." You will notice that the basic information about subjects and verbs is presented on one page. Ideally, in a minute or so you should be able to review the basic information about subjects and verbs.

● Now turn to the second page of the chapter, page 28. Write down the two headings on this page:

Understanding Subjects and Verbs

Check Your Understanding

On the second page of this chapter and all the other chapters in Part One, you are given examples of the skill in question, along with a chance to check your understanding of that skill. You are also introduced, in photos and in the text, to the person or persons featured in the chapter.

- Turn to the third, fourth, and fifth pages of the chapter (pages 29, 30, and 31). How many activities are included on those pages? ___3___

  It is through repeated and varied practice in the skill that you best learn it.

- Turn to the last five pages in the chapter (pages 32-36). How many tests are included on those pages? ___5___

Note that the last two tests are designed to resemble standardized tests, and you or your teacher can easily grade them.

PART TWO: Extending the Skills. Look again at the table of contents on page iii.

- Part Two presents some topics not included in Part One. For example, what is the first topic, on page 169? ___Preparing a Paper___

- Part Two also includes additional information about many of the topics presented in Part One. For example, what is the first "More about" section? _____ ___More about Subjects and Verbs___

PART THREE: Proofreading. An important part of becoming a good writer is learning to proofread—to carefully check the next-to-final draft of a paper for grammar, punctuation, and other mistakes. This chapter provides you with the hints and practice you need to improve your proofreading skills.

- How many proofreading tests appear at the end of the chapter? ___10___

  You'll see there are ten tests in all.

PART FOUR: Related Matters. The three chapters here include several areas that may be part of English courses: spelling tips and rules, parts of speech, and dictionary use.

A FINAL WORD

English Essentials has been designed to benefit you as much as possible. Its format is inviting, its explanations are clear, and its many activities, practices, tests, and assignments will help you learn through doing. It is a book that has been created to reward effort, and if you provide that effort, you can make yourself a competent and confident writer. We wish you luck.

John Langan   Beth Johnson

Becoming a Better Writer

What, in a nutshell, do you need to become a better writer? You need to know the basic goals in writing and to understand the writing process—as explained on the pages that follow.

TWO BASIC GOALS IN WRITING

When you write a paper, your two basic goals should be (1) to make a point and (2) to support that point. Look for a moment at the following cartoon:

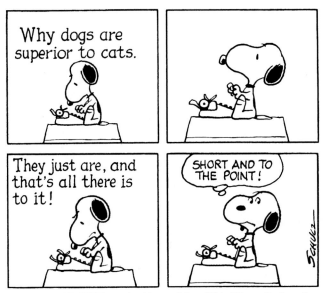

PEANUTS reproduced by permission of United Feature Syndicate, Inc.

See if you can answer the following questions:

● What is Snoopy's point in his paper?

Your answer: His point is that _____dogs are superior to cats._____

● What is his support for his point?

Your answer: _____No support is given._____

Explanation Snoopy's point, of course, is that dogs are superior to cats. But he offers no support whatsoever to back up his point! There are two jokes here. First, he is a dog and so is naturally going to believe that dogs are superior. The other joke is that his evidence ("They just are, and that's all there is to it!") is a lot of empty words. His somewhat guilty look in the last panel suggests that he knows he has not proved his point. To write effectively, you must provide real support for your points and opinions.

WRITING PARAGRAPHS

A paragraph is a series of sentences about one main idea, or point. A paragraph typically starts with a point (also called the *topic sentence*), and the rest of the paragraph provides specific details to support and develop that point.

Look at the following paragraph, written by a student named Carla.

Three Kinds of Bullies

There are three kinds of bullies in schools. First of all, there are the physical bullies. They are the bigger or meaner kids who try to hurt kids who are smaller or unsure of themselves. They'll push other kids off swings, trip them in the halls, or knock books out of their hands. They'll also wait for kids after school and slap them or yank their hair or pull out their shirts or throw them to the ground. They do their best to frighten kids and make them cry. Another kind of bully is the verbal bully. This kind tries to hurt with words rather than fists. Nursery-school kids may call each other "dummy" or "weirdo" or "fatty," and as kids get older, their words carry even more sting. "You are such a loser," those bullies will tell their victim, making sure there is a crowd near-by to hear. "Where did you get that sweater—a trash bin?" The worst kind of bully is the social bully. Social bullies realize that they can make themselves feel powerful by making others feel unwanted. Bullies choose their victims and then do all they can to isolate them. They roll their eyes and turn away in disgust if those people try to talk to them. They move away if a victim sits near them at lunch. They make sure the unwanted ones know about the games and parties they aren't invited to. Physical, verbal, and social bullies all have the same ugly goal: to hurt and humiliate others.

● What is the point of the above paragraph? _____
　　　　　　　There are three kinds of bullies in schools.

● What are the three kinds of evidence that Carla has provided to back up her point?
　　　　　　　　　　　　　　　　　　　　　　　　　　Wording of answers may vary.
1. Physical—try to hurt or frighten kids physically. _____
2. Verbal—try to hurt with words. _____
3. Social—try to make victims feel unwanted. _____

The above paragraph, like many effective paragraphs, starts by stating a main idea, or point. In this case, the clear point is that there are three kinds of bullies in schools. An effective paragraph must not only make a point but also support it with specific evidence—reasons, examples, and other details. Such specifics help prove to readers that the point is a reasonable one. Even if readers do not agree with the writer, at least they have the writer's evidence in front of them. Readers are like juries: they want to see the evidence for themselves so that they can make their own judgments.

As you have seen, the author of the paragraph provides plenty of examples to support the idea that there are physical, verbal, and social bullies. To write an effective paragraph, always aim to do what the author has done: begin by making a point, and then go on to back up that point with strong specific evidence.

WRITING ESSAYS

Like a paragraph, an essay starts with a point and then goes on to provide specific details to support and develop that point. However, a paragraph is a series of sentences about one main idea or point, while an essay is a series of paragraphs about one main idea or point—called the central point or thesis. Since an essay is much longer than one paragraph, it allows a writer to develop a topic in more detail.

Look at the following essay, written by Carla after she was asked to develop more fully her paragraph on bullies.

A Hateful Activity: Bullying

Introductory Paragraph

Eric, a new boy at school, was shy and physically small. He quickly became a victim of bullies. Kids would wait after school, pull out his shirt, and punch and shove him around. He was called such names as "Mouse Boy" and "Jerk Boy." When he sat down during lunch hour, others would leave his table. In gym games he was never thrown the ball, as if he didn't exist. Then one day he came to school with a gun. When the police were called, he told them he just couldn't take it anymore. Bullying had hurt him badly, just as it hurts so many other students. As Eric's experience shows, there are three hateful forms of bullying in schools: physical, verbal, and social.

First Supporting Paragraph

First of all, there is physical bullying. Bigger or meaner kids try to hurt kids who are smaller or unsure of themselves. They'll push kids into their lockers, knock books out of their hands, or shoulder them out of the cafeteria line. In gym class, a popular bully move is to kick someone's legs out from under him while he is running. In the classroom, bullies might kick the back of the chair or step on the foot of the kids they want to intimidate. Another classic bully move is to corner a kid in a bathroom. There the victim will be slapped around, will have his or her clothes half pulled off, and might even be shoved into a trash can. Bullies will also wait for kids after school and bump or wrestle them around, often while others are looking on. The goal is to frighten kids as much as possible and try to make them cry. The victims are left bruised, hurting, and feeling emotional pain.

Second Supporting Paragraph

Perhaps even worse than physical attack is verbal bullying, which uses words, rather than hands or fists, as weapons. We may be told that "sticks and stones may break my bones, but names can never harm me," but few of us are immune to the pain of a verbal attack. Like physical bullies, verbal bullies tend to single out certain targets. From that moment on, the victim is subjected to a hail of insults and put-downs. These are usually delivered in public, so the victim's humiliation will be greatest: "Oh, no; here comes the nerd!" "Why don't you lose some weight, blubber boy?" "You smell as bad as you look!" "Weirdo." "Fairy." "Creep." "Dork." "Slut." "Loser." Meanwhile, the victim retreats into a painful shell, hoping to escape further notice.

Third Supporting Paragraph

As bad as verbal bullying is, perhaps the most painful type of bullying is social bullying. Many students have a strong need for the comfort of being part of a group. For social bullies, the pleasure of belonging to a group is increased by the sight of someone who is refused entry into that group. So, like wolves targeting the weakest sheep in a herd, the bullies lead the pack in isolating people who they decide are different. They roll their eyes and turn away in disgust if those people try to talk to them. They move away if a victim sits near them at lunch or stands near them in a school hallway or at a bus stop. No one volunteers to work with these victims on class activities, and they are the ones that no one wants as part of gym teams. They make sure the unwanted ones know about the games and parties they aren't invited to. As the victims sink into isolation and depression, the social bullies feel all the more puffed up by their own popularity.

Concluding Paragraph

Whether bullying is physical, verbal, or social, it can leave deep and lasting scars. If parents, teachers, and other adults were more aware of the types of bullying, they might help by stepping in before the situation becomes too extreme. If students were more aware of the terrible pain that bullying causes, they might think twice about being bullies themselves.

- Which sentence in the introductory paragraph expresses the central point of the essay?
  The final sentence

- How many supporting paragraphs are provided to back up the central point? _____3_____

THE PARTS OF AN ESSAY

Each of the parts of an essay is explained below.

Introductory Paragraph

A well-written introductory paragraph will normally do the following:

- Gain the reader's interest by using one of several common methods of introduction.

- Present the thesis statement. The thesis statement expresses the central point of an essay, just as a topic sentence states the main idea of a paragraph. The central idea in Carla's essay is expressed in the last sentence of the introductory paragraph.

Four Common Methods of Introduction

Four common methods of introduction are (1) telling a brief story, (2) asking one or more questions, (3) shifting to the opposite, or (4) going from the broad to the narrow. Following are examples of all four.

1 **Telling a brief story.** An interesting anecdote is hard for a reader to resist. In an introduction, a story should be no more than a few sentences, and it should relate meaningfully to the central idea. The story can be an experience of your own, of someone you know, or of someone you have read about. Carla uses this method of introduction for her essay on bullying:

> Eric, a new boy at school, was shy and physically small. He quickly became a victim of bullies. Kids would wait after school, pull out his shirt, and punch and shove him around. He was called such names as "Mouse Boy" and "Jerk Boy." When he sat down during lunch hour, others would leave his table. In gym games he was never thrown the ball, as if he didn't exist. Then one day he came to school with a gun. When the police were called, he told them he just couldn't take it anymore. Bullying had hurt him badly, just as it hurts so many other students. Every member of a school community should be aware of bullying and the three hateful forms that it takes: physical, verbal, and social bullying.

2 **Asking one or more questions.** These questions may be ones that you intend to answer in your essay, or they may indicate that your topic is relevant to readers—it is something they care about. If Carla had used this approach, here is how her introductory paragraph might have looked:

> When you were a kid, were you ever pushed around by bigger children? Were you shoved aside in hallways or knocked out of your seat in classrooms? Were you ever called hurtful names like fatso, worm, dogface, or retard? Or were you coldly ignored by other students? Did they turn their backs on you, pretending you didn't exist? If the answer to any of these questions is "yes," then you were a victim of one of three forms of bullying: physical, verbal, or social.

3 Shifting to the opposite. Another way to gain the reader's interest is to first present an idea that is the opposite of what will be written about. Using this approach, Carla could have begun her essay like this:

> For many children, school is a happy experience. They like their teachers, they see their friends on a daily basis, and they feel comfortable and welcome. But for the victims of bullies, school is a nightmare. Every day they must face someone bigger or meaner than they are and endure humiliation in a variety of forms—physical, verbal, and social.

4 Going from the broad to the narrow. Broad, general observations can capture your reader's interest; they can also introduce your general topic and provide helpful background information. If Carla had used this method of introduction, she might have written first about typical problems in growing up and then narrowed her focus down to one problem: bullying.

> Many unpleasant parts of growing up seem unavoidable. Pimples happen, voices crack, and students worry all the time about their looks and their changing bodies. In time, the pimples disappear, the voices deepen, and the worries recede. But one all-too-common aspect of growing up, bullying, can have lasting negative results. Young people should not have to put up with bullying in any of its forms—physical, verbal, or social.

Supporting Paragraphs

The traditional school essay has three supporting paragraphs. But some essays will have two supporting paragraphs, and others will have four or more. Each supporting paragraph should have its own topic sentence stating the point to be developed in that paragraph.

Notice that the essay on bullying has clear topic sentences for each of the three supporting paragraphs.

Transitional Sentences

In a paragraph, transitional words like *First, Another, Also, In addition*, and *Finally* are used to help connect supporting ideas. In an essay, transitional sentences are used to help tie the supporting paragraphs together. Such transitional sentences often occur at the beginning of a supporting paragraph.

- Look at the topic sentences for the second and third supporting paragraphs in the essay on bullying. Explain how those sentences are also transitional sentences.

  The first two words in each sentence refer to the main idea of the paragraph

  immediately before it.

Concluding Paragraph

The concluding paragraph often summarizes the essay by briefly restating the thesis and, at times, the main supporting points. It may also provide a closing thought or two as a way of bringing the paper to a natural and graceful end.

- Look again at the concluding paragraph of the essay on bullies. Which sentence summarizes the essay? _____ first _____ Which sentences provide closing thoughts? _____ second and third _____ How many closing thoughts are there? _____ two _____

A NOTE ON A THIRD GOAL IN WRITING

A third important goal in writing (see page 3 for the first two goals) is to organize the supporting material in a paper. Perhaps the most common way to do so is to use a **listing order**. In other words, provide a list of three or more reasons, examples, or other details. Use signal words such as *First of all, Another, Secondly, Also,* and *Finally* to mark the items in your list. Signal words, better known as transitions, let your reader know that you are providing a list of items.

● Turn back to page 4 and look again at the paragraph on bullies. What signal words does Carla use to mark each of the three kinds of bullies?

First of all   Another   worst

You'll note that she uses "First of all" to introduce the first kind of bully, "Another" to introduce the second kind of bully, and "worst" to introduce the last kind of bully.

Activity: Using a Listing Order

Read the paragraph below and answer the questions that follow.

Drunk Drivers

People caught driving while drunk—even first offenders—should be jailed. For one thing, drunk driving is more dangerous than carrying a loaded gun. Drunk drivers are in charge of three-thousand-pound weapons at a time when they have little coordination or judgment. Instead of getting off with a license suspension, the drunk driver should be treated as seriously as someone who walks into a crowded building with a ticking time bomb. In addition, views on drunk driving have changed. We are no longer willing to make jokes about funny drunk drivers, to see drunk driving as a typical adolescent stunt, or to overlook repeat offenders who have been lucky enough not to hurt anybody—so far. Last of all, a jail penalty might encourage solutions to the problem of drinking and driving. People who go out for an evening that includes drinking would be more likely to select another person as the driver. That person would stay completely sober. Bars might promote more tasty and trendy nonalcoholic drinks such as fruit daiquiris and "virgin" piña coladas. And perhaps beer and alcohol advertising would be regulated so that young people would not learn to associate alcohol consumption with adulthood. By taking drunk driving seriously enough to require a jail sentence, we would surely save lives.

● What is the writer's point in this paragraph? _____
    People caught driving while drunk should be jailed.

● What transition introduces the first supporting reason for the point?   For one thing

● What transition introduces the second supporting reason?   In addition

● What transition introduces the third supporting reason?   Last of all

The author's list of reasons and use of transitions—"For one thing," "In addition," and "Last of all"—both help the author organize the supporting material and help the reader clearly and easily understand the supporting material.

Another common way to organize supporting details is to use a **time order**. In time order, supporting details are presented in the order in which they occurred. *First* this happened; *next,* this; *after* that, this; *then* this; and so on. The events that make up a story are organized in time order.

Activity: Using a Time Order

Read the paragraph below, which is organized in a time order. In the spaces provided, write appropriate transitions showing time relationships. Use each of the following transitions once: *Before, Then, When, As, After.*

An Upsetting Incident

An incident happened yesterday that made me very angry. I got off the bus and started walking the four blocks to my friend's house. _____As_____ I walked along, I noticed a group of boys gathered on the sidewalk about a block ahead of me. _____When_____ they saw me, they stopped talking. A bit nervous, I thought about crossing the street to avoid them. But as I came nearer and they began to whistle, a different feeling came over me. Instead of being afraid, I was suddenly angry. Why should I have to worry about being hassled just because I was a woman? I stared straight at the boys and continued walking. _____Then_____ one of them said, "Oooh, baby. Looking fine today." _____Before_____ I knew what I was doing, I turned on him. "Do you have a mother? Or any sisters?" I demanded. He looked astonished and didn't answer me. I went on. "Is it OK with you if men speak to them like that? Shouldn't they be able to walk down the street without some creeps bothering them?" _____After_____ I spoke, he and the other boys looked guilty and backed away. I held my head up high and walked by them. An hour later, I was still angry.

The writer makes the main point of the paragraph in her first sentence: "An incident happened yesterday that made me very angry." She then supports her point with a specific account of just what happened. Time words that could be used to help connect her details include the following: "As I walked along," "When they saw me," "Then one of them said," "Before I knew," "After I spoke."

THE WRITING PROCESS

Even professional writers do not sit down and write a paper in a single draft. Instead, they have to work on it one step at a time. Writing a paper is a process that can be divided into the following five steps:

STEP 1   **Getting Started through Prewriting**

STEP 2   **Preparing a Scratch Outline**

STEP 3   **Writing the First Draft**

STEP 4   **Revising**

STEP 5   **Editing**

STEP 1   Getting Started through Prewriting

What you need to learn, first, are methods that you can use to start working on a writing assignment. These techniques will help you think on paper. They'll help you figure out both the point you want to make and the support you need for that point. Here are three helpful prewriting techniques:

● Freewriting
● Questioning
● List making

Freewriting

Freewriting is just sitting down and writing whatever comes into your mind about a topic. Do this for ten minutes or so. Write without stopping and without worrying in the slightest about spelling, grammar, and the like. Simply get down on paper all the information that occurs to you about the topic.

Below is part of the freewriting done by Carla for her paragraph about bullies. Carla had been given the assignment "Write about the types of bullying that go on in school." She began prewriting as a way to explore her topic and generate details about it.

Example of Freewriting

> Bullying is part of school most of the time teachers dont have a clue. I really never thought about it and was just glad I wasn't part of it. At least for the most part. I'd see some phisikal stuff now and then but kind of turned my head not wanting to look at it. The worst thing with girls was words, they meant more than phisikal stuff. I rember once being called a name and it stung me so bad and it bothered me for weeks. . . .

Notice that there are lots of problems with spelling, grammar, and punctuation in Carla's freewriting. Carla is not worried about such matters, nor should she be—at this stage. She is just concentrating on getting ideas and details down on paper. She knows that it is best to focus on one thing at a time. At this point, she just wants to write out thoughts as they come to her, to do some thinking on paper.

You should take the same approach when freewriting: explore your topic without worrying at all about writing "correctly." Figuring out what you want to say should have all your attention in this early stage of the writing process.

Activity: Freewriting

On a sheet of paper, freewrite for at least ten minutes on the best or worst job or chore you ever had. Don't worry about grammar, punctuation, or spelling. Try to write—without stopping—about whatever comes into your head concerning your best or worst job or chore.

Questioning

Questioning means that you generate details about your topic by writing down a series of questions and answers about it. Your questions can start with words like *what, when, where, why,* and *how.*

Here are just some of the questions that Carla might have asked while developing her paper:

Example of Questioning

- Who was bullied?
- Who were the bullies?
- When did bullying take place?
- Where did it happen?
- Were there different kinds of bullying?
- Why were some kids teased and bullied?

Activity: Questioning

On a sheet of paper, answer the following questions about your best or worst job or chore.

- When did you have the job (or chore)?
- Where did you work?
- What did you do?
- Whom did you work for?
- Why did you like or dislike the job? (Give one reason and some details that support that reason.)
- What is another reason you liked or disliked the job? What are some details that support the second reason?
- Can you think of a third reason you liked or did not like the job? What are some details that support the third reason?

List Making

In list making (also known as brainstorming), you make a list of ideas and details that could go into your paper. Simply pile these items up, one after another, without worrying about putting them in any special order. Try to accumulate as many details as you can think of.

After Carla did her freewriting about bullies, she made up a list of details, part of which is shown below.

Example of List Making

some bullies were phisikal

boys would push kids around

kids would be tripped in hallways

some kids would cry

names would be used

"dummy" or "creep" or "fairy"

no one would sit near some kids

some kids never chosen for games

. . . .

One detail led to another as Carla expanded her list. Slowly but surely, more supporting material emerged that she could use in developing her paper. By the time she had finished her list, she was ready to plan an outline of her paragraph and to write her first draft.

Activity: List Making

On a separate piece of paper, make a list of details about the job (or chore). Don't worry about putting them in a certain order. Just get down as many details about the job as occur to you. The list can include specific reasons you liked or did not like the job and specific details supporting those reasons.

STEP 2   Preparing a Scratch Outline

A scratch outline is a brief plan for a paragraph. It shows at a glance the point of the paragraph and the support for that point. It is the logical framework on which the paper is built.

This rough outline often follows freewriting, questioning, list making, or all three. Or it may gradually emerge in the midst of these strategies. In fact, trying to outline is a good way to see if you need to do more prewriting. If a solid outline does not emerge, then you know you need to do more prewriting to clarify your main point or its support. And once you have a workable outline, you may realize, for instance, that you want to do more list making to develop one of the supporting details in the outline.

In Carla's case, as she was working on her list of details, she suddenly discovered what the plan of her paragraph could be. She realized that she could describe in turn each of three different kinds of bullies.

Example of a scratch outline

There are three kinds of bullies.
1. Physical
2. Verbal
3. Social

After all her preliminary writing, Carla sat back pleased. She knew she had a promising paper—one with a clear point and solid support. Carla was now ready to write the first draft of her paper, using her outline as a guide.

Activity: Scratch Outline

Using the list you have prepared, see if you can prepare a scratch outline made up of the three main reasons you liked or did not like the job.   *Answers will vary.*

_____ was the best (or worst) job (or chore) I ever had.

Reason 1: _____

Reason 2: _____

Reason 3: _____

STEP 3   Writing the First Draft

When you do a first draft, be prepared to put in additional thoughts and details that didn't emerge in your prewriting. And don't worry if you hit a snag. Just leave a blank space or add a comment such as "Do later" and press on to finish the paper. Also, don't worry yet about grammar, punctuation, or spelling. You don't want to take time correcting words or sentences that you may decide to remove later. Instead, make it your goal to develop the content of your paper with plenty of specific details.

Here are a few lines of Carla's first draft:

First Draft

There are different kinds of bullies that can be seen in schools. One kind of bullying that goes on is done by phisikal bullies. You see kids who will get pushed around on the playground. You see kids getting shoved into lockers and that kind of stuff. There was a girl I knew who was a real bully and a bit crazy because of a really bad home life. She would shove gum into another girl's hair and would also pull her hair. Other bullying went on with words and the calling of names. There were awful names that kids would use with each other, words included "creep" and "weirdo" and names that I don't even want to write here. . . .

Activity: First Draft

Now write a first draft of your paper. Begin with your topic sentence stating that a certain job (or chore) was the best or worst one you ever had. Then state the first reason why it was the best or the worst, followed by specific details supporting that reason. Use a transition such as *First of all* to introduce the first reason. Next, state the second reason, followed by specific details supporting that reason. Use a transition such as *Secondly* to introduce the second reason. Last, state the third reason, followed with support. Use a transition such as *Finally* to introduce the last reason.

Don't worry about grammar, punctuation, or spelling. Just concentrate on getting down on paper the details about the job.

STEP 4   Revising

Revising is as much a stage in the writing process as prewriting, outlining, and doing the first draft. *Revising* means that you rewrite a paper, building upon what has been done, to make it stronger and better. One writer has said about revision, "It's like cleaning house—getting rid of all the junk and putting things in the right order." A typical revision means writing at least one or two more drafts, adding and omitting details, organizing more clearly, and beginning to correct spelling and grammar.

Here are a few lines of Carla's second draft.

Second Draft

There are three kinds of bullies in schools. First of all, there are the physical bullies. They are the bigger kids who try to hurt smaller kids. They'll push kids off of swings in the playground or shove them into lockers. Other examples are knocking books out of the hands of kids or waiting for them after school and slapping them around or yanking their hair. Another kind of bullying is by verbal bullies. The aim here is to hurt with words rather than with fists. A victim will be called a "creep" or "weirdo" or "fatty" or will be told "You are such a loser." . . .

Notice that in redoing the draft, Carla started by more concisely stating the point of her paragraph. Also, she inserted transitions ("First of all" and "Another") to clearly set off the kinds of bullies. She omitted the detail about the crazy girl she knew because it was not relevant to a paragraph focusing on bullies. She added more details so that she would have enough supporting examples for the types of bullies.

Carla then went on to revise the second draft. Since she was doing her paper on a computer, she was able to print it out quickly. She double-spaced the lines, allowing room for revisions, which she added in longhand as part of her third draft, and eventually the paragraph on page 4 resulted. (Note that if you are not using a computer, you may want to skip every other line when writing out each draft. Also, write on only one side of a page, so that you can see your entire paper at one time.)

Activity: Revising the Draft

Ideally, you will have a chance to put the paper aside for a while before doing later drafts. When you revise, try to do all of the following:

- Omit any details that do not truly support your topic sentence.
- Add more details as needed, making sure you have plenty of specific support for each of your three reasons.
- Be sure to include a final sentence that rounds off the paper, bringing it to a close.

STEP 5   Editing

Editing, the final stage in the writing process, means checking a paper carefully for spelling, grammar, punctuation, and other errors. You are ready for this stage when you are satisfied that your point is clear, your supporting details are good, and your paper is well organized.

At this stage, you must read your paper out loud. Hearing how your writing sounds is an excellent way to pick up grammar and punctuation problems in your writing. Chances are that you will find sentence mistakes at every spot where your paper does not read smoothly and clearly. This point is so important that it bears repeating: To find mistakes in your paper, read it out loud!

At this point in her work, Carla read her latest draft out loud. She looked closely at all the spots where her writing did not read easily. She used a grammar handbook to deal with the problems at those spots in her paper, and she made the corrections needed so that all her sentences read smoothly. She also used her dictionary to check on the spelling of every word she was unsure about. She even took a blank sheet of paper and used it to uncover her paper one line at a time, looking for any other mistakes that might be there.

Activity: Editing

When you have your almost-final draft of the paper, edit it in the following ways:

- Read the paper aloud, listening for awkward wordings and places where the meaning is unclear. Make the changes needed for the paper to read smoothly and clearly. In addition, see if you can get another person to read the draft aloud to you. The spots that this person has trouble reading are spots where you may have to do some revision and correct your grammar or punctuation mistakes.

- Using your dictionary (or a spell-check program if you have a computer), check any words that you think might be misspelled.

- Finally, take a sheet of paper and cover your paper so that you can expose and carefully proofread one line at a time. Use your handbook to check any other spots where you think there might be grammar or punctuation mistakes in your writing.

Final Thoughts

When you have a paper to write, here in a nutshell is what to do:

1   Write about what you know. If you don't know much about your topic, go onto the Internet and use the helpful search engine Google. You can access it by typing this:

   www.google.com

   A screen will then appear with a box in which you can type one or more keywords. For example, if you were thinking about doing a paper on some other topic involving bullies, you could type in the keyword *bullies*. Within a second or so you will get a list of over 80,000 articles on the Web about bullies!

   You would then need to narrow your topic by adding other keywords. For instance, if you typed, "bullies in schools," you would get a list of over 20,000 items. If you narrowed your potential topic further by typing "solutions to bullies in schools," you would get a list of 2,500 items. You could then click on the items that sound most promising to you. As you read and think about bullies, you will gradually get a sense of a topic you might be able to develop.

   Keep in mind that you do not want to take other people's ideas or words—that would be stealing. The formal term is *plagiarizing*—using someone else's work and presenting it as your own. Rather, your goal is to use other people's information and thoughts as a springboard for your own words and ideas about a topic.

2   Use prewriting strategies to begin to write about your topic. Look for a point you can make, and make sure you have details to support it.

3   Write several drafts, aiming all the while for three goals in your writing: a clear point, strong support for that point, and well-organized support. Use transitions to help organize your support.

4   Then read your paper out loud. It should read smoothly and clearly. Look closely for grammar and punctuation problems at any rough spots. Check a grammar handbook or a dictionary as needed.

Writing Assignments

Writing is best done on topics about which you have information and in which you have interest. To ensure that you have a choice of topics, following are ten groups of **two** writing assignments. Your instructor may ask you, for example, to write on your choice of one of the two topics in Group A. As the semester proceeds, he or she may ask you to write paragraphs on your choice of topics from additional groups as well.

GROUP A

1 **Hometown.** If a friend wrote to you asking whether your hometown would be a good place for him or her to move to, what would be your response? Write a one-paragraph letter to your friend explaining the advantages or disadvantages of living in your hometown. Begin your remarks with a specific recommendation to your friend; it will serve as the topic sentence of the paragraph. Cover such matters as employment, recreation, housing, schools, and safety. Be sure your details are as specific and descriptive as you can make them. To connect your ideas, use transitions such as *in addition, furthermore, on the other hand,* and *however.*

2 **Best or Worst Childhood Experience.** Some of our most vivid memories are of things that happened to us as children, and these memories don't ever seem to fade. In fact, many elderly people say that childhood memories are clearer to them than things that happened yesterday. Think back to one of the best or worst experiences you had as a child. Try to remember the details of the event—sights, sounds, smells, textures, tastes.

You might begin by freewriting for ten minutes or so about good or bad childhood experiences. That freewriting may suggest to you a topic you will want to develop.

After you have decided on a topic, try to write a clear sentence stating what the experience was and whether it was one of the best or worst of your childhood. For example, "The time I was beaten up coming home from my first day in fifth grade was one of my worst childhood moments."

You may then find it helpful to make a list in which you jot down as many details as you can remember about the experience. Stick with a single experience, and don't try to describe too much. If a week you spent at summer camp was an unpleasant experience, don't try to write about the entire week. Just describe one horrible moment or event.

When you write the paper, use a time order to organize details: first this happened, then this, next this, and so on.

As you write, imagine that someone is going to make a short film based on your paragraph. Try to provide vivid details, quotations, and pictures for the filmmaker to shoot.

GROUP B

1 **A Certain Song or Movie.** Is there a certain song or movie that is especially memorable to you? If so, mention the title of the song (the title should be in quotation marks) or movie (the title should be underlined or in italics), and write about the time when the song or movie became so meaningful to you. To be convincing, you will need to include numerous details and clear explanations.

2 A Special Place or Object. Write a paragraph describing either a place or an object you respond to with strong emotion, such as love, fear, warmth, dread, joy, or sadness. Specific details and vivid descriptions will need to be provided if your emotional reaction is to be understood.

GROUP C

1 A Good or Bad Day in Your Life. Write in detail about a recent good or bad day in your life—your activities, feelings, and experiences during the day. You might begin by making a list of things that you did, felt, saw, thought, heard, and said during that day. Your aim is to accumulate a great many details that you can draw upon later as you begin writing your paper. Making a long list is an excellent way to get started.

Then select and develop those details that best support the idea that the day was a good one or a bad one. Organize your paragraph using a time order—first this happened, then this, next this, and so on.

2 Directions to a Place. Write a set of specific directions on how to get from the English classroom to your house. Imagine you are giving these directions to a stranger who has just come into the room and who wants to deliver a million dollars to your home. You want, naturally, to give exact directions, including various landmarks that may guide the way, for the stranger does not know the area.

To help you write the paper, first make up a list of all the directions involved. Also, use words like *next, then,* and *after* to help the reader follow clearly as you move from one direction to the next.

GROUP D

1 A Helpful Experience. Write an account of an experience you have had that taught you something important. It might involve a mistake you made or an event that gave you insight into yourself or others. Perhaps you have had school problems that taught you to be a more effective student, or you have had a conflict with someone that you now understand could have been avoided. Whatever experience you choose to write about, be sure to tell how it has changed your way of thinking.

2 Hindsight. Occasionally, we call someone a "Monday-morning quarterback." By this we mean that it's easy to say what should have been done after an event (or game) is over. But while we're in the midst of our daily lives, it's hard to know which is the right decision to make or what is the right course of action. We've all looked back and thought, "I wish I'd done . . ." or "I wish I'd said . . ."

Think back to a year or two ago. What is the best advice someone could have given you then? Freewrite for ten minutes or so about how your life might have changed if you had been given that advice.

Then go on to write a paper that begins with a topic sentence something like this: "I wish someone had told me a year ago to cut back a little on my work hours while I'm in school."

GROUP E

1 Parents and Children.   It has been said that the older we get, the more we see our parents in ourselves. Indeed, any of our habits (good and bad), beliefs, and temperaments can often be traced to one of our parents.

Write a paragraph in which you describe three characteristics you have "inherited" from a parent. You might want to think about your topic by asking yourself a series of questions: "How am I like my mother (or father)?" "When and where am I like her (or him)?" "Why am I like her (or him)?"

One student who did such a paper used as her topic sentence the following statement: "Although I hate to admit it, I know that in several ways I'm just like my mom." She then went on to describe how she works too hard, worries too much, and judges other people too harshly. Another student wrote, "I resemble my father in my love of TV sports, my habit of putting things off, and my reluctance to show my feelings." Be sure to include examples for each of the characteristics you mention.

2 A Matter of Survival.   Someone has written, "There are times for each of us when simple survival becomes a deadly serious matter. We must then learn to persist—to struggle through each day." What has been your worst struggle? Write a paper describing the problem, what you had to do to deal with it, and how things worked out. You may also wish to comment on how you'd handle the problem today if you had to face it again.

As you work on the drafts for this paper, consider including the following to add interest and clarity:

- Exact quotations of what people said
- Descriptions of revealing behavior, actions, and physical characteristics
- Time transitions to clarify relationships between events

GROUP F

1 Avoiding Responsibility.   M. Scott Peck, the author of several best-selling self-help books, has written, "The extent to which people will go psychologically to avoid assuming responsibility for personal problems, while always sad, is sometimes almost ludicrous." Think of times you have observed people blaming other people or circumstances for their own problems. Then write a paragraph that begins with the following topic sentence:

- I have seen someone refuse to take responsibility for his (or her) own problem.

Then go on to support that statement with an example. As you develop that example, be sure to explain what the person's problem was, how he had helped create it, and how he blamed other people or circumstances rather than accept responsibility for it.

As you think of how to develop your paragraph, ask yourself questions such as these:

- Whom do I know who usually seems to be in one kind of trouble or another?
- Does that person always seem to blame others for his or her problems?
- What are some specific problems that person has in his or her life?
- How has he or she helped to create the problems?
- Whom or what does the person blame for those problems?

2 **Dealing with a Problem.**   M. Scott Peck states that the only way to solve a problem is to solve it—in other words, to take responsibility for the problem and find a solution. When did you accept the responsibility for a problem in your own life and figure out a solution for it? Write about what happened. Be sure to answer the following questions:

- How was the problem affecting my life?

- When did I realize that I was (in part) responsible for the problem?

- What solution for the problem did I come up with?

- What happened after I put my solution to work?

In selecting a topic for this assignment, think about various kinds of problems you may have experienced: problems getting along with other people, money problems, relationship problems, problems completing work on time, difficulties in self-discipline, use of alcohol or other drugs, and so on. Then ask yourself which of these problems you have accepted responsibility for and solved. Once you have thought of a topic, you might begin with a statement like one of the following:

- This past year, I began to take responsibility for my continuing problems with my mother.

- I recently faced the fact that I have a self-discipline problem and have taken steps to deal with it.

- After years of spending my money on the wrong kinds of things, I've acted to deal with my money problems.

This statement could then be supported with one or more examples of the problem, a description of how and when you realized the problem, and a detailing of the steps you have taken to deal with the problem.

GROUP G

1 **A Key Experience in School.**   Write a paragraph about one of your key experiences in grade school. Use concrete details—actions, comments, reactions, and so on—to help your readers picture what happened. To select an event to write about, try asking yourself the following questions:

- Which teachers or events in school influenced how I felt about myself?
- What specific incidents stand out in my mind as I think back to elementary school?

Once you know which experience you'll write about, use freewriting to help you remember and record the details. Here is one student's freewriting for this assignment:

> In second grade, Richard L. sat next to me, a really good artist. When he drew something, it looked just like what it was meant to be. He was so good at choosing colors, the use of crayons, watercolors. His pictures were always picked by teacher to be shown on bulletin board. I still remember his drawing of a circus. He drew acrobats, animals, and clowns. Many colors and details. I felt pretty bad in art, even though I loved it and couldn't wait for art in class. One day the teacher read story about a boy who looked at the mountains far away, wondering what was on the other side, mountains were huge, dark. After reading, it was art time. "Paint something from the story" teacher said. I painted

those mountains, big purple brown mountains with watercolor dripping to show the slopes and coloring of sunset. Also a thin slice of very blue sky at top. Next day I sat down at my desk in the morning. Then I saw my picture was on the bulletin board! Later teacher passed by me, bent down, put hand on my shoulder and whispered good job, lovely painting. Made me feel capable, proud. The feeling lasted a long time.

Once the details of the experience are on paper, you will be free to concentrate on a more carefully constructed version of the event. The author of the above freewriting, for instance, needed to think of a topic sentence. So when writing the first draft, she began with this sentence: "A seemingly small experience in elementary school encouraged me greatly." Writing drafts is also the time to add any persuasive details you may have missed at first. When working on her second draft, the author of the above added at the end: "I felt very proud, which gave me confidence to work harder in all my school subjects."

Before writing out your final version, remember to check for grammar, punctuation, and spelling errors.

2 Finding Time for Reading. A number of authors have described how a parent or teacher has helped them become regular readers—and how that habit of reading then led to enormous positive changes in their lives. Most of us, however, don't have someone around to insist that we do a certain amount of personal reading every week. In addition, many of us don't seem to have a great deal of free time for reading. How can adults find time to read more? Write a paragraph listing several ways adults can add more reading to their lives.

A good prewriting strategy for this assignment is list making. Simply write out as many ways as you can think of. Don't worry about putting them in any special order. You will select and organize the strategies you wish to include in your paper after accumulating as many ideas as you can. Here is an example of a prewriting list for this paper:

Ways adults can increase the amount of time they spend reading
— on the bus to and from work/school
— while eating breakfast
— instead of watching some TV
— choose motivating materials (articles, books about hobbies, problems, etc.)

Feel free to use items from the above list, but add at least one or two of your own points to include in your paper.

GROUP H

1 An Embarrassing Moment.   In a paragraph, tell about a time you felt ashamed or embarrassed. Provide details that show clearly what happened. Explain what you and the other people involved said and did. Also, explain how you felt and why you were so uncomfortable.

For example, the paragraph might begin with a sentence like this:

● I was deeply ashamed when I was caught cheating on a spelling test in fifth grade.

The paragraph could continue by telling how the writer cheated and how he was caught; how the teacher and other students looked, spoke, and acted; what the writer did when he was caught; and what emotions and thoughts the writer experienced throughout the incident.

On the facing page are some other topic sentence possibilities. Develop one of them or a variation on one of them. Feel free as well to come up with and write about an entirely different idea.

- My first formal date was the occasion of an embarrassing moment in my life.
- To this day, I wince when I think of an incident that happened to me at a family party.
- I can still remember the shame I felt in my teenage body when I had to use the shower room at school.
- An event that occurred in high school makes my cheeks glow hot and red even today.

2 **A Fear of Looking Foolish.** Write a paragraph about how the fear of looking foolish affected your behavior in grade school or high school. Choose an example of a time you acted in a particular way because you were afraid of being ridiculed. Describe how you behaved, and be sure to explain just what kind of embarrassment you were trying to avoid.

Your paragraph might begin with a topic sentence like one of the following:

- Not wanting other students to turn on me, I joined them in making fun of a high school classmate who was very overweight.
- My mother's idea of how I should dress caused me a great deal of embarrassment in school.
- Because I didn't want to admit that I needed glasses, I had a lot of problems in fifth grade.

GROUP I

1 **A Special Person.** Who has helped you the most in your quest for an education? Write a paper explaining who this person is and how he or she has helped you. Here are some possible topic sentences for this paper:

- My best friend has helped me with my college education in several ways.
- If it weren't for my father, I wouldn't be in college today.
- It was my aunt who impressed upon me the importance of a college education.

To develop support for this paper, try listing the problems you faced and the ways this person has helped you deal with each problem. Alternatively, you could do some freewriting about the person you're writing about.

2 **Reaching a Goal.** Write a paragraph telling of something you wanted very badly, but were afraid you would not be able to attain. Describe the struggles you had to overcome to get to your goal. How did you finally reach it? Include some details that communicate how strongly you wanted the goal and how difficult it was to reach. In thinking about a topic for this paper, you may wish to consider the following common goals:

- A certain job
- Enough money for college
- A passing grade
- Quitting smoking or drugs
- Overcoming an illness

Once you've decided on the goal you wish to write about, use it to write a topic sentence, such as any of the following:

- After several false starts, I finally quit smoking.
- After gradually changing my attitude about school, I have begun to get good grades.
- After two years of medical treatment and support, I feel I have learned to live with my illness.
- Following a careful budget, I was finally able to afford to . . .

To develop supporting material for your topic sentence, try freewriting. For example, here is part of one person's freewriting about the struggle to quit smoking:

> The first time I tried to quit, it lasted a short time. Only a month or less. I made the mistake of not getting rid of all the cigarettes in the house, I kept a few here and there for emergencies. But there should be no emergencies when you quit. Once I took a few puffs on a cigarette I found in the silverware drawer. It was all over—I ran out that day to buy a pack. I told myself I would smoke only one or two cigarettes a day until I was ready to really quit. That type of promise is always a lie because I can't really control myself once I start smoking. It's either all or nothing, and for me, even a puff or two isn't nothing. It wasn't long before I started thinking about quitting again. I was coughing a lot and several news stories were about people with lung cancer and the father of someone in my apartment building died of lung cancer. Also I read in a magazine that smoking causes wrinkles. Finally, about a year ago . . .

GROUP J

1 Being One's Own Worst Enemy. "A lot of people are their own worst enemies" is a familiar saying. We all know people who hurt themselves. Write a paragraph describing someone you know who is his or her own worst enemy. In your paper, introduce the person and explain his or her hurtful behaviors. You may wish to conclude your paragraph with suggestions for that person. A useful way to gather ideas for this paper is to combine two prewriting techniques—outlining and listing. Begin with an outline of the general areas you expect to cover. Here's an outline that may work:

— Introduce the person

— Describe the hurtful behavior(s)

— Suggest changes

Once you have a workable outline, then use list making to produce specific details for each outline point. For example, here are one person's lists for the points in the outline:

Person

— Vanessa

— Just graduated high school

— Works at a department store

— Wants to go to college, but needs money

Hurtful behaviors

— Just moved into own apartment, which takes much of monthly income—could have stayed at home

— Spends a lot of money on clothing

— Makes no effort to find financial aid for school

Changes

— Stop spending so much and start saving

— Get information from school financial aid offices

2   A Time for Courage.   Write about a time when you had to have courage. Think of an action that frightened you, but that you felt you needed to take anyway. Perhaps you were afraid to ask someone out on a date, or to say no when someone asked you to do something you felt was wrong, or to perform a dangerous activity. In your paper, describe the frightening situation that faced you and how you made the decision to act with courage. Then tell what happened—the actions that you took, the responses of those around you, significant things people said, and how things turned out.

For example, you might begin with a statement like this:

● When I was in junior high, it required courage for me to resist the temptation to shoplift with my favorite cousin.

That passage would then continue with a description of what the cousin did and said, how you found the courage to say no to the idea, how the shoplifting cousin reacted, and how you felt throughout the whole process.

As you describe the incident, use time transition words to make the sequence of events clear, as in this example: "At *first* I didn't think I could do it. *Later*, however, I had an idea."

PART ONE Fourteen Basic Skills

PART ONE
Fourteen Basic Skills

PREVIEW

Part One presents basic information about fourteen key grammar, punctuation, and usage skills.

1   Subjects and Verbs   27–36

2   Irregular Verbs   37–46

3   Subject–Verb Agreement   47–56

4   Sentence Types   57–66

5   Fragments I   67–76

6   Fragments II   77–86

7   Run-ons and Comma Splices I   87–96

8   Run-ons and Comma Splices II   97–106

9   The Comma   107–116

10   The Apostrophe   117–126

11   Quotation Marks   127–136

12   Homonyms   137–146

13   Capital Letters   147–156

14   Parallelism   157–166

① Subjects and Verbs

Basics about Subjects and Verbs

Every complete sentence contains a **subject** and a **verb**.

SUBJECTS

The **subject** of a sentence is the person, place, thing, or idea that the sentence is about. The subject can be called the "who or what" word. To find the subject, ask yourself, "Who or what is this sentence about?" or "Who or what is doing something in this sentence?"

For example, look at the following two sentences:
- People applauded.
- Gloria wrote the answers on the board.

People is what the first sentence is about; they are the ones who applauded. So *people* is the subject of the first sentence. The second sentence answers the question, "Who is doing something in the sentence?" The answer is *Gloria*. She is the person who wrote the answers on the board. So *Gloria* is the subject of the second sentence.

A subject will always be either a noun or a pronoun. A **noun** is the name of a person, place, thing, or idea. A **pronoun** is a word—such as *I, you, he, she, it, we,* or *they*—that stands for a noun.

VERBS

Many **verbs** express action; they tell what the subject is doing. You can find an **action verb** by asking, "What does the subject do?" Look again at these sentences:
- People applauded.
- Gloria wrote the answers on the board.

You remember that *people* is the subject of the first sentence. What did they do? They *applauded. Applauded* is the verb in the first sentence. *Gloria* is the subject in the second sentence. What did Gloria do? She *wrote,* so *wrote* is the verb in the second sentence.

Some verbs do not show action; they are called **linking verbs**. Linking verbs like *is, are, was,* and *were* join (or link) the subject to something that is said about the subject. For example, in the sentence *Gloria is a teacher,* the linking verb *is* connects the subject *Gloria* with what is said about her—that she is a teacher.

> **Notes**
>
> **1** Some verbs consist of more than one word—a **helping verb** plus the main verb. Here are some examples of verbs containing more than one word:
> - Gloria has written the answer on the board.
>   The verb is *has written.*
> - The balloons were drifting slowly to earth.
>   The verb is *were drifting.*
>
> **2** The verb of a sentence never begins with *to.* For example:
> - Gloria is going to write the answer on the board.
>   The verb of the sentence is *is going.* It is not *write* or *to write.*
> - The balloons seemed to hang in the air.
>   The verb of the sentence is *seemed.* It is not *hang* or *to hang.*

27

Understanding Subjects and Verbs

In each sentence, underline the subject <u>once</u> and the verb <u>twice</u>. Then check your answers below.

¹Daisy Russell lives in Missouri. ²Her dog's name is Happy. ³Daisy is happy now, too, after an unhappy past. ⁴Daisy experienced a difficult childhood. ⁵Her father beat her. ⁶He called her worthless. ⁷He even tried to sell her to another couple. ⁸Her family moved constantly. ⁹Unable to read, Daisy felt stupid and ashamed. ¹⁰Now things are different. ¹¹Daisy has learned to read. ¹²Moreover, she teaches other adults to read. ¹³Today, Daisy has a lot to smile about.

ANSWERS

¹Daisy Russell, lives; ²name, is; ³Daisy, is; ⁴Daisy, experienced; ⁵father, beat; ⁶He, called; ⁷He, tried; ⁸family, moved; ⁹Daisy, felt; ¹⁰things, are; ¹¹Daisy, has learned; ¹²she, teaches; ¹³Daisy, has

Check Your Understanding

Underline each subject <u>once</u> and each verb <u>twice</u>.

¹Daisy often baby-sits her grandchildren. ²Their childhood is very different from hers. ³She was often lonely and afraid. ⁴They live without fear. ⁵In the photo to the left, Daisy appears with her granddaughter Tiffany. ⁶Daisy taught Tiffany to read. ⁷The two visit the library in their town often. ⁸Daisy's grandchildren both enjoy reading. ⁹They have no need to feel ashamed. ¹⁰Their grandmother feels great about that.

A Note on Prepositional Phrases

The subject of a sentence is never part of a prepositional phrase. A **prepositional phrase** is a group of words that begins with a preposition and ends with a noun. Common prepositions are *about, after, as, at, before, between, by, during, for, from, in, into, like, of, on, outside, over, through, to, toward, with,* and *without.* As you look for the subject of a sentence, it may help to cross out any prepositional phrases that you find. Here are examples:

> The coffee ~~from the leaking pot~~ stained the carpet.
> One ~~of my classmates~~ fell asleep ~~during class~~.
> The woman ~~on that motorcycle~~ has no helmet.
> The cracks and booms ~~during the thunderstorm~~ were terrifying.

Subjects and Verbs: PRACTICE 1

In each sentence below, cross out the prepositional phrases. Then underline the subject of each sentence <u>once</u> and the verb of each sentence <u>twice</u>.

1. <u>Daisy</u> is <u>looking</u> ~~through her "brag book."~~
2. <u>She</u> <u>keeps</u> special papers ~~in it.~~
3. One <u>letter</u> ~~in the book~~ <u>is</u> especially important ~~to her~~.
4. <u>She</u> <u>had entered</u> a scholarship contest ~~for college students~~.
5. Her <u>entry</u> <u>was</u> an essay ~~about her life~~.
6. The <u>letter</u> ~~from the contest officials~~ <u>awarded</u> her first prize.
7. The <u>eagle</u> ~~on the front of her brag book~~ <u>has</u> a special meaning.
8. <u>It</u> <u>tells</u> her to "fly" ~~over any obstacle to her success~~.

9. <u>Daisy</u> <u>used</u> the scholarship money ~~for a computer.~~
10. ~~On the computer~~ <u>she</u> <u>writes</u> more essays, poems, and stories.
11. Daisy's <u>life</u> <u>has changed</u> a great deal ~~during the last few years~~.
12. <u>She</u> <u>learned</u> to read ~~as an adult~~.
13. <u>She</u> <u>earned</u> her high-school diploma ~~at age 44~~.
14. <u>She</u> <u>has told</u> her life story ~~on radio and TV~~.
15. <u>Daisy</u> truly <u>has taken</u> charge ~~of her own life~~.

A Note on Helping Verbs

As already mentioned, many verbs consist of a main verb plus one or more helping verbs. Helping verbs are shown below:

Forms of *be*:	be, am, is, are, was, were, being, been
Forms of *have*:	have, has, had
Forms of *do*:	do, does, did
Special verbs:	can, could, may, might, must, ought (to), shall, should, will, would

Subjects and Verbs: PRACTICE 2

In each sentence below, cross out the prepositional phrases. Then underline the subject of each sentence once and the verb of each sentence twice.

1. Dogs ~~at the animal shelter~~ wait ~~for a good home~~.

2. The frozen fish ~~on the counter~~ defrosted quickly.

3. My computer's screen went blank ~~without warning~~.

4. The kitchen ~~in my parents' house~~ smells ~~like vanilla and cinnamon~~.

5. A very large truck stalled ~~on the bridge~~.

6. The orange ~~in the refrigerator~~ has purple spots.

7. Everyone cried ~~at one point during the movie~~.

8. Several sad-looking puppies huddled ~~in the small cage~~.

9. Two young boys ~~from the neighborhood~~ were playing catch ~~in the alley~~.

10. ~~By the end of the day~~, we had sold between 350 and 400 tickets.

Subjects and Verbs: PRACTICE 3

In each sentence below, cross out the prepositional phrases. Then underline the subject of each sentence <u>once</u> and the verb of each sentence <u>twice</u>.

1. Today, <u>Daisy</u> <u><u>is surrounded</u></u> ~~by people~~.

2. <u>All</u> ~~of them~~ <u><u>care</u></u> ~~about her.~~

3. Her husband <u>Don</u> <u><u>has encouraged</u></u> her ~~over the years~~ to pursue her dreams.

4. <u>Daisy</u> <u><u>calls</u></u> their neighbor Shorty ~~by the name of "Dad~~."

5. "<u>I</u> <u><u>was</u></u> ~~without a loving dad of my own~~."

6. "So <u>I</u> <u><u>adopted</u></u> Shorty ~~as my father~~."

7. Little <u>Bradley</u> <u><u>has</u></u> no knowledge ~~of Daisy's story~~.

8. <u>He</u> just <u><u>loves</u></u> to be ~~with his Grandma~~.

9. ~~As a child~~, <u>Daisy</u> <u><u>had</u></u> an unhappy family life.

10. But, ~~through her own efforts~~, <u>she</u> <u><u>is creating</u></u> a happy present and future.

Name _____ Section _____ Date _____

Score: (Number right) _____ x 10 = _____%

Subjects and Verbs: TEST 1

For each sentence, cross out any prepositional phrases. Then underline the subject <u>once</u> and the verb <u>twice</u>. Remember to include any helping verb(s).

NOTE To help in your review of subjects and verbs, explanations are given for three of the sentences.

1. A <u>family</u> ~~of ducks~~ <u><u>waddled</u></u> ~~toward the pond~~.

   Of ducks and *toward the pond* are prepositional phrases. The sentence is about a *family (of ducks)*; what they did was *waddled*.

2. <u>Ramona</u> <u><u>loves</u></u> to exchange e-mails ~~with her friends~~.

   Since *exchange* has a *to* in front of it, it cannot be the verb of the sentence.

3. Many park <u>visitors</u> <u><u>have complained</u></u> ~~about the new regulations~~.

   Have complained (*complained* plus the helping verb *have*) is what the sentence says the park visitors did.

4. The <u>pot</u> ~~of vegetable soup~~ <u><u>simmered</u></u> gently ~~on the stove~~.

5. Your digital <u>camera</u> <u><u>takes</u></u> very clear pictures ~~in all kinds of locations~~.

6. ~~After the party,~~ <u>we</u> <u><u>went</u></u> ~~to a diner~~ ~~for coffee~~.

7. The summer <u>concert</u> <u><u>was canceled</u></u> ~~with only one day's notice~~.

8. The <u>coffee</u> ~~from the leaking pot~~ <u><u>left</u></u> a stain ~~on the white carpet~~.

9. A German <u>shepherd</u> <u><u>waited</u></u> patiently ~~outside the drugstore~~.

10. The curious <u>child</u> <u><u>stared</u></u> silently ~~at the man~~ ~~in the Santa Claus suit~~.

Name _____ Section _____ Date _____

Score: (Number right) _____ x 10 = _____ %

Subjects and Verbs: TEST 2

For each sentence, cross out any prepositional phrases. Then underline the subject <u>once</u> and the verb <u>twice</u>. Remember to include any helping verb(s).

1. The <u>candles</u> ~~on the table~~ <u>smell</u> ~~like vanilla~~.

2. The <u>people</u> ~~in my family~~ <u>speak</u> two languages.

3. Clean <u>clothes</u> ~~on the line~~ <u>fluttered</u> ~~in the breeze~~.

4. ~~Without a word~~, <u>Hugh</u> <u>raced</u> ~~out of the house~~ and ~~into the front yard~~.

5. <u>Teams</u> ~~of cheerleaders~~ <u>yelled</u> ~~on opposite sides of the gym~~.

6. Sofia's <u>boyfriend</u> <u>is</u> good ~~with cars~~.

7. <u>I</u> <u>work</u> ~~at the computer lab~~ ~~between classes~~.

8. Huge <u>mounds</u> ~~of dirt~~ <u>surround</u> the construction site.

9. The <u>tiles</u> ~~on the bathroom floor~~ <u>look</u> gray ~~in the dim light~~.

10. <u>Movies</u> ~~about dinosaurs~~ always <u>seem</u> popular ~~with audiences~~.

Name _____   Section _____   Date _____

Score: (Number right) _____ x 10 = _____ %

Subjects and Verbs: TEST 3

In each sentence below, cross out the prepositional phrases. Then underline the subject of each sentence once and the verb of each sentence twice.

1. In present-day America, with all its wealth and resources, many adults read poorly.

2. Many, in fact, are unable to read at all.

3. Some, like Daisy Russell, never had a chance to learn during childhood.

4. In other cases, people struggle with learning disabilities.

5. Adults without the ability to read often feel hopeless about their situation.

6. In addition, they may feel ashamed about their lack of this skill.

7. It took a number of years for Daisy Russell to find the courage to ask for help.

8. Then she began to work with a tutor.

9. She learned quickly about "sounding out" words and how to understand written language.

10. Now she is happy to work with other nonreaders.

Name _____ Section _____ Date _____

Score: (Number right) _____ x 10 = _____ %

Subjects and Verbs: TEST 4

Read the sentences below. Then, in the space provided, write the letter of the correct answer to each question.

● The movie audience shrieked in terror and glee at the sight of the seven-headed monster.

___a___ **1.** In the sentence above, the subject is
  a. audience.   **b.** terror.   **c.** monster.

___a___ **2.** In the sentence above, the verb is
  a. shrieked.   **b.** glee.   **c.** sight.

● A solution to the problem suddenly popped into my head.

___c___ **3.** In the sentence above, the subject is
  a. problem.   **b.** head.   **c.** solution.

___a___ **4.** In the sentence above, the verb is
  a. popped.   **b.** suddenly.   **c.** head.

● During the long bus trip from Baltimore to Florida, many passengers slept.

___c___ **5.** In the sentence above, the subject is
  a. bus.   **b.** many.   **c.** passengers.

___c___ **6.** In the sentence above, the verb is
  a. During.   **b.** many.   **c.** slept.

● For his birthday dinner, Will had a pizza with pepperoni, mushrooms, and onions.

___c___ **7.** In the sentence above, the subject is
  a. dinner.   **b.** birthday.   **c.** Will.

___b___ **8.** In the sentence above, the verb is
  a. dinner.   **b.** had.   **c.** with.

● After my final exam, I can forget about school for a week.

___b___ **9.** In the sentence above, the subject is
  a. exam.   **b.** I.   **c.** school.

___b___ **10.** In the sentence above, the verb is
  a. can.   **b.** can forget.   **c.** forget.

Name _____ Section _____ Date _____

Score: (Number right) _____ x 10 = _____ %

Subjects and Verbs: TEST 5

Read the sentences below. Then, in the space provided, write the letter of the correct answer to each question.

● During the hot, dry summer, the farmers worried about their crops.

___c___ **1.** In the sentence above, the subject is
    a. summer.   **b.** crops.   **c.** farmers.

___c___ **2.** In the sentence above, the verb is
    a. During.   **b.** about.   **c.** worried.

● Drops of icy rain began to fall on the basketball players.

___a___ **3.** In the sentence above, the subject is
    a. Drops.   **b.** rain.   **c.** players.

___b___ **4.** In the sentence above, the verb is
    a. icy.   **b.** began.   **c.** fall.

● As a result of my father's illness, my family in the past two months has lived a nightmare.

___c___ **5.** In the sentence above, the subject is
    a. illness.   **b.** result.   **c.** family.

___b___ **6.** In the sentence above, the verb is
    a. lived.   **b.** has lived.   **c.** has.

● To catch the bus to school, Stacy awakens before sunrise.

___a___ **7.** In the sentence above, the subject is
    a. Stacy.   **b.** bus.   **c.** sunrise.

___c___ **8.** In the sentence above, the verb is
    a. catch.   **b.** to catch.   **c.** awakens.

● Tracy has been sending romantic e-mails to her boyfriend during computer lab.

___a___ **9.** In the sentence above, the subject is
    a. Tracy.   **b.** boyfriend.   **c.** e-mails.

___b___ **10.** In the sentence above, the verb is
    a. has.   **b.** has been sending.   **c.** during.

② Irregular Verbs

Basics about Irregular Verbs

Most English verbs are **regular**. That is, they form their past tense and past participle by adding *-ed* or *-d* to the basic form, as shown here:

Basic Form	Past Tense	Past Participle
ask	asked	asked
raise	raised	raised

Some English verbs are **irregular.** They do not form their past tense and past participle by adding *-ed* or *-d* to the basic form of the verb. Instead, their past tenses and past participles are formed in other ways. Here are some of the most common irregular verbs.

Basic Form	Past Tense	Past Participle	Basic Form	Past Tense	Past Participle
become	became	become	go	went	gone
begin	began	begun	grow	grew	grown
break	broke	broken	have	had	had
bring	brought	brought	hide	hid	hidden
catch	caught	caught	is	was	been
choose	chose	chosen	keep	kept	kept
come	came	come	know	knew	known
do	did	done	leave	left	left
drink	drank	drunk	read	read	read
drive	drove	driven	see	saw	seen
eat	ate	eaten	shake	shook	shaken
feel	felt	felt	spend	spent	spent
find	found	found	take	took	taken
forget	forgot	forgotten	tell	told	told
get	got	got, gotten	write	wrote	written
give	gave	given			

A word about helping verbs Sometimes the verb of a sentence consists of more than one word. In these cases, the main verb will be joined by one or more **helping verbs**. Look at the following sentence:

> I **should have gone** to bed earlier last night.

In this sentence, the main verb is *gone*. The helping verbs are *should* and *have*. Other common helping verbs include *be, can, could, do, has, may, must, will,* and *would*.

When you use the above chart, keep these two points in mind:

1 If your sentence does **not** have a helping verb, choose the past tense form.
   I **ate** a bacon, lettuce, and tomato sandwich.

2 If the sentence **does have** a helping verb, choose the past participle.
   I **had eaten** a bacon, lettuce, and tomato sandwich.

NOTE If you think a verb is irregular, and it is not in the above list, look it up in your dictionary. If it is irregular, the principal parts will be listed. See "Dictionary Use," page 337.

Understanding Irregular Verbs

In the following passage about college student Zamil Ortiz, **five** mistakes in irregular verbs are underlined. The correct forms of the verbs are then shown in the spaces below.

¹During her first semester at college, Zamil <u>becomed</u> discouraged. ²The workload nearly <u>drived</u> her crazy! ³She had always <u>did</u> well in high school. ⁴But at college, everything <u>feeled</u> so new and strange. ⁵She worried that she had <u>taked</u> on too big a job.

1. became
2. drove
3. done
4. felt
5. taken

Check Your Understanding

Underline the **five** mistakes in irregular verbs. Then write the correct form of the verbs in the spaces provided.

¹Zamil <u>knowed</u> she needed to do something. ²She decided to talk to her instructors. ³She <u>telled</u> them where she was having problems, and they <u>gived</u> her advice. ⁴She worked hard and <u>growed</u> more confident. ⁵By the end of her freshman year, she felt she had <u>beginned</u> to win at the college game.

1. knew
2. told
3. gave
4. grew
5. begun

A Note on Three Problem Verbs

Three common irregular verbs that confuse many writers are *be, do,* and *have.* Here are the correct present tense and past tense forms of these three verbs.

	Present Tense		**Past Tense**	
Be	I am	we are	I was	we were
	you are	you are	you were	you were
	he, she, it is	they are	he, she, it was	they were
Do	I do	we do	I did	we did
	you do	you do	you did	you did
	he, she, it does	they do	he, she, it did	they did
Have	I have	we have	I had	we had
	you have	you have	you had	you had
	he, she, it has	they have	he, she it had	they had

Irregular Verbs: PRACTICE 1

Underline the mistakes in irregular verbs. Then write the correct form of the verbs in the spaces provided.

¹Zamil taked an art class that she liked very much. ²While she was taking the class, she spended hours in the library, looking through art books. ³Here she has choosed a book about African art.

1. ____took____
2. ____spent____
3. ____chosen____

¹When you can find the book you want in the library, it's great. ²But sometimes that doesn't happen. ³Sometimes the last person who borrowed it never bringed it back. ⁴Maybe he or she just forgotted to return it. ⁵Maybe the person moved away and keeped it. ⁶In any case, books sometimes do disappear from the library forever.

4. ____brought____
5. ____forgot____
6. ____kept____

¹Zamil doesn't always eat in the cafeteria. ²Today she eated there because there were grilled cheese sandwiches. ³She likes them so much that she taked two. ⁴When her friends seen her sit down, they comed over to join her for lunch.

7. ____ate____
8. ____took____
9. ____saw____
10. ____came____

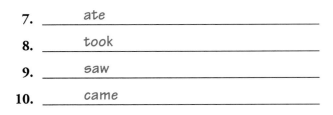

Irregular Verbs: PRACTICE 2

For each sentence below, fill in the correct form of the verb in the space provided.

broke, broken **1.** When I _____*broke*_____ my leg, my friends scribbled cheerful messages on the cast.

spended, spent **2.** Nathan _____*spent*_____ most of his teenage years dressed in black and alone in his bedroom.

catched, caught **3.** The kindergarten teacher _____*caught*_____ chicken pox from one of her students.

went, gone **4.** The sign on the barbershop door said, "Closed. I have _____*gone*_____ fishing."

wrote, writed **5.** Before he was famous, the horror author Stephen King taught high-school English and _____*wrote*_____ short stories and novels at night.

done, did **6.** When my little sister broke the living-room lamp, she told my parents that I had _____*done*_____ it.

bringed, brought **7.** Seven people _____*brought*_____ potato salad to the church picnic, and only one person made a dessert.

chose, choosed **8.** Although she was close to winning $100,000, the game-show contestant lost it all when she _____*chose*_____ the wrong answer to the final question.

drove, drived **9.** In the Fourth of July parade, the mayor _____*drove*_____ an antique Model T car that was owned by the city.

eaten, ate **10.** My friend stuck to his diet for six days. Then he _____*ate*_____ an entire gallon of ice cream and a bag of Snickers in fifteen minutes.

Irregular Verbs: PRACTICE 3

The following passage contains **ten** errors in irregular verbs. Cross out each error. Then, in the space provided, write the correct form of each verb.

¹Zamil ~~readed~~ and ~~writed~~ a lot in high school. ²Once she ~~becomed~~ a student at Haverford College, she ~~finded~~ that reading and writing were even more important in college. ³She also learned that reading in her dorm room could be difficult. ⁴Friends often ~~camed~~ by to visit her when she needed to be working. ⁵At other times, she ~~growed~~ tired working in her room. ⁶She even ~~catched~~ herself falling asleep. ⁷She ~~knowed~~ that she needed to find other places to do her school work. ⁸She ~~taked~~ her books to the library and tried studying there. ⁹The library quickly became one of her favorite places. ¹⁰It was beautiful and quiet. ¹¹She ~~getted~~ her work done more easily there. ¹²Now, you can often find Zamil hard at work in the library.

1. _____ read _____

2. _____ wrote _____

3. _____ became _____

4. _____ found _____

5. _____ came _____

6. _____ grew _____

7. _____ caught _____

8. _____ knew _____

9. _____ took _____

10. _____ got _____

Name _____ Section _____ Date _____

Score: (Number right) _____ x 10 = _____%

Irregular Verbs: TEST 1

Each of the items below contains **two** errors in irregular verbs. Find the errors and cross them out. Then, in the spaces provided, write the correct forms of the verbs.

NOTE To help you master irregular verbs, explanations are given for five of the sentences.

1. Once I ~~seen~~ a hawk dive from the top of a tall tree to capture a field mouse. The bird ~~catched~~ the tiny creature in its claws and flew back to its perch.

    a. ___saw___

    b. ___caught___

    Use the past tense of the irregular verb *see* for the first correction needed.

2. I always have ~~gave~~ my little children household chores. This month, my son sets the table, and my daughter does some dusting. Last month, they both ~~done~~ some weeding in the backyard.

    a. ___given___

    b. ___did___

    Use the past participle of the irregular verb *give* for the first correction needed.

3. My aunt ~~be~~ a big fan of Elvis Presley. Every time she hears "Love Me Tender," she becomes misty-eyed. Last year, she and my uncle ~~gone~~ on a trip to Graceland, Elvis's home. While there, she bought "Elvis Lives" bumper stickers for herself and all her friends.

    a. ___is___

    b. ___went___

    Use the past tense of the irregular verb *go* for the second correction needed.

4. It is dangerous to shake a baby. Many babies who have been ~~shook~~ have suffered brain injuries. The adults who ~~done~~ this seldom meant to cause such harm.

    a. ___shaken___

    b. ___did___

    Use the past tense of the irregular verb *do* for the second correction needed.

5. I was determined not to forget anything I needed at the store. I sat down and ~~writed~~ a long shopping list. Feeling proud of myself, I went to the store. Then I realized I had ~~forgotted~~ the list.

    a. ___wrote___

    b. ___forgotten___

    Use the past participle of the irregular verb *forget* for the second correction needed.

Name _____ Section _____ Date _____

Irregular Verbs: TEST 2

Each of the items below contains **two** errors in irregular verbs. Find the errors and cross them out. Then, in the spaces provided, write the correct forms of the verbs.

1. It really can be more fun to give than to receive. Yesterday I ~~gived~~ my sister a ring of mine that she has always loved. When she saw what I had ~~gave~~ her, her face lit up.

   a. ___gave___

   b. ___given___

2. In the winter, I drink about a quart of orange juice a week. But last week when it was so hot, I ~~drinked~~ that much in a day. Once all the orange juice was ~~drank~~, I started in on ice water and cold soda.

   a. ___drank___

   b. ___drunk___

3. I was angry that my friend ~~taked~~ the money that was lying on the dresser. She didn't know it was mine, but she ~~knowed~~ it wasn't hers.

   a. ___took___

   b. ___knew___

4. The teacher ~~becomed~~ impatient with the students who had forgotten their homework. "I thought you had ~~growed~~ up by now," he complained.

   a. ___became___

   b. ___grown___

5. Three people had ~~saw~~ the robbery take place, but no one ~~be~~ sure what the robber looked like.

   a. ___seen___

   b. ___is [OR was]___

Name _____   Section _____ Date _____

Score: (Number right) _____ x 10 = _____ %

Irregular Verbs: TEST 3

Each of the following passages contains **five** errors in irregular verbs. Cross out each error. Then, in the space provided, write the correct form of each verb.

¹Think of a time when you ~~beginned~~ something new in your life. ²Maybe it was a new school, a new job, or even a new personal relationship. ³Try to remember how you ~~feeled~~ at first. ⁴Were you nervous? ⁵Or were you confident you ~~knowed~~ what you were doing? ⁶Zamil had ~~did~~ very well in high school. ⁷But she ~~finded~~ out that college was very different. ⁸Fortunately, Zamil was willing to do the hard work of "learning the ropes" at college. ⁹Now she feels much more at home.

1. _____ began _____

2. _____ felt _____

3. _____ knew _____

4. _____ done _____

5. _____ found _____

¹"Who ~~taked~~ my food?" ²The students living on the second floor of Smith Hall ~~getted~~ used to hearing that. ³There was just one refrigerator on the floor, and many of them ~~keeped~~ snacks in it. ⁴But lately, some of that food had been disappearing. ⁵Nobody ever ~~seed~~ who took it. ⁶Some students ~~lefted~~ notes for the thief, asking her to stop. ⁷But nothing helped. ⁸Finally some students placed dead mice in brown paper bags and put them in the refrigerator. ⁹Two were stolen that night. ¹⁰After that, the thief never struck again.

6. _____ took _____

7. _____ got _____

8. _____ kept _____

9. _____ saw _____

10. _____ left _____

Name _____   Section _____ Date _____

Score: (Number right) _____ x 10 = _____%

Irregular Verbs: TEST 4

Read each sentence below. Then choose the correct verb, fill in the blank, and write the letter of your choice in the space provided in the margin.

___d___   **1.** Sandy has _____*gone*_____ to a counselor every week since her parents' divorce.
          a. went   **c.** go
          b. wented   **d.** gone

___c___   **2.** My grandmother has _____*written*_____ our family history.
          a. writed   **c.** written
          b. wrote   **d.** write

___b___   **3.** Our neighbors _____*drove*_____ us crazy when they first moved in, but now we're good friends.
          a. drived   **c.** driven
          b. drove   **d.** droved

___b___   **4.** How long have you and Stephanie _____*known*_____ each other?
          a. knew   **c.** knowed
          b. known   **d.** knewed

___c___   **5.** The lucky woman who _____*caught*_____ the home run ball got it autographed by the famous baseball player.
          a. catched   **c.** caught
          b. catch   **d.** caughted

___d___   **6.** In the middle of dinner, Stacy gasped, "I _____*forgot*_____ I was supposed to baby-sit tonight!"
          a. forget   **c.** forgotted
          b. forgotten   **d.** forgot

___b___   **7.** Trying to avoid catching a cold, everyone in the family _____*took*_____ extra vitamin C every day last winter.
          a. take   **c.** taked
          b. took   **d.** tooked

___c___   **8.** The kindergarten teacher was not thrilled when Keith _____*brought*_____ a live worm to class.
          a. bring   **c.** brought
          b. brang   **d.** bringed

___c___   **9.** The boss _____*told*_____ everyone to plan to work late Thursday night.
          a. tell   **c.** told
          b. telled   **d.** tolded

___a___   **10.** Only the people who had _____*seen*_____ the first movie understood the sequel.
          a. seen   **c.** seed
          b. saw   **d.** sawed

Name _____   Section _____   Date _____

Score: (Number right) _____ × 10 = _____%

Irregular Verbs: TEST 5

Read each sentence below. Then choose the correct verb, fill in the blank and write the letter of your choice in the space provided in the margin.

___c___   **1.** Last July, Ivan ___became___ an American citizen.
   a. become   **c.** became
   b. becomed   **d.** becamed

___d___   **2.** The tiny, cute puppy has ___grown___ into a ninety-pound monster.
   a. grow   **c.** growed
   b. grew   **d.** grown

___a___   **3.** Last night, Natalie ___spent___ nearly four hours on homework.
   a. spent   **c.** spended
   b. spends   **d.** spend

___d___   **4.** Most people who traveled to Alaska during the Gold Rush never ___found___ anything.
   a. finded   **c.** find
   b. founded   **d.** found

___b___   **5.** My father has ___done___ everything he can to keep our car in good shape.
   a. did   **c.** do
   b. done   **d.** doned

___b___   **6.** I had ___forgotten___ to do the assignment.
   a. forget   **c.** forgot
   b. forgotten   **d.** forgetted

___c___   **7.** My family had ___eaten___ the whole pie before I got home.
   a. eat   **c.** eaten
   b. ate   **d.** eated

___a___   **8.** The millionaire businessman ___left___ all his money to charity.
   a. left   **c.** lefted
   b. leave   **d.** leaved

___d___   **9.** Juanita has ___chosen___ the color gray for her bridesmaids' dresses.
   a. chose   **c.** choose
   b. choosed   **d.** chosen

___b___   **10.** The story was about a man who foolishly ___hid___ some money in an old trash barrel.
   a. hide   **c.** hided
   b. hid   **d.** hides

③ Subject-Verb Agreement

Basics about Subject-Verb Agreement

In a correctly written sentence, the subject and verb agree (match) in number. Singular subjects have singular verbs, and plural subjects have plural verbs.

In simple sentences of few words, it's not difficult to make the subject and verb agree:

● Our *baby* **sleeps** more than ten hours a day. Some *babies* **sleep** even longer.

However, not all sentences are as straightforward as the above examples. Here are two situations that can cause problems with subject-verb agreement.

WORDS BETWEEN THE SUBJECT AND VERB

A verb often comes right after its subject, as in this example:

● The sealed *boxes* **belong** to my brother.

Note Here and in the rest of the chapter, the *subject* is shown in *italic type,* and the **verb** is shown in **boldface type.**

However, at times the subject and verb are separated by a **prepositional phrase**. A prepositional phrase is a group of words that begins with a preposition and ends with a noun or pronoun. *By, for, from, in, of, on,* and *to* are common prepositions. (A longer list of prepositions is on page 226.) Look at the following sentences:

● A small *bag* of potato chips **contains** 440 calories.

   In this sentence, the subject and verb are separated by the prepositional phrase *of potato chips.* The verb must agree with the singular subject *bag*—not with a word in the prepositional phrase.

● The *tomatoes* in this salad **are** brown and mushy.

   Because the subject, *tomatoes,* is plural, the verb must also be plural. The prepositional phrase *in this salad* has no effect on subject and verb agreement.

● *Books* about baseball **fill** my son's room.

   The plural subject *books* takes the plural verb *fill. About baseball* is a prepositional phrase.

COMPOUND SUBJECTS

A **compound subject** is made up of two nouns connected by a joining word. Subjects joined by *and* generally take a plural verb.

● *Running* and *lifting* weights **are** good ways to keep in shape.

● *Fear* and *ignorance* **have** a lot to do with hatred.

Understanding Subject-Verb Agreement

The following passage contains **five** mistakes in subject-verb agreement. See if you can underline them. Then check your answers below.

¹This is Teron Ivery, a teacher at a school in Philadelphia. ²It's early in the day, and Teron has just gotten to work. ³The children in his class <u>hasn't</u> arrived yet.

⁴This is Teron's first year as a teacher. ⁵Some parts of his job still <u>surprises</u> him. ⁶For example, preparation and paperwork <u>takes</u> up more time than he expected. ⁷Those papers in Teron's hand <u>contains</u> his lesson plans for the day. ⁸Every day, Teron learns more about what it means to be a good teacher. ⁹One thing he knows is that a sense of humor and patience <u>is</u> qualities no teacher should be without.

1. The children in his class haven't arrived yet.
2. Some parts of his job still surprise him.
3. preparation and paperwork take up
4. Those papers in Teron's hand contain
5. a sense of humor and patience are

Check Your Understanding

The following passage has **five** errors in subject-verb agreement. Underline the errors. Then write the correct subject and verb in the space provided.

¹The students in Teron's class <u>is</u> very young. ²These boys and girls <u>attends</u> the school's pre-kindergarten class. ³Most of them can't read yet. ⁴But Teron and their other teachers <u>reads</u> to them every day. ⁵Being read to is one way children learn to read themselves. ⁶The boy on Teron's right <u>love</u> to read about insects. ⁷Beetles and mosquitoes <u>doesn't</u> bother him! ⁸He thinks that someday he might like to be a scientist who studies bugs.

1. The students in Teron's class are
2. These boys and girls attend
3. But Teron and their other teachers read
4. The boy on Teron's right loves
5. Beetles and mosquitoes don't

Subject-Verb Agreement: PRACTICE 1

Each of the short passages below contains errors in subject-verb agreement. Underline the errors. Then correct them in the spaces provided.

¹Recess time! ²Reading and writing <u>is</u> important parts of the school day. ³But games on the playground <u>is</u>, too. ⁴The little kids in Teron's class <u>loves</u> racing around on these scooter-boards. ⁵The exercise and fresh air <u>benefits</u> their bodies and minds.

1. <u>Reading and writing are</u>

2. <u>games on the playground are</u>

3. <u>The little kids in Teron's class love</u>

4. <u>The exercise and fresh air benefit</u>

¹It's time to head back into class. ²The smiles on the kids' faces <u>makes</u> Teron feel good. ³They remind him of why he is a teacher. ⁴Teron grew up in a poor neighborhood without his father around. ⁵Drugs and crime <u>was</u> everywhere he looked. ⁶The teachers in his own life <u>was</u> very important to him. ⁷They let him know they believed he could succeed in life. ⁸Adult support and encouragement <u>makes</u> a big difference in the life of a child. ⁹Teron wants to provide that kind of support to the children he teaches.

5. <u>The smiles on the kids' faces make</u>

6. <u>Drugs and crime were</u>

7. <u>The teachers in his own life were</u>

8. <u>Adult support and encouragement make</u>

¹Boys and girls <u>learns</u> how to be adults from observing the grownups around them. ²Teron saw lots of negative role models, such as drug dealers, as he was growing up. ³But he focused on the positive people in his life. ⁴He hopes the kids in his class <u>does</u> the same thing.

9. <u>Boys and girls learn</u>

10. <u>the kids in his class do</u>

Subject-Verb Agreement: PRACTICE 2

For each sentence below, choose the correct form of the verb from the words in the margin, and write it in the space provided.

taste, tastes   **1.** Bananas and peanut butter ____taste____ good together.

wear, wears   **2.** The members of the choir ____wear____ blue robes.

has, have   **3.** My counselor and my English instructor ____have____ agreed to write recommendations for me.

speak, speaks   **4.** Most people in this neighborhood ____speak____ Italian.

see, sees   **5.** Shantell and Justin both ____see____ better with contact lenses than they did with glasses.

surrounds, surround   **6.** Forests and lakes ____surround____ the campground.

is, are   **7.** The jokes in that movie ____are____ not at all funny.

sleep, sleeps   **8.** The cat and the dog ____sleep____ curled up together.

live, lives   **9.** Kara and her children ____live____ in a shelter.

do, does   **10.** Those piles of dirty laundry ____do____ not belong to me.

Subject-Verb Agreement: PRACTICE 3

Each of the short passages below contains **five** errors in subject-verb agreement. Underline the errors. Then correct them in the spaces provided.

¹Parents and educators sometimes <u>talks</u> about "teachable moments." ²A teachable moment can occur whenever an adult and a child <u>is</u> together. ³Here, Teron and a little girl <u>shares</u> such a moment. ⁴Teron is asking her about what she has written on the sidewalk. ⁵The number of letters in her name <u>becomes</u> a little math lesson. ⁶The color of the chalk marks <u>are</u> another mini-lesson. ⁷The little girl doesn't know she's having a "teachable moment." ⁸She just knows she's having fun.

1. Parents and educators sometimes talk
2. an adult and a child are
3. Teron and a little girl share
4. The number of letters in her name become
5. The color of the chalk marks is

¹The students in Teron's class <u>has</u> gone home, and now he can, too. ²Even though the seats on the bus <u>is</u> hard, he might fall asleep. ³A long day of little kids <u>wear</u> him out! ⁴But even when he is tired, the rewards of being a teacher <u>satisfies</u> him. ⁵He thinks teaching small children <u>are</u> the best career in the world.

6. The students in Teron's class have
7. the seats on the bus are
8. A long day of little kids wears
9. the rewards of being a teacher satisfy
10. teaching small children is

Name _____   Section _____ Date _____

Score: (Number right) _____ x 10 = _____%

Subject-Verb Agreement: TEST 1

For each sentence, fill in the correct form of the missing verb.

NOTE To help you review subject-verb agreement, explanations are given for the first two sentences.

belong, belongs   **1.** The bones in the backyard _____belong_____ to our neighbor's dog.
Bones, the subject, is a plural noun and so needs a plural verb. *In the backyard* is a prepositional phrase. The subject is never in—or affected by—a prepositional phrase.

is, are   **2.** Sunflower seeds and peanuts _____are_____ the main ingredients in this bird-food mix.
Seeds and peanuts is a compound subject requiring a plural verb.

draw, draws   **3.** Students in the art class _____draw_____ with a charcoal stick.

look, looks   **4.** The men sitting in the corner booth _____look_____ unhappy with their food.

bake, bakes   **5.** Ruby and her mother _____bake_____ cakes and cookies for a local restaurant.

play, plays   **6.** The teenager in the apartment upstairs _____plays_____ a guitar late at night.

echo, echoes   **7.** The singing of the caged canaries _____echoes_____ through the tiny pet shop.

seem, seems   **8.** The questions on this test _____seem_____ unfair to me.

is, are   **9.** E-mail and voice mail _____are_____ the only ways that some people ever communicate with each other.

attracts, attract   **10.** A colorful assortment of toys _____attracts_____ shoppers to the store's display window.

Copyright ©2005 The McGraw-Hill Companies, Inc. All rights reserved.

Name _____ Section _____ Date _____

Score: (Number right) _____ x 10 = _____ %

Subject-Verb Agreement: TEST 2

For each sentence, fill in the correct form of the missing verb.

have, has 1. The ice cubes in the punchbowl _____*have*_____ melted.

is, are 2. The old telephones in my grandparents' home _____*are*_____ still in working order.

appear, appears 3. Garlic and onions _____*appear*_____ in almost everything my grandmother cooks.

wail, wails 4. The tired, cranky baby _____*wails*_____ while his mother tries to comfort him.

belong, belongs 5. The leather cap and jacket on the desk _____*belong*_____ to our teacher.

forget, forgets 6. Members of the audience sometimes _____*forget*_____ to turn off their cell phones during a performance.

is, are 7. Goat and rabbit _____*are*_____ two of the more unusual items on the restaurant's menu.

greet, greets 8. Moans and groans _____*greet*_____ the teacher whenever she announces a pop quiz.

show, shows 9. Dirt and grease _____*show*_____ clearly on the windows when the sun shines through them.

do, does 10. Contrary to public opinion, cats and dogs _____*do*_____ not really hate each other.

Name _____   Section _____   Date _____

Score: (Number right) _____ x 10 = _____ %

Subject-Verb Agreement: TEST 3

The following passage contains **ten** errors in subject-verb agreement. Cross out each wrong verb, and write the correction above the error. The first correction has been added for you as an example.

               is

[1]The typical elementary-school teacher in most schools ~~are~~ a woman. [2]More men are

                                          remains

going into elementary teaching today, but the percentage of male teachers ~~remain~~ low. [3]One

        is   *make*

of the reasons ~~are~~ financial. [4]Men with college degrees often ~~makes~~ more money doing things

                            are

other than teaching. [5]But the stereotypes about teaching ~~is~~ at least as important. [6]Many

             consider

young men in college never ~~considers~~ elementary teaching. [7]They may assume that women

                                         are

are "just naturally better" working with young children. [8]But patience and kindness ~~is~~

qualities not found only in females. [9]Men can be wonderful elementary teachers. [10]Both the

               grow

boys and girls in their classes ~~grows~~ up knowing that men can be both strong and caring.

               learn

[11]Also, the boys in the class ~~learns~~ a lot about how to be a good father. [12]The children and

        win

the community all ~~wins~~ when there are positive male role models in the classroom.

Name _____ Section _____ Date _____

Score: (Number right) _____ x 10 = _____%

Subject-Verb Agreement: TEST 4

Read each sentence below. Then choose the correct verb, fill in the blank, and write the letter of your choice in the space provided in the margin.

__a__ 1. Our friends in the country _____get_____ rid of the insects in their yard without using poisonous sprays—they keep chickens.
a. get   **b.** gets

__a__ 2. The chickens _____eat_____ most of the insects. In addition, our friends get to enjoy fresh eggs.
a. eat   **b.** eats

__b__ 3. The children and their mother _____are_____ disappointed in the frozen dinners. The peas look wrinkled and dry.
a. is   **b.** are

__a__ 4. Also, mounds of soggy stuffing in the TV dinners ____cover____ a small piece of meat.
a. cover   **b.** covers

__a__ 5. Our kitchen is anything but quiet. The microwave and the dishwasher ____produce____ all kinds of noise.
a. produce   **b.** produces

__b__ 6. Furthermore, the refrigerator in the kitchen hums, and the clock hanging over the cabinets ____chimes____ every hour.
a. chime   **b.** chimes

__a__ 7. The coins in the jar on my dresser _____weigh_____ almost three pounds. I wonder how much money is actually there.
a. weigh   **b.** weighs

__a__ 8. Unfortunately, pennies and nickels ____make____ up most of the total in the jar.
a. make   **b.** makes

__a__ 9. The Bradleys have made their property much more attractive. Flowers and an evergreen bush now ____line____ the sidewalk.
a. line   **b.** lines

__b__ 10. Also, a birdbath near the front steps ____attracts____ robins, blue jays, and other colorful birds.
a. attract   **b.** attracts

Name _____ Section _____ Date _____

Score: (Number right) _____ x 10 = _____%

Subject-Verb Agreement: TEST 5

Read each sentence below. Then choose the correct verb, fill in the blank, and write the letter of your choice in the space provided in the margin.

___b___ **1.** Few people ever _____recall_____ seeing baby pigeons. The reason is simple.
     a. recalls   **b.** recall

___a___ **2.** Baby pigeons in the nest _____eat_____ a huge amount of food each day. Upon leaving the nest, they are nearly as large as their parents.
     a. eat   **b.** eats

___a___ **3.** The books in your book bag _____weigh_____ a ton. How can you carry them around all day?
     a. weigh   **b.** weighs

___b___ **4.** I'm afraid that book bag will hurt your back. The strain on your muscles _____is_____ enormous.
     a. are   **b.** is

___b___ **5.** Ricardo picks up his bowling ball. The pins at the end of the lane _____look_____ so defenseless. He almost feels sorry for them.
     a. looks   **b.** look

___a___ **6.** But then Ricardo releases the ball. He and his friends _____watch_____ the pins come crashing down.
     a. watch   **b.** watches

___a___ **7.** The presents under the Christmas tree _____tempt_____ the children. They want to squeeze, shake, and investigate every one.
     a. tempt   **b.** tempts

___b___ **8.** The adults _____tell_____ the children that they have to be patient.
     a. tells   **b.** tell

___a___ **9.** My friends and I _____enjoy_____ going to the movies.
     a. enjoy   **b.** enjoys

___a___ **10.** But some people in the theater really _____irritate_____ us. They talk as loudly as if they were in their own living rooms.
     a. irritate   **b.** irritates

4 Sentence Types

Basics about Sentence Types

There are three basic kinds of sentences in English:

SIMPLE SENTENCES

A **simple sentence** has only one subject-verb combination and expresses one complete thought.

- Our daughter cooked dinner tonight.
  Daughter is the subject, and *cooked* is the verb.

A simple sentence may have more than one subject or more than one verb:

- Shorts and T-shirts sway on the clothesline.
  Shorts and *T-shirts* are the two subjects; *sway* is the verb.

- The children splashed and squealed in the swimming pool.
  Children is the subject; *splashed* and *squealed* are the two verbs.

COMPOUND SENTENCES

A **compound sentence** is made up of two or more complete thoughts. Following are two complete thoughts, joined to form a compound sentence:

- Rose wants chili for dinner, but she forgot to buy beans.

By using a comma and a joining word such as *but*, we can combine what would otherwise be two simple sentences (*Rose wants chili for dinner* and *She forgot to buy beans*) into one compound sentence. In addition to *but*, the words *and* and *so* are the joining words most often used to connect two complete thoughts. Here are examples of *and* and *so* as joining words:

- The driver failed to signal, and he went through a stop sign.

- The meal was not hot, so we sent it back to the kitchen.

COMPLEX SENTENCES

A **complex sentence** is made up of one complete thought and a thought that begins with a dependent word like *after, although, as, because, before, if, since, unless, until, when, where,* and *while.*

Note A comma is placed after a dependent statement when it starts a sentence.

- Although I had a free ticket to the game, I was too tired to go.

- I set my alarm for 5 a.m. because I wanted to finish a paper.

- After the test was over, we got something to eat.

When you write, try to make your sentences varied and interesting. Using all three kinds of sentences will both help you express more complex thoughts and give your writing a lively style.

Understanding Sentence Types

Notice the different sentence types used in this passage about Vimul Ros, a Cambodian-American high-school student. Vimul's friends call him "V."

[1]Although Vimul Ros is only seventeen, he has traveled more than most people in their entire lives. [2]V's parents grew up in Cambodia. [3]They loved their country, but they had to leave upon the outset of war. [4]They fled to neighboring Thailand, where V was born. [5]After time in New York, Singapore, and Philadelphia, V is now a junior at Philadelphia's Charter School for Architecture and Design (CHAD). [6]He is at home in America, but he never wants to forget his Cambodian heritage.

Sentences 2 and 5 are simple sentences. Sentences 3 and 6 are compound sentences. Sentences 1 and 4 are complex sentences.

Check Your Understanding

Combine each group of simple sentences below into a compound or a complex sentence. Write your answers in the spaces provided. Use each of the following words in this order: **and, before, but, because,** and **so.**

1. V is excited about going to college. He is thinking carefully about where to apply.

   V is excited about going to college, and he is
   thinking carefully about where to apply.

2. He enrolled at CHAD. V attended another high school.

   Before he enrolled at CHAD, V attended another
   high school.

3. He did not work hard. He still made all A's.

   He did not work hard, but he still made all A's.

4. He felt bored and unhappy. His adviser encouraged him to find another school.

   Because he felt bored and unhappy, his adviser encouraged him to find another
   school.

5. V is interested in graphic design. CHAD is a good school for him.

   V is interested in graphic design, so CHAD is a good school for him.

Sentence Types: PRACTICE 1

Combine each group of simple sentences below into a compound or a complex sentence. Write your sentences in the spaces provided. Use each of the following words in this order: **because, and, so, but,** and **if**.

1. V has never seen Cambodia. He relies on his parents to tell him about it.

2. V's mother shares memories with her children. She also shows them sites such as the Cambodian temple in the picture.

3. "My parents want me to understand my background. They try all kinds of stuff."

4. "They put me in a group to learn Cambodian folk dance. I was really bad at that."

5. V has children of his own some day. He will want them to learn about the Cambodian culture.

1.   Because V has never seen Cambodia, he relies on his parents to tell him about it.

2.   V's mother shares memories with her children, and she also shows them sites such as the Cambodian temple in the picture.

3.   "My parents want me to understand my background, so they try all kinds of stuff."

4.   "They put me in a group to learn Cambodian folk dance, but I was really bad at that."

5.   If V has children of his own some day, he will want them to learn about the Cambodian culture.

Combine each group of simple sentences below into a compound or a complex sentence. Write your sentences in the spaces provided. Use each of the following words in this order: **when, because, and, after,** and **so**.

6. V's father returned to Cambodia. V enrolled in elementary school.
   When V's father returned to Cambodia, V enrolled in elementary school.

7. Cambodia is a poor and troubled country. It needs educated people like Mr. Ros.
   Because Cambodia is a poor and troubled country, it needs educated people like Mr. Ros.

8. Mr. Ros sees his family only about once a year. They miss him very much.
   Mr. Ros sees his family only about once a year, and they miss him very much.

9. His father left the United States. V lost interest in school for a while.
   After his father left the United States, V lost interest in school for a while.

10. V realized he was endangering his own future. He made himself start working again.
    V realized he was endangering his own future, so he made himself start working again.

Sentence Types: PRACTICE 2

A. Use a comma and a logical joining word to combine the following pairs of simple sentences into compound sentences. Choose from **and, but,** or **so**. Place a comma before the joining word.

> **HINT** Be sure to choose the logical joining word in each case. Keep in mind that
> **and** means *in addition*
> **but** means *however*
> **so** means *as a result*

Some answers may vary.

1. Kwan is quite attractive. She sees herself as ugly.
   Kwan is quite attractive, but she sees herself as ugly.

2. Jared is good at math. He writes well, too.
   Jared is good at math, and he writes well, too.

3. I lost my watch. I don't know what time it is.
   I lost my watch, so I don't know what time it is.

4. The book is four hundred pages long. The print is very small.
   The book is four hundred pages long, and the print is very small.

5. The night air was chilly. I put on a sweater.
   The night air was chilly, so I put on a sweater.

B. Use a suitable dependent word to combine the following pairs of simple sentences into complex sentences. Choose from **although, because, since,** and **when**. Place a comma after a dependent statement when it starts a sentence.

6. Strawberries are expensive. I don't often buy them.
   Because strawberries are expensive, I don't often buy them.

7. An elephant's skin is very thick. It is also very sensitive.
   Although an elephant's skin is very thick, it is also very sensitive.

8. The city pools have been crowded. The weather turned hot.
   The city pools have been crowded since the weather turned hot.

9. I quickly called the police. I heard a scream outside.
   I quickly called the police when I heard a scream outside.

10. Jessica seems unfriendly. She is really just shy.
    Although Jessica seems unfriendly, she is really just shy.

Sentence Types: PRACTICE 3

Combine each group of simple sentences below into a compound or a complex sentence. Use each of the following words in this order: **but, when, although, and**.

1. V's father cannot be with his family. They are proud of him.

2. He was living in the United States. He wrote two books for children, including *Brother Rabbit*.

3. Brother Rabbit is just a little bunny. He outwits a dangerous crocodile.

4. In a second book, *The Two Brothers*, one brother becomes rich. The other becomes king of Cambodia.

1. V's father cannot be with his family, but they are proud of him.

2. When he was living in the United States, he wrote two books for children, including Brother Rabbit.

3. Although Brother Rabbit is just a little bunny, he outwits a dangerous crocodile.

4. In a second book, The Two Brothers, one brother becomes rich, and the other becomes king of Cambodia.

Combine each group of simple sentences below into a compound or a complex sentence. Use each of the following words in this order: **because, although, but, and, if, since**.

5. V was born into one culture but raised in another. He has a foot in two worlds.

6. He lives surrounded by souvenirs of Cambodia. He wears a sweatshirt from a college in New Hampshire.

7. He is involved in Cambodian youth organizations. He is friends with "all kinds of people."

8. He doesn't pay attention to people's color. His Asian, black, white, and Hispanic friends are proof of this.

9. V gets a chance to travel to Cambodia some day. He would like to be of help there.

10. He was a little boy. V has seen himself as a citizen of the world.

5. Because V was born into one culture but raised in another, he has a foot in two worlds.

6. Although he lives surrounded by souvenirs of Cambodia, he wears a sweatshirt from a college in New Hampshire.

7. He is involved in Cambodian youth organizations, but he is friends with "all kinds of people."

8. He doesn't pay attention to people's color, and his Asian, black, white, and Hispanic friends are proof of this.

9. If V gets a chance to travel to Cambodia some day, he would like to be of help there.

10. Since he was a little boy, V has seen himself as a citizen of the world.

Name _____   Section _____   Date _____

Score: (Number right) _____ x 10 = _____ %

Sentence Types: TEST 1

A. Use a comma and a suitable joining word to combine the following pairs of simple sentences into compound sentences. Choose from **and** (which means *in addition*), **but** (which means *however*), or **so** (which means *as a result*).

NOTE To help you master sentence combining, hints are given for the first two sentences.

Some answers may vary.

1. The coffee is cold. It is also too strong.
   The coffee is cold; *in addition*, it is also too strong.
   The coffee is cold, and it is also too strong.

2. Our car runs well. Its body is dented and rusty.
   Our car runs well; *however*, its body is dented and rusty.
   Our car runs well, but its body is dented and rusty.

3. The book was very expensive. I didn't buy it.
   The book was very expensive, so I didn't buy it.

4. Gene laughed throughout the movie. His date didn't laugh once.
   Gene laughed throughout the movie, but his date didn't laugh once.

5. The electricity was out. We had no candles.
   The electricity was out, and we had no candles.

B. Use a suitable dependent word to combine the following pairs of simple sentences into complex sentences. Choose from **although, because, since**, and **when**. Place a comma after a dependent statement when it starts a sentence.

6. The ball game was postponed. It began to rain heavily.
   The ball game was postponed because it began to rain heavily.

7. Sam practices his saxophone. The dog howls.
   When Sam practices his saxophone, the dog howls.

8. The house looks beautiful. It seems cold and unfriendly to me.
   Although the house looks beautiful, it seems cold and unfriendly to me.

9. She doesn't drive. Mia must walk or take the bus to work.
   Since she doesn't drive, Mia must walk or take the bus to work.

10. The beautiful fireworks exploded. The audience gasped and applauded.
   When the beautiful fireworks exploded, the audience gasped and applauded.

Name _____ Section _____ Date _____

Score: (Number right) _____ x 10 = _____ %

Sentence Types: TEST 2

A. Use a comma and a suitable joining word to combine the following pairs of simple sentences into compound sentences. Choose from **and, but,** or **so.**   *Some answers may vary.*

1. Eddie was tired of his appearance. He shaved all the hair off his head.

   Eddie was tired of his appearance, so he shaved all the hair off his head.

2. Eddie bought new clothing in bright colors. He added an earring as well.

   Eddie bought new clothing in bright colors, and he added an earring as well.

3. Twenty students were enrolled in the class. Only eight were present that stormy day.

   Twenty students were enrolled in the class, but only eight were present that stormy day.

4. Thirty percent of M&M's are brown. Twenty percent of them are red.

   Thirty percent of M&M's are brown, and twenty percent of them are red.

5. The stain did not wash out of my white pants. I dyed the pants tan.

   The stain did not wash out of my white pants, so I dyed the pants tan.

B. Use a suitable dependent word to combine the following pairs of simple sentences into complex sentences. Choose from **although, because, since,** and **when.** Place a comma after a dependent statement when it starts a sentence.

6. I need to improve my grades. I will start taking more notes in class.

   Because I need to improve my grades, I will start taking more notes in class.

7. There used to be many small stores downtown. They are gone now.

   Although there used to be many small stores downtown, they are gone now.

8. The bus came into sight. Connie shouted "Goodbye!" and rushed out the door.

   When the bus came into sight, Connie shouted "Goodbye!" and rushed out the door.

9. Mental illness is so little understood. It has always frightened people.

   Since mental illness is so little understood, it has always frightened people.

10. I'm allergic to most animals. Siamese cats don't bother me.

    Although I'm allergic to most animals, Siamese cats don't bother me.

Name _____ Section _____ Date _____

Score: (Number right) _____ x 10 = _____%

Sentence Types: TEST 3

Combine each group of simple sentences into compound or complex sentences. Combine the first two sentences into one sentence, and combine the last two sentences into another sentence. Use any of the following joining words and dependent words.

Joining words	**and**	**but**	**so**	
Dependent words	**after**	**although**	**because**	**when**

> **Two comma hints**
> 1   Use a comma between two complete thoughts joined by **and, but,** or **so**.
> 2   Place a comma after a dependent statement when it starts a sentence.

Some answers may vary.

1. It had rained for three days. The sun finally came out.

   We wanted to have a picnic. The ground was too wet.

   After it had rained for three days, the sun finally came out.

   We wanted to have a picnic, but the ground was too wet.

2. Roy saw a bright rainbow. He ran to get his camera.

   He rushed back to take a picture. The rainbow had gone.

   Roy saw a bright rainbow, so he ran to get his camera.

   When he rushed back to take a picture, the rainbow had gone.

3. A long-winded neighbor was at my door. I pretended not to be home.

   She rang the bell several times. She knocked on the door repeatedly.

   Because a long-winded neighbor was at my door, I pretended not to be home.

   She rang the bell several times, and she knocked on the door repeatedly.

4. Nadine hates her job. She won't leave it.

   She likes the pension plan. She will stay until retirement.

   Although Nadine hates her job, she won't leave it.

   She likes the pension plan, so she will stay until retirement.

5. I had to meet my girlfriend's mother. I was very nervous.

   I was afraid of her opinion of me. She was very warm and friendly.

   When I had to meet my girlfriend's mother, I was very nervous.

   I was afraid of her opinion of me, but she was very warm and friendly.

Name _____ Section _____ Date _____

Score: (Number right) _____ x 10 = _____%

Sentence Types: TEST 4

In the space provided, write the letter of the combined sentence that reads most smoothly, clearly, and logically.

_c_ **1. a.** Because my parents are both quite short, we kids are all on the tall side.
    b. My parents are both quite short, so we kids are all on the tall side.
    c. Although my parents are both quite short, we kids are all on the tall side.

_c_ **2. a.** My cousin was falling behind in algebra class, but he decided to work with a tutor.
    b. My cousin was falling behind in algebra class because he decided to work with a tutor.
    c. Because my cousin was falling behind in algebra class, he decided to work with a tutor.

_c_ **3. a.** The thunderstorm rattled the windows, but the dog hid in the closet.
    b. Although the thunderstorm rattled the windows, the dog hid in the closet.
    c. While the thunderstorm rattled the windows, the dog hid in the closet.

_a_ **4. a.** The movie turned out to be too scary, so I took the children home.
    b. The movie turned out to be too scary, but I took the children home.
    c. Although the movie turned out to be too scary, I took the children home.

_a_ **5. a.** Although the baby goat was cute and fluffy, it had a vicious temper.
    b. The baby goat was cute and fluffy, and it had a vicious temper.
    c. Because the baby goat was cute and fluffy, it had a vicious temper.

_b_ **6. a.** Nobody was very hungry Thanksgiving night, but we ate cereal for dinner.
    b. Nobody was very hungry Thanksgiving night, so we ate cereal for dinner.
    c. Nobody was very hungry Thanksgiving night because we ate cereal for dinner.

_b_ **7. a.** The mechanic called about our car, so he didn't have good news.
    b. When the mechanic called about our car, he didn't have good news.
    c. Before the mechanic called about our car, he didn't have good news.

_a_ **8. a.** Alan is limping badly because he twisted his ankle playing basketball.
    b. Because Alan is limping badly, he twisted his ankle playing basketball.
    c. Alan is limping badly, and he twisted his ankle playing basketball.

_a_ **9. a.** Before I met my new neighbor, I had never been friends with a blind person.
    b. I met my new neighbor, but I had never been friends with a blind person.
    c. I met my new neighbor, so I had never been friends with a blind person.

_c_ **10. a.** You put masking tape around the windows and doors, but I'll get the paint and brushes.
    b. Although you put masking tape around the windows and doors, I'll get the paint and brushes.
    c. While you put masking tape around the windows and doors, I'll get the paint and brushes.

Name _____ Section _____ Date _____

Score: (Number right) _____ x 10 = _____ %

Sentence Types: TEST 5

In the space provided, write the letter of the combined sentence that reads most smoothly, clearly, and logically.

_c_   **1. a.** After I have an exam in the morning, I'd better get to bed early.
        b. Although I have an exam in the morning, I'd better get to bed early.
        c. I have an exam in the morning, so I'd better get to bed early.

_c_   **2. a.** Because these shoes are comfortable, their price is reasonable.
        b. These shoes are comfortable, but their price is reasonable.
        c. These shoes are comfortable, and their price is reasonable.

_b_   **3. a.** Although the clothes were being washed, we sat in the laundromat reading magazines.
        b. While the clothes were being washed, we sat in the laundromat reading magazines.
        c. The clothes were being washed, but we sat in the laundromat reading magazines.

_b_   **4. a.** I am afraid of heights, and flying in an airplane doesn't bother me.
        b. Although I am afraid of heights, flying in an airplane doesn't bother me.
        c. Because I am afraid of heights, flying in an airplane doesn't bother me.

_a_   **5. a.** After rain began falling heavily, the umpires cancelled the game.
        b. Although rain began falling heavily, the umpires cancelled the game.
        c. Rain began falling heavily while the umpires cancelled the game.

_c_   **6. a.** When I always hang up on telemarketers, they keep calling.
        b. Because I always hang up on telemarketers, they keep calling.
        c. Although I always hang up on telemarketers, they keep calling.

_a_   **7. a.** When my mother was a young girl, she quit school to help support her family.
        b. Because my mother was a young girl, she quit school to help support her family.
        c. My mother was a young girl, so she quit school to help support her family.

_c_   **8. a.** The towels look soft and fluffy, so they feel scratchy.
        b. When the towels look soft and fluffy, they feel scratchy.
        c. Although the towels look soft and fluffy, they feel scratchy.

_b_   **9. a.** We went to a movie last night until we stopped for ice cream.
        b. After we went to a movie last night, we stopped for ice cream.
        c. We went to a movie last night, but we stopped for ice cream.

_a_   **10. a.** The newlyweds are trying to save money, so they clip coupons and buy items on sale.
        b. Although the newlyweds are trying to save money, they clip coupons and buy items on sale.
        c. The newlyweds are trying to save money, but they clip coupons and buy items on sale.

⑤ Fragments I

Basics about Fragments

To be a complete sentence, a group of words must contain a subject and a verb. It must also express a complete thought. If it lacks a subject, verb, or a complete thought, it is a **fragment**.

The most common kind of fragment is the **dependent-word fragment**, which has a subject and verb but does not express a complete thought. Here is an example:

● Because Laura was tired.

Although this word group contains a subject (*Laura*) and a verb (*was*), it is an incomplete thought. The reader wants to know **what happened** because Laura was tired. A word group that begins with *because* or another dependent word cannot stand alone; another idea is needed to complete the thought. For example, we could correct the above fragment like this:

● Because Laura was tired, **she took a nap**.
  The words *she took a nap* complete the thought.

Here are two more dependent-word fragments.

● When the man pointed the gun at us.

● After I turned off the television set.

Each of these word groups begins with a dependent word (*when, after*) and expresses an incomplete idea. See if you can add words to each fragment that would complete the thought.

● When the man pointed the gun at us, _____.

● _____ after I turned off the television set.

Here are some ways to complete the above fragments:

● When the man pointed the gun at us, **we gave him our money**.

● **I picked up a book** after I turned off the television set.

Punctuation note When a dependent-word group starts a sentence, follow it with a comma.

When you use a dependent word, take care that you complete the thought in the same sentence. Otherwise, a fragment may result. Here is a list of common dependent words:

after	even though	unless	wherever
although	even when	until	whether
as	if	what	which
because	since	when	while
before	that	whenever	who
even if	though	where	

Note that very often the way to correct a dependent-word fragment will be to connect it to the sentence that comes before or after it.

Understanding Fragments

The following passage about Donna Atkinson, a wife, mother, college student, and jobholder, contains **five** dependent-word fragments. See if you can underline the five fragments. Then look at how they are corrected.

¹Although Donna is a wife and mother. ²She is also a college student. ³She wants to be an elementary teacher. ⁴When she has earned her degree. ⁵Since she is very busy with her son, her husband, her job, and her other duties. ⁶She has decided to take college courses online, using her computer. ⁷She is happy with her decision. ⁸Because she does not have to travel to campus. ⁹In order to take her classes, she reads assignments from her textbooks and then reads lectures online. ¹⁰She has the option of taking tests online. ¹¹She is even able to ask her instructor questions. ¹²Which she can do using e-mail.

1. Although Donna is a wife and mother, she is also a college student.

2. She wants to be an elementary teacher when she has earned her degree.

3. Since she is very busy with her son, her husband, her job, and her other duties, she has decided to take college courses online, using her computer.

4. She is happy with her decision because she does not have to travel to campus.

5. She is even able to ask her instructor questions, which she can do using e-mail.

Check Your Understanding

Underline the **five** dependent-word fragments. Then correct them in the spaces provided.

¹Before she goes to bed at night, Donna gets ready for the next day. ²Which will begin very early. ³She will get up before sunrise. ⁴Even if she stays up late studying. ⁵She wakes up so early because she has her own office-cleaning business. ⁶She does the cleaning jobs early in the morning. ⁷Before the employees arrive at the office. ⁸In the evening, she makes sure she has all her supplies together. ⁹Because she doesn't want to forget anything. ¹⁰Donna can't do everything she needs to do. ¹¹Unless she is well organized.

1. Before she goes to bed at night, Donna gets ready for the next day, which will begin very early.

2. She will get up before sunrise, even if she stays up late studying.

3. She does the cleaning jobs early in the morning before the employees arrive at the office.

4. In the evening, she makes sure she has all her supplies together because she doesn't want to forget anything.

5. Donna can't do everything she needs to do unless she is well organized.

Fragments I: PRACTICE 1

Each of the short passages below contains dependent-word fragments. Underline each fragment. Then correct it on or above the line, crossing out unneeded periods, replacing unneeded capital letters with lowercase letters, and so on.

[1]After Donna returns from her cleaning ~~jobs. [2]It's~~ time to study.
jobs, it's

[3]Fortunately, it's a beautiful ~~day. [4]Which~~ makes it nice to read on the
day, which

porch. [5]Today she will prepare for an algebra test. [6]When her son

and husband get ~~home. [7]The~~ family will have dinner together.
home, the

[8]Donna will then study some ~~more. [9]Until~~ it is time to go to bed.
more until

[1]Although it's hard to work and go to school at the same ~~time. [2]Many~~ people do it. [3]They get up
time, many

early and stay up ~~late. [4]Until~~ they've finished all their work. [5]It's amazing what people can
late until

~~accomplish. [6]When~~ they are determined.
accomplish when

[1]After she gets ~~home. [2]Donna~~ has to do some more
home, Donna

cleaning up. [3]Her son John Paul and his friends have left

toys on the ~~floor. [4]Even~~ though they said the room was fine.
floor even

[5]Children often see a room as neat and ~~clean. [6]When~~ it still
clean when

looks messy to an adult.

Fragments I: PRACTICE 2

Underline the dependent-word fragment in each of the following items. Then correct it in the space provided. Add a comma after a dependent-word group that begins a sentence.

1. Because the movie was so violent. Some people left the theater.

Because the movie was so violent, some people left the theater.

2. Everything was peaceful. Before Martha stormed into the room.

Everything was peaceful before Martha stormed into the room.

3. Unless the refrigerator is fixed soon. All the food will spoil.

Unless the refrigerator is fixed soon, all the food will spoil.

4. The batter argued with the umpire. While the crowd booed.

The batter argued with the umpire while the crowd booed.

5. When two guests began to argue. The hostess moved the party outside.

When two guests began to argue, the hostess moved the party outside.

6. After he bought some donuts. Virgil hurried to school.

After he bought some donuts, Virgil hurried to school.

7. We jumped up from the sofa. When we heard the crash in the kitchen.

We jumped up from the sofa when we heard the crash in the kitchen.

8. Although the car was totaled. The passengers were unharmed.

Although the car was totaled, the passengers were unharmed.

9. Classes ended early today. Because of a leak in the water main.

Classes ended early today because of a leak in the water main.

10. Our neighbor is a quiet man. Who works as a nurse on a night shift.

Our neighbor is a quiet man who works as a nurse on a night shift.

Fragments I: PRACTICE 3

Each passage below contains **five** dependent-word fragments. Underline each fragment. Then correct it on or above the line, crossing out unneeded periods, replacing unneeded capital letters with lowercase letters, and so on.

¹When Donna's son John Paul was ~~born.~~ *born, a* ²~~A~~ friend gave the family a book. ³It was *The Read-Aloud Handbook. Handbook, which* ⁴~~Which~~ was written by Jim Trelease. ⁵The book explains why reading aloud to a child is so ~~important.~~ *important even* ⁶~~Even~~ if the child is very young. ⁷It says that children who are read to become better readers themselves. ⁸It also provides a long list of good stories and books. ⁹Because Donna and her husband Tom took the book's message ~~seriously.~~ *seriously, they* ¹⁰~~They~~ began to read out loud to John Paul every day. ¹¹Now John Paul is a second-grader who loves to read. ¹²Here he is reading the latest Harry Potter book. ¹³If Tom and Donna could give other parents one important ~~message.~~ *message, it* ¹⁴~~It~~ would be, "Read to your kids."

¹Even when her days are ~~busy.~~ *busy, Donna* ²~~Donna~~ finds time to play with John Paul. ³Here they are in their backyard. ⁴In the yard is an aboveground ~~pool.~~ *pool that* ⁵~~That~~ has a little "beach." ⁶The beach was made by John Paul's dad, Tom. ⁷The neighborhood children often come over to play, and Donna and Tom like that even though sand ends up in the pool. ⁸Until John Paul and his friends are a little ~~older.~~ *older, Tom* ⁹~~Tom~~ will rebuild the beach every summer. ¹⁰After their son is bigger in a few ~~years.~~ *years, Tom* ¹¹~~Tom~~ and Donna will probably replace the beach with a deck. ¹²But right now they have the only beach on the ~~street.~~ *street, which* ¹³~~Which~~ John Paul certainly enjoys.

Name _____ Section _____ Date _____

Score: (Number right) _____ x 10 = _____ %

Fragments I: TEST 1

Underline the dependent-word fragment in each of the following items. Then correct it in the space provided. Add a comma after a dependent-word group that begins a sentence.

NOTE To help you correct fragments, directions are given for the first two sentences.

1. <u>Because we have smoke detectors.</u> We survived the fire.
    The first word group begins with the dependent word *because*.
    Correct the fragment by adding it to the second word group.

    Because we have smoke detectors, we survived the fire.

2. The kitchen looked like new. <u>After we painted it.</u>
    The second word group begins with the dependent word *after*.
    Correct the fragment by adding it to the first word group.

    The kitchen looked like new after we painted it.

3. My sister is always out of money. <u>Although she has a good job.</u>

    My sister is always out of money although she has a good job.

4. <u>Before the game even started.</u> I could tell team morale was low.

    Before the game even started, I could tell team morale was low.

5. I wouldn't date him again. <u>If he begged me on his knees.</u>

    I wouldn't date him again if he begged me on his knees.

6. Our car is making a chugging noise. <u>That sounds ominous.</u>

    Our car is making a chugging noise that sounds ominous.

7. Young elephants stay with their mothers. <u>Until they are about sixteen years old.</u>

    Young elephants stay with their mothers until they are about sixteen years old.

8. <u>After this rain stops.</u> The children can play outside.

    After this rain stops, the children can play outside.

9. A crowd showed up to meet the author. <u>Who had written a best-selling novel at the age of nineteen.</u>

    A crowd showed up to meet the author who had written a best-selling novel at the age of nineteen.

10. <u>Until the tornado warning ended.</u> Everyone stayed in the basement.

    Until the tornado warning ended, everyone stayed in the basement.

Name _____ Section _____ Date _____

Score: (Number right) _____ x 10 = _____ %

Fragments I: TEST 2

Underline the dependent-word fragment in each of the following items. Then correct it in the space provided. Add a comma after a dependent-word group that begins a sentence.

1. Although the sign said "No Parking." A rude driver parked there.

   Although the sign said "No Parking," a rude driver parked there.

2. I'll never be ready for the test tomorrow. Even if I study all night.

   I'll never be ready for the test tomorrow even if I study all night.

3. Because pearls are quite soft. They are easily scratched.

   Because pearls are quite soft, they are easily scratched.

4. I wasn't able to sleep. Until I found out how the book ended.

   I wasn't able to sleep until I found out how the book ended.

5. People at the movie house screamed. When the monster appeared.

   People at the movie house screamed when the monster appeared.

6. After running a block to catch his bus. Mack missed it by seconds.

   After running a block to catch his bus, Mack missed it by seconds.

7. We all have a few pet peeves. Which especially irritate us.

   We all have a few pet peeves which especially irritate us.

8. You won't enjoy dinner. Unless you like burned chicken and soggy beans.

   You won't enjoy dinner unless you like burned chicken and soggy beans.

9. If the weather is bad tomorrow. We'll have to reschedule the reunion.

   If the weather is bad tomorrow, we'll have to reschedule the reunion.

10. When the huge dog rushed up to him. Troy almost stopped breathing.

    When the huge dog rushed up to him, Troy almost stopped breathing.

Name _____ Section _____ Date _____

Score: (Number right) _____ x 10 = _____%

Fragments I: TEST 3

Each passage below contains **five** dependent-word fragments. Underline each fragment. Then correct it on or above the line, crossing out unneeded periods, replacing unneeded capital letters with lowercase letters, and so on.

twenties, many
¹Although most college students are in their teens or ~~twenties. ²Many~~ are a good deal older.

younger, they
³Such people are often called "nontraditional students." ⁴When they were ~~younger. ⁵They~~ may

have been too busy raising children to attend college. ⁶Or maybe they have decided that going to

college would be good for their careers. ⁷Going to school as a "nontraditional" student has its own

difficulties which
~~difficulties. ⁸Which~~ often include a job and family duties. ⁹But older adults generally do very well

school because   sacrifices, they
in ~~school. ¹⁰Because~~ they have strong goals. ¹¹Even if it means making personal ~~sacrifices. ¹²They~~

are willing to do whatever it takes to get an education.

invented, a
¹Since the Internet was ~~invented. ²A~~ real social revolution has taken place. ³That revolution

has affected many of our lives. ⁴Going shopping in stores is a thing of the past for some

people who
~~people. ⁵Who~~ now order clothing, books, and supplies online. ⁶Because e-mail is so fast and

easy, some
~~easy. ⁷Some~~ people don't use the telephone anymore. ⁸Through online chat rooms, people form

other even
close relationships with each ~~other. ⁹Even~~ though they've never met. ¹⁰Before the "computer

place, none
revolution" took ~~place. ¹¹None~~ of these things would have been possible.

Name _____ Section _____ Date _____

Fragments I: TEST 4

Read each group below. Then write the letter of the item that contains a fragment.

_____c_____ **1. a.** Leon was very nervous. He had not studied for the exam. A failing grade could result in his failing the course.

        b. Leon was very nervous because he had not studied for the exam. A failing grade could result in his failing the course.

        c. Because Leon had not studied for the exam. He was very nervous. A failing grade could result in his failing the course.

_____a_____ **2. a.** In 1969, the Oscar for Best Actor went to John Wayne. Who had appeared in nearly 250 movies by then.

        b. In 1969, the Oscar for Best Actor went to John Wayne. He had appeared in nearly 250 movies by then.

        c. In 1969, the Oscar for Best Actor went to John Wayne, who had appeared in nearly 250 movies by then.

_____b_____ **3. a.** Before Tracy went to the party, she tried on six different outfits. She finally chose the one she'd tried on first.

        b. Before Tracy went to the party. She tried on six different outfits. She finally chose the one she'd tried on first.

        c. Tracy tried on six different outfits before she went to the party. She finally chose the one she'd tried on first.

_____a_____ **4. a.** On our drive into the city, we came across an accident. Which had closed three of the four lanes of traffic. It added an extra hour to our trip.

        b. On our drive into the city, we came across an accident which had closed three of the four lanes of traffic. It added an extra hour to our trip.

        c. On our drive into the city, we came across an accident. It had closed three of the four lanes of traffic, and it added an extra hour to our trip.

_____a_____ **5. a.** Unless you are ready to work hard. Don't even think of enrolling in Dr. Reynold's class. She is a very demanding teacher.

        b. Don't even think of enrolling in Dr. Reynold's class unless you are ready to work hard. She is a very demanding teacher.

        c. Unless you are ready to work hard, don't even think of enrolling in Dr. Reynold's class. She is a very demanding teacher.

Name _____ Section _____ Date _____

Score: (Number right) _____ x 20 = _____%

Fragments I: TEST 5

Read each group below. Then write the letter of the item that contains a fragment.

___a___ **1. a.** When a flock of birds is resting in the trees. One seems to act as the lookout. If it sees danger, it will alert the others to fly away.

        b. When a flock of birds is resting in the trees, one seems to act as the lookout. If it sees danger, it will alert the others to fly away.

        c. A flock of birds is resting in the trees, with one acting as the lookout. If it sees danger, it will alert the others to fly away.

___b___ **2. a.** Karen hung a big mirror at the end of her living room because it made the room look larger. She painted the dark walls a light color for the same reason.

        b. Karen hung a big mirror at the end of her living room. Because it made the room look larger. She painted the dark walls a light color for the same reason.

        c. Because it made the room look larger, Karen hung a big mirror at the end of her living room. She painted the dark walls a light color for the same reason.

___a___ **3. a.** Our dog loves to retrieve sticks. He will beg you to throw them for hours. Even if it's clear that he is exhausted.

        b. Our dog loves to retrieve sticks. He will beg you to throw them for hours even if it's clear that he is exhausted.

        c. Our dog loves to retrieve sticks. Even if it's clear that he is exhausted, he will beg you to throw them for hours.

___c___ **4. a.** Unless Nate apologizes, I am not going to speak to him again. What he said was unforgivable.

        b. I am not going to speak to Nate again unless he apologizes. What he said was unforgivable.

        c. Unless Nate apologizes. I am not going to speak to him again because what he said was unforgivable.

___c___ **5. a.** The police believed the witness until she picked the wrong person out of a lineup. Then they began to have their doubts about her story.

        b. Until the witness picked the wrong person out of a lineup, the police believed her. Then they began to have their doubts about her story.

        c. The police believed the witness. Until she picked the wrong person out of a lineup. Then they began to have their doubts about her story.

6 Fragments II

More about Fragments

In addition to dependent-word fragments, there are three other common types of fragments:

FRAGMENTS WITHOUT A SUBJECT

Some fragments do have a verb, but lack a subject.

Fragment	Joe Davis lowered himself from the van into his wheelchair. And then rolled up the sidewalk ramp.
	The second word group lacks a subject, so it is a fragment.

You can often fix such a fragment by adding it to the sentence that comes before it.

Sentence	Joe Davis lowered himself from the van into his **wheelchair and** then rolled up the sidewalk ramp.

–*ING* AND *TO* FRAGMENTS

When *-ing* appears at or near the beginning of a word group, a fragment may result.

Fragment	Hoping to furnish their new home cheaply. The newlyweds go to garage sales.
	The first word group lacks both a subject and a verb, so it is a fragment.

A fragment may also result when a word group begins with *to* followed by a verb:

Fragment	Leo jogged through the park. To clear his mind before the midterm.
	The second word group is a fragment that lacks both a subject and a complete verb. (A word that follows *to* cannot be the verb of a sentence.)

You can often fix such fragments by attaching them to the sentence that comes before or after.

Sentence	Hoping to furnish their new home **cheaply, the** newlyweds go to garage sales.
Sentence	Leo jogged through the **park to** clear his mind before the midterm.

Punctuation note When an *-ing* or *to* word group starts a sentence, follow it with a comma.

EXAMPLE FRAGMENTS

Word groups that begin with words like *including, such as, especially,* and *for example* are sometimes fragments.

Fragment	For class, we had to read several books. Including *The Diary of Anne Frank.*
Fragment	My grandfather has many interests. For example, playing poker and watching old cowboy movies.

You can often fix such fragments by attaching them to the sentence that comes before, or by adding a subject and a verb.

Sentence	For class we had to read several **books, including** *The Diary of Anne Frank.*
Sentence	My grandfather has many interests. For example, **he plays** poker and **watches** old cowboy movies.

Understanding Fragments

The following passage about Charlene Clarke, a single parent and student living in rural Virginia, contains five fragments. See if you can find and underline the five fragments. Then look at how they are corrected.

¹This is Charlene Clarke. ²Taking a moment to relax with her Boston terrier, Diamond. ³Charlene doesn't have a lot of time to do things she enjoys. ⁴Such as playing with her dog. ⁵Working on her degree at the local business college. ⁶She has a great deal of reading and studying to do. ⁷In addition, she has other responsibilities. ⁸Especially as the mother of four active young children. ⁹There are plenty of days that Charlene feels overwhelmed. ¹⁰But knows she must keep on going.

1. This is Charlene Clarke, taking a moment to relax with her Boston terrier, Diamond.

2. Charlene doesn't have a lot of time to do things she enjoys, such as playing with her dog.

3. Working on her degree at the local business college, she has a great deal of reading and studying to do.

4. In addition, she has other responsibilities, especially as the mother of four active young children.

5. There are plenty of days that Charlene feels overwhelmed but knows she must keep on going.

Check Your Understanding

Underline the **five** fragments in the following passage. Then correct them in the spaces provided.

¹Charlene is studying to become a pharmacy technician. ²She has to learn some very challenging material. ³Such as the names of dozens of drugs and medical disorders. ⁴Sometimes Charlene is amazed to find herself in school at all. ⁵Considering how much she disliked school as a child. ⁶She had trouble reading and spelling. ⁷And was in special ed until seventh grade. ⁸She has never forgotten how cruel other students could be. ⁹Calling her names and making fun of her. ¹⁰But she worked hard on her reading skills. ¹¹And was able to get back into regular classes. ¹²Now she is earning A's and B's in school. ¹³She even works part-time in the school library.

Methods of correction may vary.

1. She has to learn some very challenging material, such as the names of dozens of drugs and medical disorders.

2. Sometimes Charlene is amazed to find herself in school at all, considering how much she disliked school as a child.

3. She had trouble reading and spelling and was in special ed until seventh grade.

4. She has never forgotten how cruel other students could be. They called her names and made fun of her.

5. But she worked hard on her reading skills and was able to get back into regular classes.

Fragments II: PRACTICE 1

Each of the short passages below contains fragments. Underline the fragments and then correct each in the space provided.   *Methods of correction may vary.*

¹Charlene has a number of reasons for enrolling in her job-training program. ²Especially her four children, Kimmie, Nicole, Josh, and Sarah. ³In the past, Charlene worked as an aide in a nursing home. ⁴Handing out medications and feeding and helping residents. ⁵She and her husband, Woodie, shared the job of raising the children. ⁶But driving to work one morning. ⁷Woodie was in a terrible automobile accident. ⁸Charlene lost her husband, and the children lost their father. ⁹Having to be a single parent. ¹⁰Charlene has more responsibilities than ever. ¹¹She realized she needed a better job. ¹²To provide for her children.

1. Charlene has a number of reasons for enrolling in her job-training program, especially her four children, Kimmie, Nicole, Josh, and Sarah.

2. In the past, Charlene worked as an aide in a nursing home, handing out medications and feeding and helping residents.

3. But driving to work one morning, Woodie was in a terrible automobile accident.

4. Having to be a single parent, Charlene has more responsibilities than ever.

5. She realized she needed a better job to provide for her children.

¹The children are all in school now. ²Remembering her own hard time in school. ³Charlene is determined that her children will have a better experience. ⁴She stays in touch with their teachers. ⁵To learn about little problems before they become big ones. ⁶She knows that teachers have their hands full with many students. ⁷And wants to make sure her kids get the attention they need.

6. Remembering her own hard time in school, Charlene is determined that her children will have a better experience.

7. She stays in touch with their teachers to learn about little problems before they become big ones.

8. She knows that teachers have their hands full with many students and wants to make sure her kids get the attention they need.

¹But being a parent isn't all about stress. ²There are lots of fun times, too. ³Such as reading about dinosaurs with Josh. ⁴Charlene likes to see her children spend time with books. ⁵Learning to enjoy reading for its own sake.

9. There are lots of fun times, too, such as reading about dinosaurs with Josh.

10. Charlene likes to see her children spend time with books, learning to enjoy reading for its own sake.

Fragments II: PRACTICE 2

Underline the fragment in each item that follows. Then rewrite and correct the fragment in the space provided.

Methods of correction may vary.

1. Jan is talking out loud in her bedroom. Practicing a speech for her English class.

    Jan is talking out loud in her bedroom. She is practicing a speech for her English class.

2. Puffing on a bad-smelling cigar. Mr. Bloom said, "You ought to take better care of your health."

    Puffing on a bad-smelling cigar, Mr. Bloom said, "You ought to take better care of your health."

3. I hung a sweater in the bathroom as the shower ran. To steam out the wrinkles.

    I hung a sweater in the bathroom as the shower ran to steam out the wrinkles.

4. Ticking loudly. The clock reminded me how little time I had to get ready.

    Ticking loudly, the clock reminded me how little time I had to get ready.

5. We get forty-two channels on our TV. But don't have anything we want to watch.

    We get forty-two channels on our TV but don't have anything we want to watch.

6. Hank runs four miles every day after school. To get ready for track season.

    Hank runs four miles every day after school to get ready for track season.

7. Staring at me with an icy look on her face. The clerk refused to answer my question.

    Staring at me with an icy look on her face, the clerk refused to answer my question.

8. I eat only healthy snacks. Such as ice cream made with natural ingredients.

    I eat only healthy snacks such as ice cream made with natural ingredients.

9. Crowds of fans hung around the theater all day. Hoping to see the famous actor.

    Crowds of fans hung around the theater all day. They were hoping to see the famous actor.

10. Some nursery rhymes have unpleasant stories. One example, "Three Blind Mice."

    Some nursery rhymes have unpleasant stories. One example is "Three Blind Mice."

Fragments II: **PRACTICE 3**

Each of the short passages below contains **five** fragments. Underline the fragments, and then correct each fragment in the space provided.

Methods of correction may vary.

¹A single mom in school has a lot of challenges. ²Especially finding time for studying. ³After school, the kids all want her attention. ⁴To fix them a snack or listen to their stories. ⁵Charlene then helps them with their homework and prepares dinner. ⁶Then there are other chores to do. ⁷Such as giving the younger children their baths. ⁸Once the children are settled for the night, it's time for Charlene to sit down. ⁹To do her own schoolwork. ¹⁰Charlene admits that life is often difficult. ¹¹However, she knows that by going to school and working hard, she sets a good example for her kids. ¹²And that Woodie would be proud of her.

1. A single mom in school has a lot of challenges, especially finding time for studying.

2. They want her to fix them a snack or listen to their stories.

3. Then there are other chores to do, such as giving the younger children their baths.

4. Once the children are settled for the night, it's time for Charlene to sit down to do her own schoolwork.

5. However, she knows that by going to school and working hard, she sets a good example for her kids and that Woodie would be proud of her.

¹Pet nicknames are often used for Charlene's children. ²Including Nicole and Sarah. ³The family calls them "Noodie" and "Baby Sarah." ⁴The two girls are six and five years old. ⁵And are both in kindergarten. ⁶They like to play with all kinds of toys. ⁷Such as the sticker books they are holding. ⁸When they see Charlene studying, they sometimes get out their books as well. ⁹Wanting to imitate their mom. ¹⁰It's a big responsibility for parents. ¹¹To realize how much influence they have over their children.

6. These include Nicole and Sarah.

7. The two girls are six and five years old and are both in kindergarten.

8. They like to play with all kinds of toys such as the sticker books they are holding.

9. They want to imitate their mom.

10. It's a big responsibility for parents to realize how much influence they have over their children.

Fragments II: TEST 1

Underline the fragment in each item that follows. Then correct the fragment in the space provided.

Note To help you correct fragments, directions are given for the first three sentences.

1. Glancing at his watch frequently. The man seemed anxious to leave.

   The first word group lacks a subject and verb. Connect it to the complete statement that follows it.

   Glancing at his watch frequently, the man seemed anxious to leave.

2. There are many healthful desserts. Including sherbet and fruit salad.

   The second word group lacks a subject and verb. Connect it to the complete statement that comes before it.

   There are many healthful desserts, including sherbet and fruit salad.

3. Our instructor sometimes loses her temper. However, always apologizes afterward.

   Add a subject to the second word group to make it a complete thought.

   However, she always apologizes afterward.

4. To keep his bike from being stolen. Gilbert bought a padlock.

   To keep his bike from being stolen, Gilbert bought a padlock.

5. The small town is a beautiful place to visit. Especially in the spring.

   The small town is a beautiful place to visit, especially in the spring.

6. Thomas lost the key to the front door. As a result, had to call a locksmith.

   As a result, he had to call a locksmith.

7. Certain dogs are well suited to be guide dogs. Including German shepherds and golden retrievers.

   Certain dogs are well suited to be guide dogs, including German shepherds and golden retrievers.

8. To get to school on time. I keep the clock in my room set ten minutes ahead.

   To get to school on time, I keep the clock in my room set ten minutes ahead.

9. Relaxing on the beach. Anna said, "I want to be a lifeguard."

   Relaxing on the beach, Anna said, "I want to be a lifeguard."

10. Many towns in the United States have amusing names. Such as Boring, Oregon; Peculiar, Missouri; and Okay, Oklahoma.

    Many towns in the United States have amusing names, such as Boring, Oregon; Peculiar, Missouri; and Okay, Oklahoma.

Name _____   Section _____   Date _____

Score: (Number right) _____ x 10 = _____%

Fragments II: TEST 2

Underline the fragment in each item that follows. Then correct the fragment in the space provided.

Methods of correction may vary.

1. Walking is excellent exercise. <u>Especially when you walk at a brisk pace.</u>

   Walking is excellent exercise, especially when you walk at a brisk pace.

2. Diane sat down with her boyfriend. <u>Then gently said, "I can't marry you."</u>

   Then she gently said, "I can't marry you."

3. <u>To get her brother's attention.</u> Lydia stood up on the stands and waved.

   To get her brother's attention, Lydia stood up on the stands and waved.

4. <u>Sweating from the workout.</u> Kyle grabbed his water bottle and drank deeply.

   Sweating from the workout, Kyle grabbed his water bottle and drank deeply.

5. Mother elephants devote much of their time to childcare. <u>Nursing their babies up to eight years.</u>

   They nurse their babies up to eight years.

6. Hamburgers come with your choice of cheese. <u>Including Swiss, cheddar, American, provolone, or mozzarella.</u>

   Hamburgers come with your choice of cheese, including Swiss, cheddar, American, provolone, or

   mozzarella.

7. A mouse popped out from under our sofa. <u>Then scurried back quickly.</u>

   Then he scurried back quickly.

8. Sam was helpful to his mother all afternoon. <u>Hoping to borrow her car that night.</u>

   He hoped to borrow her car that night.

9. I look terrible in certain colors. <u>Such as baby blue and pale yellow.</u>

   I look terrible in certain colors, such as baby blue and pale yellow.

10. We do what we can to save money. <u>For example, renting a video instead of going to the movie theater.</u>

    For example, we rent a video instead of going to the movie theater.

Name _____ Section _____ Date _____

Score (Number right)_____ x 20 = _____%

Fragments II: TEST 3

The passage that follows contains **five** fragments. Underline the fragments and then correct them in the
spaces provided.   *Methods of correction may vary.*

[1]Throughout our lives, we humans have a deep need for affectionate touching. [2]That need begins
as soon as we are born. [3]Infants can survive near-starvation, but they can actually die from lack of
affection. [4]When they are regularly held and cuddled, they grow and thrive. [5]Sensing that they are
loved.

[6]Children also need lots of loving touch from their parents, although they may seem to withdraw
from it around age eight. [7]For instance, saying that hugs and kisses are "icky." [8]Parents must be
sensitive to a child's growing need for independence. [9]But ready to give physical affection as needed.

[10]Teenagers often feel confused about touching. [11]Feeling a need for affection, but being
embarrassed by it as well. [12]Some teens even turn to drugs or alcohol. [13]To fill that need. [14]Parents
can help a self-conscious teen by providing as much friendly, casual touching as the teen can accept.

[15]The need for human touch never ends. [16]Surveys of successful marriages show that touching
and hugging are key factors in a happy relationship.

1. When they are regularly held and cuddled, they grow and thrive, sensing that they are loved.

    _____

2. For instance, they say that hugs and kisses are "icky."

    _____

3. Parents must be sensitive to a child's growing need for independence but ready to give physical

    affection as needed.

4. They feel a need for affection but are embarrassed by it as well.

    _____

5. Some teens even turn to drugs or alcohol to fill that need.

    _____

Name _____ Section _____ Date _____

Score (Number right)_____ x 20 = _____ %

Fragments II: TEST 4

Read each group below. Then write the letter of the item in each group that contains a fragment.

_____*a*_____ **1. a.** Rolling slowly backwards. The car had no driver. People nearby began to jump out of the way.

    b. Rolling slowly backwards, the car had no driver. People nearby began to jump out of the way.

    c. The car that was rolling slowly backwards had no driver. People nearby began to jump out of the way.

_____*b*_____ **2. a.** To keep squirrels off their birdfeeders, people have tried all kinds of things. They have even smeared Vaseline on the pole on which the feeder is mounted.

    b. To keep squirrels off their birdfeeders. People have tried all kinds of things. They have even smeared Vaseline on the pole on which the feeder is mounted.

    c. People have tried all kinds of things to keep squirrels off their birdfeeders. They have even smeared Vaseline on the pole on which the feeder is mounted.

_____*c*_____ **3. a.** Cynthia has developed wrist pain from spending so many hours using her computer. She is going to see her doctor about it.

    b. Cynthia is going to see her doctor about her wrist pain. She developed it from spending so many hours at her computer.

    c. Spending so many hours using her computer. Cynthia has developed wrist pain. She is going to see her doctor about it.

_____*a*_____ **4. a.** That instructor does not have a good fashion sense. He puts together odd clothing combinations. Such as a red flowered shirt with purple striped pants.

    b. That instructor does not have a good fashion sense. He puts together odd clothing combinations, such as a red flowered shirt with purple striped pants.

    c. That instructor puts together odd clothing combinations, such as a red flowered shirt with purple striped pants. He does not have a good fashion sense.

_____*c*_____ **5. a.** To try to hear the conversation going on in the room, Irina put her ear to the keyhole. She was embarrassed when the door opened suddenly.

    b. Irina put her ear to the keyhole to try to hear the conversation going on in the room. She was embarrassed when the door opened suddenly.

    c. Irina put her ear to the keyhole. To try to hear the conversation going on in the room. She was embarrassed when the door opened suddenly.

Name _____   Section _____   Date _____

Score (Number right)_____ x 20 = _____%

Fragments II: TEST 5

Read each group below. Then write the letter of the item in each group that contains a fragment.

_____b_____   **1. a.** Staring at the people standing outside, the tiger paced from one end of its cage to the other. It looked hungry.
      b. The tiger paced from one end of its cage to the other. Staring at the people standing outside. It looked hungry.
      c. The tiger paced from one end of its cage to the other, staring at the people standing outside. It looked hungry.

_____c_____   **2. a.** Calling every half-hour, the man seemed extremely anxious to reach my father. "I have to talk to him," he kept saying.
      b. The man who called every half-hour seemed extremely anxious to reach my father. "I have to talk to him," he kept saying.
      c. Calling every half-hour. The man seemed extremely anxious to reach my father. "I have to talk to him," he kept saying.

_____a_____   **3. a.** Robbie ran at full speed down the street. To try to get the letter in the mail before 5 p.m. He reached the post office at 5:02.
      b. Robbie ran at full speed down the street to try to get the letter in the mail before 5 p.m. He reached the post office at 5:02.
      c. Trying to get the letter in the mail before 5 p.m., Robbie ran at full speed down the street. He reached the post office at 5:02.

_____a_____   **4. a.** There's an item on the dessert menu that contains most of my favorite ingredients. Such as chocolate, caramel, coconut, and nuts. I wonder if it's low in calories.
      b. There's an item on the dessert menu that contains most of my favorite ingredients, such as chocolate, caramel, coconut, and nuts. I wonder if it's low in calories.
      c. There's an item on the dessert menu that contains chocolate, caramel, coconut, and nuts, which are my favorite ingredients. I wonder if it's low in calories.

_____b_____   **5. a.** People who can't read well run into constant problems. For example, they may have problems filling out a job application. They are often too embarrassed to admit they can't read it.
      b. People who can't read well run into constant problems. For example, filling out a job application. They are often too embarrassed to admit they can't read it.
      c. People who can't read well run into constant problems. Filling out a job application, for example, they are often too embarrassed to admit they can't read it.

⑦ Run-Ons and Comma Splices I

Basics about Run-Ons and Comma Splices

A **run-on** is made up of two complete thoughts that are incorrectly run together without a connection between them. Here is an example of a run-on:

- Dolphins have killed sharks they never attack humans.

  The complete thoughts are *dolphins have killed sharks* and *they never attack humans.*

A **comma splice** is made up of two complete thoughts that are incorrectly joined (or spliced) together with only a comma. A comma alone is not enough to connect two complete thoughts. Here's an example of a comma splice:

- Dolphins have killed sharks, they never attack humans.

How to Correct Run-Ons and Comma Splices

There are two common ways to correct run-ons and comma splices.

- **METHOD 1   Use a Period and a Capital Letter**

  Put each complete thought into its own sentence.

Run-on	The computer hummed loudly the sound was annoying.
Comma splice	The computer hummed loudly, the sound was annoying.
Correct version	The computer hummed **loudly. The** sound was annoying.

- **METHOD 2   Use a Comma and a Joining Word**

  Connect two complete thoughts into one sentence with a comma and a joining word. Perhaps the most common joining words are *and, but,* and *so.*

Run-on	Dolphins have killed sharks they never attack humans.
Comma splice	Dolphins have killed sharks, they never attack humans.
Correct version	Dolphins have killed **sharks, but they** never attack humans.

Run-on	The garden is overgrown the fence is falling down.
Comma splice	The garden is overgrown, the fence is falling down.
Correct version	The garden is **overgrown, and the** fence is falling down.

Run-on	The little boy appeared to be lost several women stopped to help him.
Comma splice	The little boy appeared to be lost, several women stopped to help him.
Correct version	The little boy appeared to be **lost, so** several women stopped to help him.

Understanding Run-Ons and Comma Splices

See if you can find and put a line (|) between the two complete thoughts in each run-on or comma splice.

¹It's Monday morning at the Cardenas home. ²Everyone is rushing to get out of the house early|it's a busy time of day. ³Alphonso, an air-conditioning installer, can give Korak a ride to high school,|Jasmine will have to take the school bus to her middle school. ⁴Maria wishes the family could have a quiet breakfast together|their busy schedules don't allow time for that.

● "Everyone is rushing to get out of the house early" and "it's a busy time of day" are both complete thoughts. To connect them, use a comma plus the logical joining word *so,* which means "as a result."

  Correct   Everyone is rushing to get out of the house **early, so** it's a busy time of day.

● "Alphonso, an air-conditioning installer, can give Korak a ride to high school" and "Jasmine will have to catch the bus to her middle school" are both complete thoughts. To connect them, use the logical joining word *but,* which means 'however":

  Correct   Alphonso, an air-conditioning installer, can give Korak a ride to high **school, but** Jasmine will have to catch the bus to her middle school.

● "Maria wishes the family could have a quiet breakfast together" and "their busy schedules don't allow time for that" are both complete thoughts. To correct the run-on, put each complete thought into its own sentence.

  Correct   Maria wishes the family could have a quiet breakfast **together. Their** busy schedules don't allow time for that.

Check Your Understanding

Put a line (|) between the two complete thoughts in each run-on or comma splice in the following passage. Then correct the errors in the spaces provided.

¹The family tries to rush out the door|the photographer begs them to wait. ²They won't be together again until late tonight,|he wants to get a family photo. ³"Give your brother a hug!" he teases Jasmine,|she throws her arms around Korak. ⁴How does Korak feel about this?

1.   The family tries to rush out the door, but the photographer begs them to wait.

2.   They won't be together again until late tonight, and he wants to get a family photo.

3.   "Give your brother a hug!" he teases Jasmine, so she throws her arms around Korak.

Run-Ons and Comma Splices I: PRACTICE 1

Draw a line (|) between the two complete thoughts in each of the run-ons and comma splices that follow. Then rewrite each sentence. Correct it in one of two ways:

1 Use a period and a capital letter to create two sentences.

2 Use a comma and a logical joining word to connect the two complete thoughts. Choose from the following joining words:

     and (which means *in addition*)   **but** (which means *however*)   **so** (which means *as a result*)

Do not use the same correction technique for all the sentences.

¹The family is a happy one,|they have a big problem. ²Maria has a serious liver disease|she has to take a lot of medicine. ³Her liver cannot heal itself,|she needs a liver transplant.

Methods of correction may vary.

1. The family is a happy one, but they have a big problem.

2. Maria has a serious liver disease, and she has to take a lot of medicine.

3. Her liver cannot heal itself. She needs a liver transplant.

¹Thousands of people are waiting for organ transplants|Maria is just one of them. ²Some of them need livers|some of them need hearts or lungs. ³Many healthy people have signed up to be organ donors when they die,|many more are needed. ⁴It's simple to become an organ donor,|you just fill out a form on your driver's license.

4. Thousands of people are waiting for organ transplants. Maria is just one of them.

5. Some of them need livers, and some of them need hearts or lungs.

6. Many healthy people have signed up to be organ donors when they die, but many more are needed.

7. It's simple to become an organ donor. You just fill out a form on your driver's license.

¹Antonietta could not be in the family picture|she wasn't awake yet. ²She worked late last night,|she will leave for school in a few minutes. ³She needs to give her parrot some attention first,|he gets angry if she ignores him.

8. Antonietta could not be in the family picture. She wasn't awake yet.

9. She worked late last night, and she will leave for school in a few minutes.

10. She needs to give her parrot some attention first. He gets angry if she ignores him.

Run-Ons and Comma Splices I: PRACTICE 2

Draw a line (|) between the two complete thoughts in each of the run-ons and comma splices that follow. Then rewrite each sentence. Correct it in one of two ways:

1 Use a period and a capital letter to create two sentences.

2 Use a comma and a logical joining word to connect the two complete thoughts. Choose from the following joining words:

and (which means *in addition*)   **but** (which means *however*)   **so** (which means *as a result*)

Do not use the same correction technique for all the sentences.

Methods of correction may vary.

1. Some people are morning people|I'm not one of them.

Some people are morning people, but I'm not one of them.

2. I was out of jelly and butter|I spread yogurt on my toast.

I was out of jelly and butter, so I spread yogurt on my toast.

3. The dog walks on three legs|its ear is chewed up.

The dog walks on three legs, and its ear is chewed up.

4. The sun was shining brightly,|I didn't bring a jacket.

The sun was shining brightly, so I didn't bring a jacket.

5. Someone unplugged the freezer|all the ice cream has melted.

Someone unplugged the freezer, and all the ice cream has melted.

6. I backed away from the growling dog,|I also looked for its owner.

I backed away from the growling dog, but I also looked for its owner.

7. Rain fell steadily outside,|it was a good day to stay indoors.

Rain fell steadily outside, so it was a good day to stay indoors.

8. My brother runs like the wind at track meets|he moves like a turtle at home.

My brother runs like the wind at track meets, but he moves like a turtle at home.

9. Fast-food restaurants are changing|they now offer healthier food choices.

Fast-food restaurants are changing. They now offer healthier food choices.

10. The button fell off the waist of my pants|I fastened them with a safety pin.

The button fell off the waist of my pants. I fastened them with a safety pin.

Run-Ons and Comma Splices I: PRACTICE 3

The following passage contains **ten** run-ons or comma splices. Correct each error in the space provided by using either **1)** a period and capital letter, or **2)** a comma and the joining word *and, so,* or *but.* Be sure to use both methods.   *Methods of correction may vary.*

[1] When Maria was a little girl, she was a migrant worker|her family traveled all the time. [2] She was never in the same school for very long|sometimes she didn't go to school at all. [3]In classes she didn't understand what was going on|she was too shy to ask for help. [4] Maria fell far behind in her studies,|she had to work hard as an adult to catch up. [5] Now Maria is a wife and a mother|she is also a college student. [6] She wants to be an elementary teacher,|she will be able to help migrant children learn. [7] Here she is with one of her professors|the professor's name is Dr. Olliff. [8] Dr. Olliff teaches a special kind of class,|she shows students how to teach children to read. [9] She and Maria are looking at a very large book,|books like these are used in elementary classrooms. [10] This class will help prepare Maria for teaching|she is looking forward to her first classroom of students.

1. When Maria was a little girl, she was a migrant worker. Her family traveled all the time.

2. She was never in the same school for very long, and sometimes she didn't go to school at all.

3. In classes she didn't understand what was going on, but she was too shy to ask for help.

4. Maria fell far behind in her studies, so she had to work hard as an adult to catch up.

5. Now Maria is a wife and a mother, and she is also a college student.

6. She wants to be an elementary teacher, so she will be able to help migrant children learn.

7. Here she is with one of her professors. The professor's name is Dr. Olliff.

8. Dr. Olliff teaches a special kind of class. She shows students how to teach children to read.

9. She and Maria are looking at a very large book. Books like these are used in elementary classrooms.

10. This class will help prepare Maria for teaching, and she is looking forward to her first classroom of students.

Name _____ Section _____ Date _____

Score: (Number right) _____ x 10 = _____ %

Run-Ons and Comma Splices I: TEST 1

Put a line (|) between the two complete thoughts in each of the following run-ons or comma splices. Then rewrite the sentences, using either **1)** a period and a capital letter or **2)** a comma and a joining word (*and, but,* or *so*). *Methods of correction may vary.*

Note To help you correct run-ons, directions are given for the first two sentences.

1. The sun was going down | the air was growing chilly.
   Use a logical joining word (*and, but* or *so*) to connect the two complete thoughts.
   The sun was going down, and the air was growing chilly.

2. Rick is not a good babysitter | he treats his little brother like an insect.
   Put each complete thought into its own sentence.
   Rick is not a good babysitter. He treats his little brother like an insect.

3. My throat is very sore | a gallon of ice cream will relieve it.
   My throat is very sore, but a gallon of ice cream will relieve it.

4. The plumber repaired the water heater, | the family can shower again.
   The plumber repaired the water heater, so the family can shower again.

5. Saturday is the worst day of the week to shop | people fill up many of the stores.
   Saturday is the worst day of the week to shop. People fill up many of the stores.

6. The phone rang | someone knocked on the door at the same time.
   The phone rang, and someone knocked on the door at the same time.

7. The movie was boring at first | it suddenly became interesting.
   The movie was boring at first, but it suddenly became interesting.

8. A burglar alarm went off | three men raced away from the store.
   A burglar alarm went off, and three men raced away from the store.

9. The bear looked at me hungrily, | I decided not to photograph him.
   The bear looked at me hungrily, so I decided not to photograph him.

10. We decided to leave the restaurant, | we were tired of waiting in line.
    We decided to leave the restaurant. We were tired of waiting in line.

Name _____   Section _____   Date _____

Run-Ons and Comma Splices I: TEST 2

Put a line (|) between the two complete thoughts in each of the following run-ons or comma splices. Then rewrite the sentences, using either **1)** a period and a capital letter or **2)** a comma and a joining word (*and*, *but*, or *so*).

Methods of correction may vary.

1. Omar started writing the paper at 9 p.m.|he finished it at 4 a.m.

   Omar started writing the paper at 9 p.m. He finished it at 4 a.m.

2. This coffee is several hours old|it probably tastes like mud.

   This coffee is several hours old, so it probably tastes like mud.

3. I called Kendra three times last night|she never answered.

   I called Kendra three times last night, but she never answered.

4. We lost our electricity last night|all the food in our freezer thawed.

   We lost our electricity last night, and all the food in our freezer thawed.

5. Mia looked tired and miserable|I asked her what was wrong.

   Mia looked tired and miserable, so I asked her what was wrong.

6. Thousands of actors go to Hollywood|few ever become stars.

   Thousands of actors go to Hollywood, but few ever become stars.

7. Coupons help shoppers save money|they also help stores sell products.

   Coupons help shoppers save money. They also help stores sell products.

8. The fortuneteller offered to read my palm|I said, "No, thanks."

   The fortuneteller offered to read my palm, but I said, "No, thanks."

9. I never eat the hamburgers in the cafeteria|they taste like rubber tires.

   I never eat the hamburgers in the cafeteria. They taste like rubber tires.

10. There was an accident on the bridge today|traffic was stopped for an hour.

    There was an accident on the bridge today, and traffic was stopped for an hour.

Name _____ Section _____ Date _____

Run-Ons and Comma Splices I: TEST 3

Each of the short passages below contains **five** run-ons and comma splices. In the space between the lines, correct each error by using **1)** a period and capital letter, or **2)** a comma and the joining word *and*, *so*, or *but*. Be sure to use both methods. The first one is done for you as an example.

Methods of correction may vary.

A. ¹There are many migrant workers in the United ~~States their~~ children face special problems. [*States, and their*]

²Many of them speak Spanish at ~~home, they~~ struggle with English at school. ³They change [*home, so they*]

schools ~~often they~~ get behind in their classes. ⁴Some communities are trying to do a better job [*often, and they*]

of helping migrant children get a good education. ⁵They try this in a variety of ~~ways, one~~ of [*ways. One*]

them is by hiring Spanish-speaking counselors to work with the families. ⁶Another way is to

help families get more involved in school ~~activities, this~~ can be done by offering child care and [*activities. This*]

transportation. ⁷A third is to develop classes that students can easily "drop in" and "drop out"

of as they move. ⁸It is good for everyone if migrant children can become well-educated citizens.

B. ¹Do you speak Spanish? ²Maybe you say you ~~don't you~~ might know more Spanish than you [*don't, but you*]

think. ³The English language has borrowed many words from ~~Spanish, you~~ probably use some [*Spanish, and you*]

of them every day. ⁴Many food words were originally ~~Spanish they~~ include words such as *taco,* [*Spanish. They*]

burrito, and *tortilla.* ⁵Old-time Mexican and American cowboys often worked ~~together, from~~ [*together. From*]

them we borrowed Spanish words including *lasso, rodeo,* and *ranch.* ⁶We use many other words

that have the same meaning in Spanish and ~~English a few~~ of them are *tornado, mosquito,* [*English. A*]

tobacco, vanilla, and *patio.*

Name _____   Section _____   Date _____

Score: (Number right) _____ x 10 = _____%

Run-Ons and Comma Splices I: TEST 4

In each group below, **one** sentence is punctuated correctly. Write the letter of that sentence in the space provided.

_____c_____   1. **a.** The cat slept on the windowsill she was wrapped in warm sunlight.
             b. The cat slept on the windowsill, she was wrapped in warm sunlight.
             c. The cat slept on the windowsill. She was wrapped in warm sunlight.

_____a_____   2. **a.** The motorcycle wouldn't start, so the man called a taxi.
             b. The motorcycle wouldn't start, the man called a taxi.
             c. The motorcycle wouldn't start the man called a taxi.

_____c_____   3. **a.** Mom is grumpy early in the morning, she is cheerful after drinking her coffee.
             b. Mom is grumpy early in the morning she is cheerful after drinking her coffee.
             c. Mom is grumpy early in the morning, but she is cheerful after drinking her coffee.

_____a_____   4. **a.** One remedy always works for my hiccups. I swallow a teaspoon of white sugar.
             b. One remedy always works for my hiccups, I swallow a teaspoon of white sugar.
             c. One remedy always works for my hiccups I swallow a teaspoon of white sugar.

_____c_____   5. **a.** The alarm clock fell on the floor, then it started to ring.
             b. The alarm clock fell on the floor then it started to ring.
             c. The alarm clock fell on the floor. Then it started to ring.

_____b_____   6. **a.** Gina is allergic to animals she can't have a pet.
             b. Gina is allergic to animals, so she can't have a pet.
             c. Gina is allergic to animals, she can't have a pet.

_____a_____   7. **a.** The flowers in that yard look wonderful, but the grass needs cutting.
             b. The flowers in that yard look wonderful, the grass needs cutting.
             c. The flowers in that yard look wonderful the grass needs cutting.

_____b_____   8. **a.** Mr. Dobbs is friendly with his customers, he is rude to his workers.
             b. Mr. Dobbs is friendly with his customers, but he is rude to his workers.
             c. Mr. Dobbs is friendly with his customers he is rude to his workers.

_____b_____   9. **a.** My back itched in a hard-to-reach place I scratched it on the doorpost.
             b. My back itched in a hard-to-reach place, so I scratched it on the doorpost.
             c. My back itched in a hard-to-reach place, I scratched it on the doorpost.

_____c_____   10. **a.** June is a month of nice weather it is also the most popular month for weddings.
             b. June is a month of nice weather, it is also the most popular month for weddings.
             c. June is a month of nice weather. It is also the most popular month for weddings.

Name _____ Section _____ Date _____

Score: (Number right) _____ x 10 = _____ %

Run-Ons and Comma Splices I: TEST 5

In each group below, **one** sentence is punctuated correctly. Write the letter of that sentence in the space provided.

_____a_____   1. **a.** Raoul is colorblind, so his wife lays out his clothes every morning.
            b. Raoul is colorblind his wife lays out his clothes every morning.
            c. Raoul is colorblind, his wife lays out his clothes every morning.

_____c_____   2. **a.** The weatherman predicted a sunny day, it is cold and cloudy.
            b. The weatherman predicted a sunny day it is cold and cloudy.
            c. The weatherman predicted a sunny day, but it is cold and cloudy.

_____b_____   3. **a.** The hammer and saw began to rust they had been left out in the rain.
            b. The hammer and saw began to rust. They had been left out in the rain.
            c. The hammer and saw began to rust, they had been left out in the rain.

_____b_____   4. **a.** My final exams are next week, I am very worried about passing.
            b. My final exams are next week, and I am very worried about passing.
            c. My final exams are next week I am very worried about passing.

_____c_____   5. **a.** I was sick a lot at the start of the semester, I was not able to keep up with the work.
            b. I was sick a lot at the start of the semester I was not able to keep up with the work.
            c. I was sick a lot at the start of the semester, so I was not able to keep up with the work.

_____c_____   6. **a.** I do not enjoy feeling stress I never intend to get so far behind in class again.
            b. I do not enjoy feeling stress, I never intend to get so far behind in class again.
            c. I do not enjoy feeling stress. I never intend to get so far behind in class again.

_____a_____   7. **a.** The children have been eating chocolate. It is smeared all over their faces.
            b. The children have been eating chocolate it is smeared all over their faces.
            c. The children have been eating chocolate, it is smeared all over their faces.

_____a_____   8. **a.** The air is very stale in the library, and the lighting is poor.
            b. The air is very stale in the library the lighting is poor.
            c. The air is very stale in the library, the lighting is poor.

_____c_____   9. **a.** My ancestors came from Greece, they arrived in this country in 1912.
            b. My ancestors came from Greece they arrived in this country in 1912.
            c. My ancestors came from Greece. They arrived in this country in 1912.

_____c_____ 10. **a.** The magician locked his assistant in a box then he cut her in half with a chainsaw.
            b. The magician locked his assistant in a box, then he cut her in half with a chainsaw.
            c. The magician locked his assistant in a box. Then he cut her in half with a chainsaw.

8 Run-Ons and Comma Splices II

Another Way to Correct Run-Ons and Comma Splices

The previous chapter described two ways to correct run-ons and comma splices:

- Use a period and a capital letter, dividing the thoughts into two sentences.
- Use a joining word (*and, but,* or *so*) to logically connect the two complete thoughts.

A third way is to add a **dependent word** to one of the complete thoughts. The sentence will then include one thought that depends upon the remaining complete thought for its full meaning. Here are some common dependent words:

after	because	since	when
although	before	unless	where
as	if, even if	until	while

For example, look at a run-on and comma splice considered in the previous chapter.

Run-on	Dolphins have killed sharks they never attack humans.
Comma splice	Dolphins have killed sharks, they never attack humans.

Using the dependent word *although,* the sentence can be corrected as follows:

Although dolphins have killed sharks, they never attack humans.

Below are other run-ons or comma splices that have been corrected by adding dependent words. In each case, a dependent word that logically connects the two thoughts has been chosen.

Punctuation note When a dependent thought begins a sentence, it is followed by a comma.

Run-on	The roads are covered with ice school has been canceled.
Corrected	**Because** the roads are covered with ice**,** school has been canceled.

Comma splice	The water began to boil, I added ears of corn.
Corrected	**After** the water began to boil, I added ears of corn.

Run-on	The fish was served with its head on Carlo quickly lost his appetite.
Corrected	**When** the fish was served with its head on**,** Carlo quickly lost his appetite.

Comma splice	You better not store cereal in the basement, there are mice there.
Corrected	You better not store cereal in the basement **since** there are mice there.

Understanding Run-Ons and Comma Splices II

See if you can find and put a line (|) between the two complete thoughts in each run-on or comma splice in the following passage.

¹This is Fern Bertram, an 87-year-old woman with two sons and many grandchildren and great-grandchildren. ²She stays in contact with everyone,|her relatives call Fern "the glue that holds the family together." ³Her sons were born,|Fern made a career as a homemaker. ⁴She likes to say that she's "just an ordinary person." ⁵"There were three of us girls," she says. ⁶"One was an excellent nurse; the other could do anything with her hands. ⁷Me, I'm just ordinary." ⁸But other people say that Fern is an extraordinary person. ⁹She maintains a cheerful attitude,|her life has not been easy. ¹⁰Her husband died when he was only 52, and she has dealt with serious illness. ¹¹Yet she insists, "I've had a good life. ¹²We face struggles, but there are so many good things in the world." ¹³The people who know Fern are inspired by her strength and optimism. ¹⁴One nephew likes to say that Fern is made of "sunshine and steel."

1. The first run-on is in sentence 2. You can correct it by adding the dependent word *because:*
   Because she stays in touch with everyone, her relatives call Fern "the glue that holds the family together."

2. The second run-on is in sentence 3. You can correct it by adding the dependent word *after:*
   After her sons were born, Fern made a career as a homemaker.

3. The third run-on is in sentence 9. You can correct it by adding the dependent word *although:*
   She maintains a cheerful attitude **although** her life has not been easy.

Check Your Understanding

Draw a line (|) between the two complete thoughts in each of the **three** run-ons or comma splices that follow. Then correct the errors by adding a dependent word to one of the complete thoughts. Choose from these words: **when, after, although**.

¹Fern has always loved to read,|she doesn't choose books that are "heavy" or "educational." ²She says, "At my age, I just read for entertainment." ³Her favorite authors include Danielle Steele and Norah Roberts.

⁴Fern was about ten,|she read a book that influenced her outlook on life. ⁵The book, called *Pollyanna*, is about a girl who always manages to be happy. ⁶At one point in the book, Pollyanna explains what she calls "the glad game." ⁷Her family received a barrel of hand-me-downs from a missionary-aid society. ⁸Pollyanna hoped there would be a doll in the barrel but found only a pair of child's crutches. ⁹At first Pollyanna was disappointed. ¹⁰She then decided to be happy because she was healthy and didn't need the crutches.

¹¹Fern finished the book|she decided to try to be like Pollyanna. ¹²"She found something to be happy about, and I figured I could do the same. ¹³I've tried to look at life that same way."

1. _Although Fern has always loved to read, she doesn't choose books that are "heavy" or "educational."_

2. _When Fern was about ten, she read a book that influenced her outlook on life._

3. _After Fern finished the book, she decided to try to be like Pollyanna._

Run-Ons and Comma Splices II: PRACTICE 1

Draw a line (|) between the two complete thoughts in each of the **five** run-ons or comma splices that follow. Then correct each sentence by adding a dependent word to one of the complete thoughts. Choose from these words: **because, before, when, since, if.**   *Methods of correction may vary.*

¹When Fern isn't reading, you can often find her writing. ²Here she is making a list of things she needs from the grocery store. ³She goes to bed tonight,| she will write a letter or two to family members. ⁴She says the letters are "nothing special," but her relatives enjoy receiving them. ⁵Instead of writing back, she says, her younger relatives will usually telephone. ⁶She prefers writing letters herself|she thinks letters are somehow more personal. ⁷"Letters are an emotional outlet," she says. ⁸"You say things in letters you wouldn't say on the phone."

1. Before she goes to bed tonight, she will write a letter or two to family members.

2. She prefers writing letters herself because she thinks letters are somehow more personal.

¹In addition to her letters, Fern has written a short autobiography. ²She described the differences between her early years and now. ³She was a child,| her house had no electricity. ⁴She had to read by candlelight. ⁵Family members wanted a bath,| they had to heat water on the kitchen stove. ⁶Her sons asked her why she didn't write about her later life, after she was married. ⁷She said, "There's too much to say. ⁸I wouldn't know where to start!"

3. When she was a child, her house had no electricity.

4. If family members wanted a bath, they had to heat water on the kitchen stove.

¹These days, Fern keeps busy at the retirement home where she lives. ²She often walks over to the Senior Center,| people gather there to eat lunch and play Bingo. ³Fern is often inspired by the people she meets. ⁴For example, one friend needs kidney dialysis three times a week. ⁵"When she comes, she walks in laughing and greeting everyone because she is so happy to be there," Fern says. ⁶"She has courage and optimism that I really admire."

5. She often walks over to the Senior Center since people gather there to eat lunch and play Bingo.

Run-Ons and Comma Splices II: PRACTICE 2

Correct each run-on or comma splice by adding the dependent word shown to one of the complete thoughts. Include a comma if the dependent word starts the sentence.

1. *(although)* These boots are supposed to be waterproof my feet are soaked.

   Although these boots are supposed to be waterproof, my feet are soaked.

2. *(when)* The driver jumped out quickly the car burst into flames.

   The driver jumped out quickly when the car burst into flames.

3. *(when)* We waded into the lake tadpoles swirled around our ankles.

   When we waded into the lake, tadpoles swirled around our ankles.

4. *(if)* You need to make a call you can borrow my cell phone.

   If you need to make a call, you can borrow my cell phone.

5. *(since)* Ricardo was late to school, he had briefly lost his contact lens.

   Ricardo was late to school since he had briefly lost his contact lens.

6. *(while)* It was still raining, a beautiful rainbow appeared in the west.

   While it was still raining, a beautiful rainbow appeared in the west.

7. *(until)* The wet paint on the woodwork dries, you should not touch it.

   Until the wet paint on the woodwork dries, you should not touch it.

8. *(after)* The players looked depressed the team lost the game.

   The players looked depressed after the team lost the game.

9. *(as)* The sky darkened bats began to appear in the air.

   As the sky darkened, bats began to appear in the air.

10. *(because)* That pain killer has serious side effects you should take it only when needed.

    Because that pain killer has serious side effects, you should take it only when needed.

Run-Ons and Comma Splices II: PRACTICE 3

Draw a line (|) between the two complete thoughts in each of the **five** run-ons or comma splices that follow. Then correct each sentence by adding a dependent word to one of the complete thoughts. Choose from these words: **when, although, if, after, because**.

[1]Fern often remembers the past at times when she is alone. [2]Her husband died many years ago|she thinks about him every day. [3]The photograph over Fern's bed was taken,|he was only one year old. [4]You look very closely,|you might see the tiny gold ring on his finger. [5]Fern still has that tiny ring. [6]He died,|she put it in a glass case to keep it safe. [7]Fern wants to pass on her love of family memories,|she has made a photo album for each of her grandchildren. [8]In addition, she has put together histories of her own parents and grandparents for the younger generation.

1. Although her husband died many years ago, she thinks about him every day.

2. When the photograph over Fern's bed was taken, he was only one year old.

3. If you look very closely, you might see the tiny gold ring on his finger.

4. After he died, she put it in a glass case to keep it safe.

5. Because Fern wants to pass on her love of family memories, she has made a photo album for each of her grandchildren.

Name _____   Section _____   Date _____

Score: (Number right) _____ x 10 = _____%

Run-Ons and Comma Splices II: TEST 1

Put a line (|) between the two complete thoughts in each of the following run-ons or comma splices. Then rewrite the sentences, correcting each one by adding a logical dependent word to one of the thoughts. Include a comma if the dependent word starts the sentence. Choose from these words: **because, after, although, if, when**.

NOTE   To help you correct run-ons, directions are given for the first three sentences.

Corrections in items 4–10 may vary.

1. Nuts are high in protein|they are a healthier snack than chips.
   Because nuts are high in protein, they are a healthier snack than chips.

   Use *because* to begin the first complete thought.

2. Many people are afraid of spiders,|most spiders are quite harmless.
   Many people are afraid of spiders although most spiders are quite harmless.

   Use *although* to begin the second complete thought.

3. It starts to rain,|bring in the clothes hanging on the line.
   If it starts to rain, bring in the clothes hanging on the line.

   Use *if* to begin the first complete thought.

4. The dishes were done|we relaxed by watching some TV.
   When the dishes were done, we relaxed by watching some TV.

5. Elaine laid down the sleeping baby,|she tiptoed out of the room.
   After Elaine laid down the sleeping baby, she tiptoed out of the room.

6. You will be late to the party,|let the host know ahead of time.
   If you will be late to the party, let the host know ahead of time.

7. I haven't spent much time outdoors,|it has been very cold.
   I haven't spent much time outdoors because it has been very cold.

8. Geneva apologized for yelling at Evan,|she felt better.
   After Geneva apologized for yelling at Evan, she felt better.

9. You win the contest,|what will you do with the prize money?
   If you win the contest, what will you do with the prize money?

10. I could not open the childproof bottle,|I was following the directions carefully.
    I could not open the childproof bottle although I was following the directions carefully.

Name _____   Section _____   Date _____

Score: (Number right) _____ x 10 = _____ %

Run-Ons and Comma Splices II: TEST 2

Correct each run-on or comma splice by adding the dependent word shown to one of the complete thoughts. Include a comma if the dependent word starts the sentence.

1. *(because)* Nobody answered the phone the whole family had gone to bed early.

   Nobody answered the phone because the whole family had gone to bed early.

2. *(after)* Debbi took a self-defense course, she felt more strong and confident.

   After Debbi took a self-defense course, she felt more strong and confident.

3. *(before)* You start answering a multiple-choice question, read every one of the possible answers.

   Before you start answering a multiple-choice question, read every one of the possible answers.

4. *(because)* My brother was tired of worrying how his hair looked, he shaved his head.

   Because my brother was tired of worrying how his hair looked, he shaved his head.

5. *(although)* Garlic may smell bad it tastes delicious.

   Although garlic may smell bad, it tastes delicious.

6. *(after)* I finished watching the sad movie my eyes were red for hours.

   After I finished watching the sad movie, my eyes were red for hours.

7. *(although)* Mrs. Hunter is not an easy teacher her students love her.

   Although Mrs. Hunter is not an easy teacher, her students love her.

8. *(because)* I am more alert in the morning, early classes are better for me.

   Because I am more alert in the morning, early classes are better for me.

9. *(after)* We had three hours of cleaning up to do, the party ended at 1 a.m.

   We had three hours of cleaning up to do after the party ended at 1 a.m.

10. *(if)* You want to be a rock star, you'd better have a second career plan just in case.

    If you want to be a rock star, you'd better have a second career plan just in case.

Name _____ Section _____ Date _____

Score: (Number right) _____ x 20 = _____ %

Run-Ons and Comma Splices II: TEST 3

Draw a line (|) between the two complete thoughts in each of the **five** run-ons or comma splices in the following paragraph. Then correct each sentence by adding a dependent word to one of the complete thoughts. Use each of the following dependent words once: **after, although, because, if, when.**

¹How much do you know about your own family history? ²Gathering family stories, photos, and keepsakes can be a fascinating hobby, and it can bring your whole family closer together. ³Young people may not be interested in such things, | they may regret their lack of knowledge later. ⁴People reach middle age, | they often begin to wish they knew more about their family history. ⁵That's why it is a great idea to get an early start on your own family's stories. ⁶Probably the best way to begin is to interview older relatives, | they're such good sources of information. ⁷Chances are you'll have a good time doing it. ⁸You're concerned about bothering people, | you probably shouldn't worry. ⁹Elderly family members are usually pleased and surprised when younger relatives ask questions about the past. ¹⁰The questions don't have to be complicated ones. ¹¹You might start by asking things like, "Where were you born? ¹²Where did your parents come from? ¹³What kind of work did they do? ¹⁴What kind of school did you go to?" ¹⁵You do a few such interviews, | you'll be on your way to becoming the family historian.

1. ___Although young people may not be interested in such things, they may regret their lack of___

___knowledge later.___

2. ___When people reach middle age, they often begin to wish they knew more about their family history.___

___

3. ___Probably the best way to begin is to interview older relatives because they're such good sources___

___of information.___

4. ___If you're concerned about bothering people, you probably shouldn't worry.___

___

5. ___After you do a few such interviews, you'll be on your way to becoming the family historian.___

___

Name _____ Section _____ Date _____

Score: (Number right) _____ x 10 = _____%

Run-Ons and Comma Splices II: TEST 4

In each group below, **one** sentence is punctuated correctly. Write the letter of that sentence in the space provided.

_b_   **1. a.** I locked all the doors and windows, I still felt too nervous to sleep.
     b. Although I locked all the doors and windows, I still felt too nervous to sleep.
     c. Although I locked all the doors and windows. I still felt too nervous to sleep.

_a_   **2. a.** Our local elementary school closed for three days because many students had the flu.
     b. Our local elementary school closed for three days. Because many students had the flu.
     c. Our local elementary school closed for three days, many students had the flu.

_c_   **3. a.** The engine has started to cool, you can add more water to the radiator.
     b. When the engine has started to cool. You can add more water to the radiator.
     c. When the engine has started to cool, you can add more water to the radiator.

_a_   **4. a.** Nita played with every puppy before she picked out the one she liked best.
     b. Nita played with every puppy. Before she picked out the one she liked best.
     c. Nita played with every puppy she picked out the one she liked best.

_b_   **5. a.** Our instructor starts class promptly. After she takes attendance.
     b. Our instructor starts class promptly after she takes attendance.
     c. Our instructor starts class promptly, she takes attendance.

_b_   **6. a.** Because Yoko wants to help her community. She works as a volunteer translator.
     b. Because Yoko wants to help her community, she works as a volunteer translator.
     c. Yoko wants to help her community, she works as a volunteer translator.

_c_   **7. a.** You should talk to a counselor. Before you decide on what courses to take.
     b. You should talk to a counselor, decide on what courses to take.
     c. You should talk to a counselor before you decide on what courses to take.

_a_   **8. a.** Emma is a Democrat although both her parents are Republicans.
     b. Emma is a Democrat. Although both her parents are Republicans.
     c. Emma is a Democrat, both her parents are Republicans.

_a_   **9. a.** Because the movie was scary, I turned on all the lights in the house.
     b. Because the movie was scary. I turned on all the lights in the house.
     c. The movie was scary, I turned on all the lights in the house.

_c_   **10. a.** Follow the instructions carefully, the computer will be set up and working in no time.
     b. If you follow the instructions carefully. The computer will be set up and working in no time.
     c. If you follow the instructions carefully, the computer will be set up and working in no time.

Name _____   Section _____   Date _____

Score: (Number right) _____ x 10 = _____%

Run-Ons and Comma Splices II: TEST 5

In each group below, **one** sentence is punctuated correctly. Write the letter of that sentence in the space provided.

_____*a*_____   **1. a.** Although friends had told us the restaurant was very good, we had a dreadful meal.
        b. Friends had told us the restaurant was very good, we had a dreadful meal.
        c. Although friends had told us the restaurant was very good. We had a dreadful meal.

_____*b*_____   **2. a.** You don't enjoy the party, we can leave early.
        b. If you don't enjoy the party, we can leave early.
        c. If you don't enjoy the party. We can leave early.

_____*c*_____   **3. a.** I nearly had a heart attack. When the smoke alarm started shrieking at 2 a.m.
        b. I nearly had a heart attack, the smoke alarm started shrieking at 2 a.m.
        c. I nearly had a heart attack when the smoke alarm started shrieking at 2 a.m.

_____*c*_____   **4. a.** I let myself eat that chocolate cake, I will finish my homework.
        b. Before I let myself eat that chocolate cake. I will finish my homework.
        c. Before I let myself eat that chocolate cake, I will finish my homework.

_____*b*_____   **5. a.** Kristen came back from her blind date, she said, "Never, ever, ever again."
        b. After Kristen came back from her blind date, she said, "Never, ever, ever again."
        c. After Kristen came from her blind date. She said, "Never, ever, ever again."

_____*b*_____   **6. a.** Although I love spicy Mexican food. I do not love the heartburn it gives me.
        b. Although I love spicy Mexican food, I do not love the heartburn it gives me.
        c. I love spicy Mexican food, I do not love the heartburn it gives me.

_____*a*_____   **7. a.** The two brothers seldom speak because they had an argument ten years ago.
        b. The two brothers seldom speak. Because they had an argument ten years ago.
        c. Because they had an argument ten years ago. The two brothers seldom speak.

_____*c*_____   **8. a.** You are afraid of snakes, you might not want to go on the hike with us.
        b. You might not want to go on the hike with us. If you are afraid of snakes.
        c. If you are afraid of snakes, you might not want to go on the hike with us.

_____*c*_____   **9. a.** The soup was too hot to eat, I dropped in two ice cubes to cool it off.
        b. Because the soup was too hot to eat. I dropped in two ice cubes to cool it.
        c. Because the soup was too hot to eat, I dropped in two ice cubes to cool it.

_____*b*_____   **10. a.** The neighbors saw a police car pull up outside. They turned off their lights and watched through the window.
        b. When the neighbors saw a police car pull up outside, they turned off their lights and watched through the window.
        c. When the neighbors saw a police car pull up outside. They turned off their lights and watched through the window.

9 The Comma

,

Basics about the Comma

Here are three main uses of the comma:

1 The comma is used to separate three or more items in a series.

- The school cafeteria has learned not to serve broccoli, spinach, or Brussels sprouts.
- The letters *k, j, x, z,* and *q* are the least frequently used letters of the alphabet.
- Our tasks for the party are blowing up balloons, setting the table, and planning the music.

2 The comma is used to separate introductory material from the rest of the sentence.

- After taking a hot shower, Vince fell asleep on the sofa.
- When covered with chocolate syrup, frozen yogurt is not a diet food.
- As the movie credits rolled, we stretched and headed toward the exits.

3 The comma is used between two complete thoughts connected by *and, but,* or *so.*

- Lee broke her leg in the accident, and her car was badly damaged.
- The forecast called for rain, but it's a beautiful sunny day.
- My glasses broke, so I mended them with duct tape.

Notes

- A comma often marks a slight pause, or break, in a sentence. When you read a sentence aloud, you can often hear the points where slight pauses occur.

- In general, use a comma only when a comma rule applies or when a comma is otherwise needed to help a sentence read clearly.

- Regarding Rule 3 above, do not use a comma just because a sentence contains *and, but,* or *so.* Use a comma only when the *and, but,* or *so* comes between two complete thoughts. Each of the two thoughts must have its own subject and verb.

  - **Comma** Lee broke her leg in the accident, and her car was badly damaged.
    Each complete thought has a subject and a verb: *Lee broke* and *car was damaged.*

  - **No comma** Lee broke her leg in the accident and badly damaged her car.
    This sentence expresses only one complete thought. The subject *Lee* has two verbs: *broke* and *damaged.*

107

Understanding the Comma

See if you can find the **three** sentences where commas are needed in the following passage about Julia Burney, a retired police officer and community leader in Racine, Wisconsin. Then look below to see the corrections.

¹Julia Burney's family was very poor when she was a little girl. ²This photograph shows Julia her mother her father and her baby sister. ³If you look closely you can see the hem is hanging out of four-year-old Julia's dress. ⁴Her little coat is missing most of its buttons. ⁵Her parents had to work hard for a living and there wasn't extra money for books. ⁶That was the worst thing of all about being poor for a book-lover like Julia.

1. This photograph shows Julia, her mother, her father, and her baby sister.
    Commas are needed to separate items in a series.

2. If you look closely, you can see the hem is hanging out of four-year-old Julia's dress.
    A comma is needed after introductory words.

3. Her parents had to work hard for a living, and there wasn't extra money for books.
    A comma is needed between complete thoughts joined by *and, but,* or *so.*

Check Your Understanding

Insert commas where needed in the following passage. **Five** commas are missing.

"Tell the kids I love them"
- *GOD*

¹When she grew up Julia became a police officer. ²She would often meet children without books in their homes so she decided to ask people in the community to donate children's books. ³She began handing the books out to kids in their homes in the parks at the police station and anywhere else she met them. ⁴Other police officers were inspired by what Julia was doing and joined her in the effort to get books into the hands of kids.

The Comma: **PRACTICE 1**

Insert commas where needed in each of the short passages below. **Ten** commas are needed.

¹The idea for the "Cops 'n Kids Reading Program" began to take off. ²After a business owner heard about the program, he donated an old building. ³The building needed a good deal of work, so many volunteers pitched in to help clean and repair it. ⁴They wanted to help Julia turn it into a reading center where kids could come in to read, relax, and learn.

¹As the work got underway, the producers of the Oprah Winfrey program heard about the project. ²Oprah invited Julia to appear on her TV show. ³While Julia was in Chicago, the Oprah people sprang into action. ⁴They installed beautiful carpets, furniture, a crafts center, a computer lab, and a piano. ⁵Artists even painted a giant mural on the wall. ⁶Julia then appeared on the show, and Oprah surprised her with pictures of what they had done. ⁷Julia was so happy that she cried.

¹Julia's idea is not just a dream anymore. ²In the city of Racine today, the Cops 'n Kids Reading Center is a wonderful reality. ³It provides an after-school program, a summer program, and lots of special events for the local children. ⁴The kids can borrow from a library of more than 5,000 books. ⁵If the books are late or lost, there are no overdue fines or fees. ⁶Julia has retired from the police force to become the Center's full-time director. ⁷The picture shows Julia and a staff member sorting through some of the newest books people have donated.

The Comma: PRACTICE 2

On the lines provided, write the word or words in each sentence that need to be followed by a comma. Include each missing comma as well.

1. Although she is 75 my grandmother can do thirty pushups.

   75,
   _____

2. The zookeeper fed raw meat to the lions gave fresh hay to the horses and conducted a guided tour.

   lions, . . . horses,
   _____

3. Our apartment walls are very thin so we hear most of our neighbors' conversations.

   thin,
   _____

4. False names that students have used when substitute teachers were in class include Sandy Beech Frank Furter and Ben Dover.

   Beech, . . . Furter,
   _____

5. In horror movies characters often do incredibly stupid things.

   movies,
   _____

6. The bookcase was filled with magazines paperback novels and CDs.

   magazines, . . . novels,
   _____

7. The sign said, "No Smoking" but many people were ignoring it.

   Smoking,"
   _____

8. I like everything about housework except vacuuming dusting making beds and washing dishes.

   vacuuming, dusting, making beds,
   _____

9. I let the dog go outside after her bath and she immediately rolled in a mud puddle.

   bath,
   _____

10. Sinking down in her chair my mother looked exhausted.

    chair,
    _____

The Comma: PRACTICE 3

Passage A   Insert commas where needed in the following passage. **Thirteen** commas are missing.

[1]As Julia thinks about her childhood, she remembers that no one ever read stories to her. [2]She is now in her 50s, but that memory still hurts. [3]She is making sure the kids at the Reading Center have better memories. [4]Every day, those children sit down, get comfortable, and enjoy a story. [5]Julia often sits down and listens, too.

[6]Although a staff member reads the story today, that is not often the case. [7]Much of the time, volunteers from the community come in to read. [8]"Guest readers" have included local teachers, school principals, police officers, news photographers, and others.

[9]This group of children is of kindergarten age. [10]This picture was taken close to Mother's Day, so some of the children were making cards for their moms. [11]Others were painting pictures or practicing upper-case and lower-case letters. [12]Older children who attend the Center might read newspapers, talk about current events, or take part in a book club.

Passage B   Insert commas where needed in the following passage. **Seven** commas are missing.

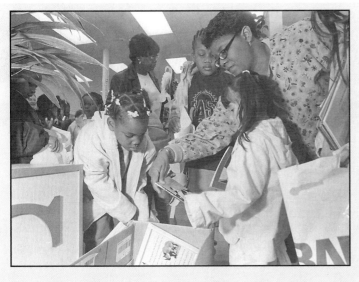

[1]The day's program is over, and it's time to go home. [2]The children always borrow books to take home, read, and return. [3]But on days when the Center has plenty of extra books, children are invited to select books to keep. [4]Today is one of those days. [5]As you can see in this photo, the children are enjoying picking out books of their own.

[6]When Julia Burney sees scenes like this, she almost cries with joy. [7]She grew up in a home without books, but she has brought books into the homes of the children in her community.

Name _____ Section _____ Date _____

Score: (Number right) _____ x 10 = _____%

The Comma: TEST 1

Add commas where needed in each sentence. Then refer to the box below and, in the space provided, write the letter of the comma rule that applies.

> **a**   Between items in a series
>
> **b**   After introductory material
>
> **c**   Between complete thoughts

NOTE To help you master the comma, explanations are given for the first three sentences.

_____c_____   1. My neighbor's dog dislikes children, and it hates the mail carrier.

  A comma is needed before the word that joins two complete thoughts.

_____b_____   2. Before the video started, there were ten minutes of commercials.

  Use a comma after introductory material.

_____a_____   3. This recipe calls for a can of tuna, a bag of frozen peas, a box of noodles, and a can of mushroom soup.

  A comma is needed after each item in a series.

_____c_____   4. Our apartment was too small after the twins were born, so we started looking for a house.

_____b_____   5. Because of the bad weather, school was delayed by two hours today.

_____a_____   6. The travel brochure showed lots of sunny skies, blue water, gorgeous beaches, and tropical sunsets.

_____b_____   7. If you have a fever, you should not go out today.

_____a_____   8. Evan came to the door stretching, yawning, and rubbing his eyes.

_____b_____   9. Carrying sodas and popcorn, the couple looked for a seat in the theater.

_____c_____ 10. The movie was in Spanish, so I had to read the subtitles.

Name _____   Section _____   Date _____

The Comma: TEST 2

Add commas where needed in each sentence. Then refer to the box below and, in the space provided, write the letter of the comma rule that applies.

> **a**   **Between items in a series**
> **b**   **After introductory material**
> **c**   **Between complete thoughts**

_c_   **1.** These shoes are my usual size, but they are still too small for me.

_b_   **2.** If you ask me, that milk has gone bad.

_c_   **3.** The car is badly rusted, and the rear window is cracked.

_a_   **4.** Lainie's chills, fever, and headache warned her she was coming down with something.

_b_   **5.** While I enjoy reading books, I hate having to write a book report.

_a_   **6.** The dog bared its teeth, flattened its ears, and snarled when it saw me.

_b_   **7.** Unused to the silence of the forest, the campers found it hard to sleep.

_a_   **8.** Every day starts with bringing in the newspaper, turning on a morning news show, and feeding the cat.

_b_   **9.** Because it increases unrest among inmates, prison overcrowding is dangerous.

_c_   **10.** I had forgotten my glasses, so I could not read the fine print on the test.

Name _____ Section _____ Date _____

Score: (Number right) _____ x 10 = _____%

The Comma: TEST 3

In each sentence, do two things: **1)** Add the comma or commas that are needed. **2)** In the space provided, write the letter of the rule that applies for the comma(s) you added.

> **a**   Between items in a series
> **b**   After introductory material
> **c**   Between complete thoughts

___b___   **1.** When Andrew Carnegie was thirteen years old, he and his parents moved from Scotland to Pennsylvania.

___c___   **2.** Andrew wanted to go to school, but he had to work in a factory instead.

___c___   **3.** Andrew's family was too poor to own many books, so Andrew was grateful when a local businessman let factory workers borrow books from his collection.

___a___   **4.** Andrew later worked as a messenger boy, a telegraph operator, a secretary, and a railroad executive.

___a___   **5.** He became known as an intelligent, hard-working, and daring businessman.

___b___   **6.** After he founded the Carnegie Steel Company, he became a very wealthy man.

___b___   **7.** As Carnegie thought about how to use his wealth, he remembered the businessman who lent books to poor factory boys.

___a___   **8.** Carnegie believed that reading had helped him to become educated, successful, and happy.

___c___   **9.** He wanted to share what had been done for him, so he used his money to establish 2,509 Carnegie libraries all over the English-speaking world.

___b___   **10.** When people use them, they should remember the poor Scottish factory boy who wanted everyone to have access to books.

Name _____   Section _____   Date _____

Score: (Number right) _____ x 10 = _____%

The Comma: TEST 4

In each group below, **one** sentence uses the comma correctly. Write the letter of that sentence in the space provided.

____*b*____   **1. a.** The smoke detector was buzzing and we, could smell something burning.
                    b. The smoke detector was buzzing, and we could smell something burning.
                    c. The smoke detector was, buzzing, and we could smell something burning.

____*c*____   **2. a.** When my sister was little she thought lima beans, were stuffed with mashed potatoes.
                    b. When my sister was little she thought lima beans were stuffed, with mashed potatoes.
                    c. When my sister was little, she thought lima beans were stuffed with mashed potatoes.

____*a*____   **3. a.** The driving instructor asked me to turn on my headlights, windshield wipers, and emergency flashers.
                    b. The driving instructor, asked me to turn on my headlights windshield wipers and emergency flashers.
                    c. The driving instructor asked, me to turn on my headlights windshield wipers, and emergency flashers.

____*a*____   **4. a.** I woke up feeling cheerful, but my mood soon changed.
                    b. I woke up, feeling cheerful but my mood soon changed.
                    c. I woke up feeling cheerful but, my mood soon changed.

____*a*____   **5. a.** Many people are afraid of spiders, and I can certainly understand why.
                    b. Many people are afraid of spiders and I, can certainly understand why.
                    c. Many people, are afraid of spiders and I can certainly understand why.

____*c*____   **6. a.** Looking embarrassed the man asked, if he could borrow bus fare.
                    b. Looking embarrassed the man asked if he could, borrow bus fare.
                    c. Looking embarrassed, the man asked if he could borrow bus fare.

____*c*____   **7. a.** You'll need to have some onions, garlic carrots tomatoes, and parsley.
                    b. You'll need to have some, onions garlic carrots tomatoes and parsley.
                    c. You'll need to have some onions, garlic, carrots, tomatoes, and parsley.

____*b*____   **8. a.** If you are approached, by a vicious dog you should stand still.
                    b. If you are approached by a vicious dog, you should stand still.
                    c. If you are approached by a vicious dog you should, stand still.

____*c*____   **9. a.** The little boy said that, his favorite subjects were lunch gym and recess.
                    b. The little boy said that his favorite subjects were lunch gym, and recess.
                    c. The little boy said that his favorite subjects were lunch, gym, and recess.

____*a*____   **10. a.** Without a sound, the thief quickly emptied the cash register.
                     b. Without a sound the thief, quickly emptied the cash register.
                    c. Without a sound the thief quickly, emptied the cash register.

Name _____ Section _____ Date _____

Score: (Number right) _____ x 10 = _____ %

The Comma: TEST 5

In each group below, **one** sentence uses the comma correctly. Write the letter of that sentence in the space provided.

_a_ 1. **a.** No one volunteered to read his or her paper out loud, so the instructor called on Amber.
  b. No one volunteered, to read his or her paper out loud so the instructor called on Amber.
  c. No one volunteered to read his or her paper out loud so, the instructor called on Amber.

_b_ 2. **a.** On most television shows people live in beautiful homes.
  b. On most television shows, people live in beautiful homes.
  c. On most television shows people live, in beautiful homes.

_c_ 3. **a.** Politics money, and religion are topics that people often argue about.
  b. Politics, money and religion are topics, that people often argue about.
  c. Politics, money, and religion are topics that people often argue about.

_a_ 4. **a.** During a thunderstorm, it's best not to use the telephone.
  b. During a thunderstorm it's best, not to use the telephone.
  c. During a thunderstorm, it's best not to use, the telephone.

_c_ 5. **a.** A customer was waiting but, the clerk kept chatting with her friend.
  b. A customer was waiting but the clerk, kept chatting with her friend.
  c. A customer was waiting, but the clerk kept chatting with her friend.

_b_ 6. **a.** The Seven Dwarfs had silly names, like Sneezy Grumpy Bashful and Dopey.
  b. The Seven Dwarfs had silly names like Sneezy, Grumpy, Bashful, and Dopey.
  c. The Seven Dwarfs had silly names like Sneezy, Grumpy, Bashful, and, Dopey.

_c_ 7. **a.** Her courtesy compassion and patience, help make Sarah very good at her job.
  b. Her courtesy compassion and patience help make Sarah, very good, at her job.
  c. Her courtesy, compassion, and patience help make Sarah very good at her job.

_b_ 8. **a.** Greg has to work, the night of his birthday so we will celebrate the night before.
  b. Greg has to work the night of his birthday, so we will celebrate the night before.
  c. Greg has to work the night of his birthday so, we will celebrate the night before.

_a_ 9. **a.** By the end of the day, we had painted the entire apartment.
  b. By the end of the day we had painted, the entire apartment.
  c. By the end, of the day, we had painted the entire apartment.

_b_ 10. **a.** The drinks on the menu include, coffee, tea soda lemonade, orange juice and milk.
  b. The drinks on the menu include coffee, tea, soda, lemonade, orange juice, and milk.
  c. The drinks on the menu, include coffee tea soda, lemonade orange juice and milk.

10 The Apostrophe

Basics about the Apostrophe

There are two main uses of the apostrophe:

1 The apostrophe takes the place of one or more missing letters in a contraction. (A **contraction** is a word formed by combining two or more words, leaving some of the letters out.)

- I am sleepy. —> **I'm** sleepy.
  The letter *a* in *am* has been left out.

- Hank did not know the answer. —> Hank **didn't** know the answer.
  The letter *o* in *not* has been left out.

- They would keep the secret. —> **They'd** keep the secret.
  The letters *woul* in *would* have been left out.

Here are a few more common contractions:

it + is = **it's** (the *i* in *is* has been left out)
does + not = **doesn't** (the *o* in *not* has been left out)
do + not = **don't** (the *o* in *not* has been left out)
she + will = **she'll** (the *wi* in *will* has been left out)
he + is = **he's** (the *i* in *is* has been left out)
we + have = **we've** (the *ha* in *have* has been left out)
could + not = **couldn't** (the *o* in *not* has been left out)
will + not = **won't** (the *o* replaces *ill*; the *o* in *not* has been left out)

2 The apostrophe shows that something belongs to someone or something. (This is called **possession**.)

- the fin of the shark —> the **shark's** fin
  The apostrophe goes after the last letter of the name of the owner, *shark*. The *'s* added to *shark* tells us that the fin belongs to the shark.

- the grades of Nina —> **Nina's** grades
  The apostrophe goes after the last letter of the name of the owner, *Nina*. The *'s* added to *Nina* tells us that the grades belong to Nina.

  Note No apostrophe is used with simple plurals such as *grades,* which simply means "more than one grade."

- the cheering of the crowd —> the **crowd's** cheering
  The apostrophe goes after the last letter of the name of the owner, *crowd*. The *'s* added to *crowd* tells us that the cheering belongs to the crowd.

For added information about the apostrophe, see page 271.

117

Understanding the Apostrophe

Notice how the apostrophe is used in the following passage about Beth Johnson's three children.

¹The day's work for this suburban family begins over breakfast. ²Isaac is finishing his Spanish homework. ³Sam notices that the calculator's batteries are getting low. ⁴Because Maddie's bus doesn't come until after the boys leave, she's still in her bathrobe.

1. **The day's work** means "the work of the day."
2. The second apostrophe, in **calculator's batteries**, means "the batteries belonging to the calculator."
3. The third apostrophe, in **Maddie's bus**, means "the bus for Maddie."
4. The fourth apostrophe, in **doesn't**, takes the place of the missing letter in *does not*.
5. The fifth apostrophe, in **she's**, takes the place of the missing letter in *she is*.

Check Your Understanding

Read the passage below. Then fill in the missing word or words in each sentence.

¹After the boys have gone, Maddie plays school. ²She pretends her dolls haven't learned to read, and she's teaching them by reading a book out loud. ³At night, the little girl's bed is so covered with dolls that there's hardly room for her to sleep. ⁴She never removes any dolls despite her mom's suggestion that she do so.

1. The apostrophe in **haven't** takes the place of the missing letter in the word _____not_____.
2. The apostrophe in **she's** takes the place of the missing letter in the word _____is_____.
3. The apostrophe in **girl's bed** means *the bed belonging to the* _____girl_____.
4. The apostrophe in **there's** takes the place of the missing letter in the word _____is_____.
5. The apostrophe in **her mom's suggestion** means *the suggestion belonging to* _____her mom_____.

The Apostrophe: PRACTICE 1

Each of the short passages below contains words that need apostrophes. Underline the words that need apostrophes. Then write each word, with its apostrophe, in the space provided.

¹Those dogs <u>shouldnt</u> be on the bed! ²<u>Logans</u> dirty paws and <u>Alexs</u> long hair will make a mess.

1. shouldn't

2. Logan's

3. Alex's

¹A <u>dogs</u> life <u>isnt</u> so bad—dogs <u>dont</u> need to worry about getting anywhere on time.

4. dog's

5. isn't

6. don't

¹Before she goes to school, Maddie changes her <u>birds</u> food and water. ²The bird is a cockatiel named Feathers. ³<u>Hes</u> so tame that he eats from his <u>owners</u> hand. ⁴<u>Maddies</u> job is to take care of Feathers.

7. bird's

8. He's

9. owner's

10. Maddie's

The Apostrophe: PRACTICE 2

Each of the sentences below contains **one** word that needs an apostrophe. Write each word, with its apostrophe, in the space provided.

1. A lobsters claws are used to crush prey and then tear it apart.
   lobster's

2. We havent seen our waitress since she gave us menus twenty minutes ago.
   haven't

3. My cousins know the stores owner, a man named Mr. Sherwin.
   store's

4. The mystery books final ten pages were missing.
   book's

5. School wont be opening until noon because of the power failure.
   won't

6. A dogs collar should not be too tight.
   dog's

7. We watched a TV movie about an adult who couldnt read.
   couldn't

8. For Halloween, Barry dressed up in a cheerleaders outfit.
   cheerleader's

9. There was a rumor that some employees would be laid off, but it wasnt true.
   wasn't

10. The models teeth were so white that they did not look real.
    model's

The Apostrophe: PRACTICE 3

Each sentence in the following passage contains **one** word that requires an apostrophe. Underline the ten words. Then, on the lines following the passage, write the corrected form of each word.

Note To help you master the apostrophe, explanations are given for five of the sentences.

¹Although the kids are brothers and sister, they <u>arent</u> at all alike in some ways. ²For instance, they <u>dont</u> like the same foods at all. ³<u>Sams</u> favorite meals are made up of basic meat and potatoes. ⁴If every meal were made up of pot roast, mashed potatoes, and gravy, <u>hed</u> be happy. ⁵But brother <u>Isaacs</u> tastes are much more adventurous. ⁶<u>Hes</u> been known to eat sushi, eel, octopus, and even liver. ⁷When it comes to Maddie, no one quite knows what <u>shell</u> eat. ⁸One day she <u>cant</u> get enough of chicken noodle soup. ⁹The next day she <u>wont</u> touch the stuff. ¹⁰<u>Its</u> a challenge for their mother to fix meals for this family.

1. __aren't__   The contraction of *are not* needs an apostrophe.

2. __don't__

3. __Sam's__   The writer means "the favorite meals of Sam."

4. __he'd__

5. __Isaac's__   The writer means "the tastes belonging to Isaac."

6. __He's__

7. __she'll__   The contraction of *she will* needs an apostrophe.

8. __can't__

9. __won't__   The contraction of *will not* needs an apostrophe.

10. __It's__

Name _____ Section _____ Date _____

The Apostrophe: TEST 1

Each of the sentences below contains **one** word that needs an apostrophe. Underline the word.
Then write the word, with its apostrophe, in the space provided.

NOTE To help you master the apostrophe, explanations are given for the first three sentences.

1. My fathers thunderous snores can be heard all over the house.
    The snores belong to the father. *Snores* is a simple plural; no apostrophe is used.
    _____father's_____

2. The movie star wore a hat and dark glasses, but she couldnt fool her waiting fans.
    An apostrophe should take the place of the missing *o* in the contraction.
    _____couldn't_____

3. The tigers pacing never stopped as it watched the crowd of zoo visitors.
    The pacing belongs to the tiger. *Visitors* is a simple plural; no apostrophe is used.
    _____tiger's_____

4. Some students are unhappy about the schools decision to remove soft-drink machines.
    _____school's_____

5. Even though they didnt finish elementary school, my grandparents want me to get a
    college degree.
    _____didn't_____

6. The grasshoppers powerful hind legs allow the insect to jump many times its own height.
    _____grasshopper's_____

7. Sheer white curtains and fresh lilacs added to the rooms simple charm.
    _____room's_____

8. The hypnotists only tools are a soothing voice and a watch that ticks very loudly.
    _____hypnotist's_____

9. If you keep eating the cheese dip, there wont be enough to serve our guests.
    _____won't_____

10. Since lemons are so cheap right now, Im going to buy enough to make lemonade, lemon
    cake, and lemon chicken.
    _____I'm_____

Name _____   Section _____   Date _____

Score: (Number right) _____ x 10 = _____ %

The Apostrophe: TEST 2

Each of the sentences below contains **one** word that needs an apostrophe. Underline the word. Then write the word, with its apostrophe, in the space provided.

1. In American culture, it <u>isnt</u> considered polite to point at someone.

   isn't _____

2. The doodles in <u>Andys</u> notebook show just how much he pays attention in his history class.

   Andy's _____

3. Yolanda and Marco <u>werent</u> speaking six months ago, but now they are getting married.

   weren't _____

4. Smudges on the <u>CDs</u> surface made it skip while it was playing.

   CD's _____

5. The sun <u>hasnt</u> shone for eight days in a row.

   hasn't _____

6. The chocolates in the silver box were a gift from my <u>mothers</u> best friend.

   mother's _____

7. The <u>coachs</u> daughter is one of the best runners on the track team.

   coach's _____

8. The men <u>couldnt</u> explain what they were doing inside the bank at 2 a.m.

   couldn't _____

9. Gina plucked the <u>daisys</u> petals, saying, "He loves me, he loves me not."

   daisy's _____

10. <u>Randys</u> alarm clock can buzz, play music, or make sounds like a babbling brook.

    Randy's _____

Name _____   Section _____   Date _____

Score: (Number right) _____ x 10 = _____%

The Apostrophe: TEST 3

Each sentence in the passages below contains a word that needs an apostrophe. Underline the **ten** words that need apostrophes. Then, on the lines following the passages, write the corrected form of each word.

A. ¹Some students are morning people, and some just <u>arent</u>. ²The morning people are awake as soon as the <u>suns</u> rays hit the window, so they are ready to hop out of bed and get ready for school. ³But given a choice, many people would prefer a <u>beds</u> warmth for a few more hours. ⁴Their brains <u>dont</u> start functioning until about 10 a.m. ⁵<u>Couldnt</u> there be one school for the morning people and another for the rest of us?

1.   aren't _____

2.   sun's _____

3.   bed's _____

4.   don't _____

5.   Couldn't _____

B. ¹If you could choose, would you rather be your <u>familys</u> only child, or would you want to have siblings? ²Sherry, an only child I once knew, never had to share her toys or her <u>mothers</u> attention. ³When I first realized that, I wanted to put my <u>brothers</u> photograph on a "for sale" sign. ⁴But later I decided I <u>didnt</u> really want to be an "only." ⁵Without my brother, I <u>wouldnt</u> have had anybody to blame when I did something wrong!

6.   family's _____

7.   mother's _____

8.   brother's _____

9.   didn't _____

10. wouldn't _____

Name _____ Section _____ Date _____

Score: (Number right) _____ × 10 = _____ %

The Apostrophe: TEST 4

In each group below, **one** sentence uses apostrophes correctly. Write the letter of that sentence in the space provided.

_b___ 1. **a.** It shouldn't take more than ten minute's to reach Phil's house.
　　　　 b. It shouldn't take more than ten minutes to reach Phil's house.
　　　　 c. It shouldn't take more than ten minutes to reach Phils house.

_c___ 2. **a.** The patients eye's havent opened since the surgery.
　　　　 b. The patients eyes haven't opened since the surgery.
　　　　 c. The patient's eyes haven't opened since the surgery.

_c___ 3. **a.** Emily won't wear anything made from an animals fur.
　　　　 b. Emily wont wear anything made from an animal's fur.
　　　　 c. Emily won't wear anything made from an animal's fur.

_c___ 4. **a.** I dont have half of this recipe's ingredient's.
　　　　 b. I dont have half of this recipe's ingredients.
　　　　 c. I don't have half of this recipe's ingredients.

_a___ 5. **a.** You'll either love or hate the movie's surprise ending.
　　　　 b. You'll either love or hate the movies surprise ending.
　　　　 c. Youll either love or hate the movie's surprise ending.

_b___ 6. **a.** My sisters taste in music and my brother's taste in friend's drive me crazy.
　　　　 b. My sister's taste in music and my brother's taste in friends drive me crazy.
　　　　 c. My sister's taste in music and my brothers taste in friend's drive me crazy.

_c___ 7. **a.** The kitchens warmth and the coffee's aroma were very welcoming.
　　　　 b. The kitchen's warmth and the coffees aroma were very welcoming.
　　　　 c. The kitchen's warmth and the coffee's aroma were very welcoming.

_a___ 8. **a.** My jacket's zipper is broken, so I can't take the jacket off.
　　　　 b. My jacket's zipper is broken, so I cant take the jacket off.
　　　　 c. My jackets zipper is broken, so I can't take the jacket off.

_b___ 9. **a.** The houses window's are shattered, and the lawn hasn't been mowed for years.
　　　　 b. The house's windows are shattered, and the lawn hasn't been mowed for years.
　　　　 c. The house's windows are shattered, and the lawn hasnt been mowed for year's.

_a___ 10. **a.** Our parrot's loud shrieks haven't made him popular with our neighbors.
　　　　 b. Our parrot's loud shrieks havent made him popular with our neighbor's.
　　　　 c. Our parrots loud shrieks haven't made him popular with our neighbor's.

Name _____ Section _____ Date _____

Score: (Number right) _____ x 10 = _____ %

The Apostrophe: TEST 5

In each group below, **one** sentence uses apostrophes correctly. Write the letter of that sentence in the space provided.

___c___   **1.** **a.** My aunts hairstyle hasnt changed in twenty years.
               b. My aunt's hairstyle hasnt changed in twenty year's.
               c. My aunt's hairstyle hasn't changed in twenty years.

___a___   **2.** **a.** The veterinarian's assistant quickly examined our puppy's hurt paws.
               b. The veterinarian's assistant quickly examined our puppys hurt paw's.
               c. The veterinarians assistant quickly examined our puppy's hurt paws.

___a___   **3.** **a.** The romance novel's cover showed a woman fainting in a man's arms.
               b. The romance novel's cover showed a woman fainting in a man's arm's.
               c. The romance novels cover showed a woman fainting in a man's arm's.

___c___   **4.** **a.** Sheila's boyfriend work's part-time in his fathers barbershop.
               b. Sheilas boyfriend work's part-time in his father's barbershop.
               c. Sheila's boyfriend works part-time in his father's barbershop.

___b___   **5.** **a.** The police didn't show up until four hour's after wed called them.
               b. The police didn't show up until four hours after we'd called them.
               c. The police didnt show up until four hour's after we'd called them.

___b___   **6.** **a.** I can't believe youve never eaten in a Chinese restaurant.
               b. I can't believe you've never eaten in a Chinese restaurant.
               c. I cant believe you've never eaten in a Chinese restaurant.

___a___   **7.** **a.** The witch's gingerbread house wasn't visible to grownups.
               b. The witch's gingerbread house wasnt visible to grownups.
               c. The witchs gingerbread house wasn't visible to grownup's.

___c___   **8.** **a.** The oceans floor isn't flat, but contains mountain's, plains, and ridges.
               b. The ocean's floor isnt flat, but contains mountain's, plains, and ridges.
               c. The ocean's floor isn't flat, but contains mountains, plains, and ridges.

___b___   **9.** **a.** An ostrich eggs shell is as thick as a nickel and can't be easily broken.
               b. An ostrich egg's shell is as thick as a nickel and can't be easily broken.
               c. An ostrich egg's shell is as thick as a nickel and cant be easily broken.

___c___   **10.** **a.** The homeless man's feet were wrapped in page's of yesterdays newspaper.
               b. The homeless mans feet were wrapped in page's of yesterday's newspaper.
               c. The homeless man's feet were wrapped in pages of yesterday's newspaper.

Basics about Quotation Marks

Use quotation marks to set off all exact words of a speaker or writer.

- The little girl's mother said, "It wasn't nice to fill up the sugar bowl with salt."
  The mother's exact words are enclosed within quotation marks.

- "I'm afraid," the mechanic muttered to Fred, "that your car is in big trouble."
  The mechanic's exact words are enclosed within quotation marks.

- "Our math teacher is unfair," complained Wanda. "He assigns two hours of homework for each class. Does he think we have nothing else to do?"
  Wanda's exact words are enclosed within quotation marks. Note that even though Wanda's second set of exact words is more than one sentence, only one pair of quotation marks is used. Do not use quotation marks for each new sentence as long as the quotation is not interrupted.

- "We cannot solve a problem by hoping that someone else will solve it for us," wrote psychiatrist M. Scott Peck.
  The exact words that Dr. Peck wrote are enclosed in quotation marks.

Punctuation Notes

- Quoted material is usually set off from the rest of the sentence by a comma. When the comma comes at the end of quoted material, it is included inside the quotation marks. The same is true for a period, exclamation point, or question mark that ends quoted material:

  Incorrect   "Watching golf", complained Rosie, "is like watching grass grow".
  Correct   "Watching golf," complained Rosie, "is like watching grass grow."

  Incorrect   "Aren't you ready yet"? Dad yelled. "Hurry up, or we're leaving without you"!
  Correct   "Aren't you ready yet?" Dad yelled. "Hurry up, or we're leaving without you!"

- Notice, too, that a quoted sentence begins with a capital letter, even when it is preceded by other words:

  Incorrect   The diner asked suspiciously, "is this fish fresh?"
  Correct   The diner asked suspiciously, "Is this fish fresh?"

Understanding Quotation Marks

Notice how quotation marks are used in the following interview with Dr. Richard Kratz, president of Reading Area Community College in Reading, Pennsylvania. All of the words Dr. Kratz actually spoke aloud are set off in quotation marks.

¹If you had told Dr. Kratz when he was a teenager that he would someday be a college president, he would have laughed at you.

²"My family believed in education. ³In fact, my father was superintendent of schools, and my mother was a teacher," Dr. Kratz says. ⁴"But somehow, I didn't get on board at first."

⁵He was a poor student in high school.

⁶"I think I was fifth in my class," he says, "but I mean fifth from the bottom." ⁷He didn't like to read, and he didn't write well. ⁸But then in college, something happened to Dr. Kratz.

⁹"I took a course in which we read some amazing novels," he remembers. ¹⁰"The ones I remember best are *Brave New World* and *1984*. ¹¹I discovered a passion for reading, and I've been a reader ever since."

¹²Dr. Kratz doesn't mean that he never had any more trouble in school. ¹³"I had to take basic English in college," he says, "and I still don't write as well as I would like. ¹⁴But I realized that writing was a skill I could acquire, if I worked at it."

Check Your Understanding

Use **five** sets of quotation marks (" ") to enclose the words that Dr. Kratz says out loud.

¹Here is Dr. Kratz in the cafeteria with some students. ²Dr. Kratz has a lot of respect for his students. ³According to him, many of them are dealing with difficult obstacles.

"⁴Many of our students are the first in their families to go to college," he says. ⁵That can make it tough. ⁶When I got back my first college English paper, it was so covered with red marks it looked like a Christmas tree. ⁷My parents told me not to worry, that the same thing had happened to them. ⁸If I hadn't had anybody at home to tell me that, I might have panicked and given up."

⁹Dr. Kratz also explains that community-college students face other challenges, too. ¹⁰He says, "The average age of our students is 28. ¹¹For many of them, school is about the fourth priority. ¹²I hear them talking about job problems, transportation problems, and family problems."

¹³Dr. Kratz then continues, "Women students have their own special issues. ¹⁴Too often, there's no support at home. ¹⁵If nobody is offering extra help with the kids or the housework, I can understand how they end up feeling they can't handle it all."

¹⁶Finally, Dr. Kratz cites the special problems of minority students: "Some people criticize them for working hard in school. ¹⁷They accuse them of thinking they're better than their friends."

¹⁸For all these reasons, Dr. Kratz is very proud of his students for being in college and doing their best there.

Quotation Marks: PRACTICE 1

Each of the short passages below contains words that need quotation marks. Add the **four** sets of missing quotation marks in the passage below.

¹Dr. Kratz loves to tell success stories about his former and current students.

²One of his favorites is about the college's commencement speaker several years ago. ³She had been a student at the college, and one day her biology instructor got into a conversation with her.

"⁴What are you majoring in?" he asked.

"⁵I'm going to be a legal secretary," she answered. "⁶I'm not really interested in it, but I'm a single mother on welfare, and I just need to get some job training quickly. ⁷I'd really like to work in medical research, but someone like me can't do that."

⁸The biology instructor encouraged the woman not to settle for a career she wasn't excited about. ⁹She decided to find a way to make her education a priority. ¹⁰She graduated from community college, went on to earn a bachelor's degree, and is now finishing her doctorate at a major medical center. ¹¹When she spoke at the community college's commencement, she said, "Don't accept the idea that you can't. ¹²Find out what you *can* do, and do it."

Add the **five** sets of missing quotation marks.

¹These students are looking forward to their own graduations. ²Commencement at the college is always an exciting day.

"³It's the greatest thing in the world," says Dr. Kratz. "⁴Everybody is hooting and hollering for their friends and relatives."

⁵He says the enthusiasm is very contagious. ⁶He then tells this story: "A few years ago, the mayor of Philadelphia came to speak at commencement. ⁷I expected he would just give his speech and leave early. ⁸But the mayor got so caught up in the excitement that he ended up hanging around for the whole evening."

⁹Dr. Kratz gets caught up in the excitement, too. "¹⁰I know many of these students have sacrificed in order to make it to this day," he says. "¹¹I'm as proud of them as if they were my own kids."

Add the **one** set of missing quotation marks.

¹Here Dr. Kratz stands nearby as a library staff member helps a student do computer research. ²He explains, "Cooperation is at the heart of what community college is all about. ³We will meet you wherever you are and help you become the best that you can be."

Quotation Marks: PRACTICE 2

Insert quotation marks where needed in the following sentences. Look at the example below.

Example   The game announcer called out, "Looks like we have a winner!"

1.   "I won't take any more criticism," Kylie said to her boyfriend. "Our relationship is over."

2.   The operator stated, "Please deposit another quarter in order to continue this call."

3.   "Let's all turn on our computers," the instructor said.

4.   The label on the chlorine bleach says, "Do not mix this product with other cleansers."

5.   "This is a movie that will scare everyone in the family," the reviewer said.

6.   The boat captain said sternly, "Please keep your arms and legs inside the boat. Failure to do so will make the alligators very happy."

7.   In his book *Think Big*, Dr. Benjamin Carson writes, "I had been in the fifth grade not even two weeks before everyone considered me the dumbest kid in the class and frequently made jokes about me."

8.   "Cut the onions into thin slices," the cooking instructor explained. "Then place them in the hot skillet."

9.   "Could you turn the radio down just a little?" the passenger shouted to the taxi driver.

10.   Anne Frank wrote the following in her diary: "It's a wonder I haven't abandoned all my ideals, which seem so absurd and impractical. Yet I cling to them because I still believe, in spite of everything, that people are truly good at heart."

Quotation Marks: PRACTICE 3

Five sets of quotation marks are missing from each of the following passages. Insert the quotation marks where needed.

Passage 1

[1]Dr. Richard Kratz knows that, of course, college isn't only about studying.

[2]"Let's go see if anyone's in the student union," Dr. Kratz says.

[3]When he gets there, he finds a number of students watching TV, talking, and playing pool.

[4]"Hey, how are you guys doing?" Dr. Kratz says to the pool players. [5]"Do you mind if we take some pictures here?"

[6]The guys don't mind at all. [7]"Put me in the picture!" says one student.

[8]Another jokes, "Why would you put him in when you can have my good-looking self in it?"

[9]In the end, all the guys get in the picture.

Passage 2

[1]Community colleges have been part of America since 1901. [2]Today, the more than one thousand community colleges educate over half the undergraduate college students in the United States. [3]Community colleges are gaining in popularity for a number of reasons. [4]According to *U.S. News and World Report,* "Some students have started off at two-year schools because they aren't ready, either academically or emotionally, for big universities."

[5]But the magazine goes on to say that many students who could go directly to a four-year college are choosing a community college instead. [6]Here's an excerpt from the magazine: "Chantel Bain wanted a college with small classes, caring professors, and diverse course offerings. [7]She found her perfect match at Santa Barbara City College, a two-year college."

[8]One person posting on an online message board had this to say about the advantages of community colleges: "My student loans are going to be only a quarter of what they would have been, thanks to my attending a community college rather than a four-year school." [9]She went on to praise the flexibility she found at her school: "Community colleges attract students who have other full-time obligations, such as work or family. [10]Most instructors understand this and are willing to accommodate."

[11]In an interview, Dr. Richard Kratz notes, "Community colleges are the only sector of American education that is truly American. [12]Everything else has been borrowed from British education."

[13]For all the above reasons, it is likely that community colleges will continue growing in importance in the American educational system.

Name _____   Section _____ Date _____

Score: (Number right) _____ x 10 = _____%

Quotation Marks: TEST 1

On the lines provided, rewrite the following sentences, adding quotation marks as needed.

Note To help you master quotation marks, explanations are given for the first three sentences.

1. My mother said, Take some vitamin C for your cold.

The mother's words and the period at the end of the sentence should be included within quotation marks.

My mother said, "Take some vitamin C for your cold."

2. Do not discuss the trial during your break, the judge reminded the jury.

The judge's words and the comma at the end of his words should be enclosd within quotation marks.

"Do not discuss the trial during your break," the judge reminded the jury.

3. That movie, my friend complained, is full of nonstop violence.

Each of the two parts of the friend's words requires a set of quotation marks. The words *my friend complained* do not get quotation marks because he did not speak them aloud.

"That movie," my friend complained, "is full of nonstop violence."

4. The children's voices sang, Row, row, row your boat, gently down the stream.

The children's voices sang, "Row, row, row your boat, gently down the stream."

5. My computer screen is frozen, I said to the instructor.

"My computer screen is frozen," I said to the instructor.

6. Let's eat, Rochelle said, before we go to the movie.

"Let's eat," Rochelle said, "before we go to the movie."

7. A sign on my father's desk reads, In the rat race, only the rats win.

A sign on my father's desk reads, "In the rat race, only the rats win."

8. Who would like another slice of turkey? Mr. Brandon asked the dinner guests.

"Who would like another slice of turkey?" Mr. Brandon asked the dinner guests.

9. Keep your voice down! the little boy shouted loudly to the woman using a cell phone.

"Keep your voice down!" the little boy shouted loudly to the woman using a cell phone.

10. Take a lot of notes, my friend warned, if you want to do well on tests.

"Take a lot of notes," my friend warned, "if you want to do well on tests."

Name _____ Section _____ Date _____

Score: (Number right) _____ x 10 = _____%

Quotation Marks: TEST 2

On the lines provided, rewrite the following sentences, adding quotation marks as needed.

1. It can't be time to get up yet, Isaac groaned as his alarm clock rang.

"It can't be time to get up yet," Isaac groaned as his alarm clock rang.

2. The waitress said, What'll it be, folks?

The waitress said, "What'll it be, folks?"

3. Get away from that hot stove! Maria ordered her daughter.

"Get away from that hot stove!" Maria ordered her daughter.

4. The tag on the hair dryer said, Do not use this product while taking a bath.

The tag on the hair dryer said, "Do not use this product while taking a bath."

5. Where did you buy that great bag? a woman on the bus asked me.

"Where did you buy that great bag?" a woman on the bus asked me.

6. The crowd chanted loudly, Defense! Defense! Defense!

The crowd chanted loudly, "Defense! Defense! Defense!"

7. On the front page of the *New York Times* are these words: All the news that's fit to print.

On the front page of the New York Times are these words: "All the news that's fit to print."

8. To pass this class, the instructor said, you must be here every day.

"To pass this class," the instructor said, "you must be here every day."

9. My grandfather used to say, Sometimes you eat the bear. Sometimes the bear eats you.

My grandfather used to say, "Sometimes you eat the bear. Sometimes the bear eats you."

10. Jan's voice-mail message says, I'm not home, or else I'm pretending not to be home.

Jan's voice-mail message says, "I'm not home, or else I'm pretending not to be home."

Name _____ Section _____ Date _____

Score (Number right)_____ x 10 = _____ %

Quotation Marks: TEST 3

Place quotation marks where needed in the short passages that follow. Each passage needs **two** sets of quotation marks.

1. After serving the couple expensive lobster dinners, the waitress was upset to find that they had left her only fifty cents for a tip. "Wait, mister," she called after the man. "You can use this more than I can."

2. The interviewer poked her head out of the office door and called out, "Please come in, Mr. Taylor." She asked him a few questions about his experience. Then she said, "We've had twenty-five applicants for this position. Tell me why you deserve to be hired rather than any of those others."

3. Pointing to a headline in the tabloid newspaper at the supermarket counter, the boy said, "It looks as if space aliens have landed in Minnesota."
   "You'd have to be from outer space to believe those newspapers," stated his father.

4. My uncle and aunt have different ways of dealing with guests who stay too long. My aunt will hint politely, "Well, it sure has been nice having you folks over." My uncle is much more direct. He says, "Let's call it a night, Norma, and let these nice people go home."

5. The Hollywood tourist asked the handsome man in the coffee shop for his autograph. He graciously signed her menu. When she read the signature, she sputtered, "James Dixon? You're nobody famous! "
   The man shrugged. "I didn't say I was. You're the one who asked for my autograph."

Name _____ Section _____ Date _____

Score: (Number right) _____ x 10 = _____ %

Quotation Marks: TEST 4

In each group below, **one** sentence uses quotation marks correctly. Write the letter of that sentence in the space provided.

_c_ 1. **a.** "My grades are going downhill, Laura whispered.
   b. My grades are going downhill," Laura whispered.
   c. "My grades are going downhill," Laura whispered.

_c_ 2. **a.** The movie star said, "I only ride in limousines.
   b. "The movie star said, I only ride in limousines."
   c. The movie star said, "I only ride in limousines."

_b_ 3. **a.** "Why are your eyes closed? the instructor asked Simon."
   b. "Why are your eyes closed?" the instructor asked Simon.
   c. "Why are your eyes closed? the instructor asked Simon.

_a_ 4. **a.** The instructions say, "Open the battery compartment. Insert 4 AA batteries."
   b. The instructions say, "Open the battery compartment." Insert 4 AA batteries.
   c. "The instructions say, Open the battery compartment. Insert 4 AA batteries."

_c_ 5. **a.** "It says right here in our lease," "The landlord is responsible for taking care of the yard."
   b. "It says right here in our lease," The landlord is responsible for taking care of the yard.
   c. It says right here in our lease, "The landlord is responsible for taking care of the yard."

_b_ 6. **a.** "I hate that music, said my brother, "and you know it.
   b. "I hate that music," said my brother, "and you know it."
   c. "I hate that music, said my brother, and you know it."

_a_ 7. **a.** The sign in the restaurant window reads, "Breakfast served anytime."
   b. "The sign in the restaurant window reads, "Breakfast served anytime."
   c. The sign in the restaurant window reads, "Breakfast served anytime.

_a_ 8. **a.** As I sat at the baseball game, I heard someone call, "Get your fresh hot peanuts."
   b. As I sat at the baseball game, "I heard someone call, Get your fresh hot peanuts."
   c. "As I sat at the baseball game, I heard someone call," Get your fresh hot peanuts.

_b_ 9. **a.** Dale said, "If that salesman were covered in gravy and dropped into a pit of lions, he could talk them into becoming vegetarians.
   b. Dale said, "If that salesman were covered in gravy and dropped into a pit of lions, he could talk them into becoming vegetarians."
   c. "Dale said, If that salesman were covered in gravy and dropped into a pit of lions, he could talk them into becoming vegetarians."

_b_ 10. **a.** "The first line in the novel *1984* reads," It was a bright cold day in April, and the clocks were striking thirteen.
   b. The first line in the novel *1984* reads, "It was a bright cold day in April, and the clocks were striking thirteen."
   c. "The first line in the novel *1984* reads," It was a bright cold day in April, and the clocks were striking thirteen."

Quotation Marks: TEST 5

In each group below, **one** sentence uses quotation marks correctly. Write the letter of that sentence in the space provided.

_____b_____ **1. a.** I don't like your lollipops, "the little girl said to the dentist."
          b. "I don't like your lollipops," the little girl said to the dentist.
          c. "I don't like your lollipops, the little girl said to the dentist."

_____c_____ **2. a.** Rachel announced, "I can open the locked door with a bent coat hanger.
          b. "Rachel announced, I can open the locked door with a bent coat hanger."
          c. Rachel announced, "I can open the locked door with a bent coat hanger."

_____a_____ **3. a.** The boss advised, "Don't be late again. If you are, I'll fire you."
          b. The boss advised, Don't be late again. If you are, I'll fire you."
          c. The boss advised, "Don't be late again. If you are, I'll fire you.

_____b_____ **4. a.** "Albert Einstein wrote, Will it matter that I was?"
          b. Albert Einstein wrote, "Will it matter that I was?"
          c. Albert Einstein wrote, "Will it matter that I was?

_____b_____ **5. a.** How do you like it? "Cindy asked, showing off her new purple fake-fur jacket."
          b. "How do you like it?" Cindy asked, showing off her new purple fake-fur jacket.
          c. "How do you like it? Cindy asked, showing off her new purple fake-fur jacket."

_____a_____ **6. a.** Her mother paused and then said, "Well, it certainly is a cheerful color."
          b. Her mother paused and then said, "Well, it certainly is a cheerful color.
          c. Her mother paused and then said, Well, it certainly is a cheerful color."

_____c_____ **7. a.** Her brother was less tactful. You look like a giant purple marshmallow, he said.
          b. Her brother was less tactful. "You look like a giant purple marshmallow, he said."
          c. Her brother was less tactful. "You look like a giant purple marshmallow," he said.

_____c_____ **8. a.** Most people don't plan to fail, "the counselor said," but they fail to plan.
          b. "Most people don't plan to fail," the counselor said, but they fail to plan.
          c. "Most people don't plan to fail," the counselor said, "but they fail to plan."

_____a_____ **9. a.** "Reading is to the mind what exercise is to the body," wrote Richard Steele.
          b. "Reading is to the mind what exercise is to the body, wrote Richard Steele."
          c. Reading is to the mind what exercise is to the body, "wrote Richard Steele."

_____a_____ **10. a.** Mother Teresa said, "Kind words can be easy to speak, but their echoes are truly endless."
          b. Mother Teresa said, "Kind words can be easy to speak, but their echoes are truly endless.
          c. "Mother Teresa said, "Kind words can be easy to speak, but their echoes are truly endless."

⑫ Homonyms

Basics about Homonyms

Homonyms are two or more words that have the same sound but different spellings and meanings.
The following four groups of homonyms cause writers the most trouble.

its   belonging to it
it's   contraction of *it is*

● **It's** a shame that the shiny car lost **its** muffler and now roars like an old truck.

    It is a shame that the shiny car lost *the muffler belonging to it* and now roars like an old truck.

    Spelling hint   In *it's,* the apostrophe takes the place of the *i* in the word *is.*

their   belonging to them
there   (1) in or to that place; (2) used with *is, are, was, were,* and other forms of the verb *to be*
they're contraction of *they are*

● Our neighbors are health-food addicts. When we attend parties at **their** home, they serve pizza with broccoli florets on top. **They're** also fond of serving carrot juice. I hope they won't be offended if we don't go **there** very often.

    Our neighbors are health-food addicts. When we attend parties at the home *belonging to them,* they serve pizza with broccoli florets on top. *They are* also fond of serving carrot juice. I hope they won't be offended when we don't go *to that place* very often.

    Spelling hints   *There, where,* and *here,* which all end in *-ere,* all refer to places.
                          In *they're,* the apostrophe takes the place of the *a* in *are.*

to   (1) used before a verb, as in "to serve"; (2) so as to reach
too   (1) overly or extremely; (2) also
two   the number 2

● I'll take these **two** letters **to** the post office for you, but you'll need **to** put more postage on one of them. It is **too** heavy for only one stamp.

    I'll take these *2* letters *so as to reach* the post office for you, but you'll need *to put* more postage on one of them. It is *overly* heavy for only one stamp.

    Spelling hint   *Too* has one *o,* and it **also** has another one.

your   belonging to you
you're contraction of *you are*

● **You're** going to need a first-aid kit and high boots for **your** camping trip.

    You are going to need a first-aid kit and high boots for the camping trip *belonging to you.*

    Spelling hint   In *you're,* the apostrophe takes the place of the *a* in *are.*

Understanding Homonyms

In the following passage about a married couple, Joe and Terri Davis, **five** homonym mistakes are underlined. The correct spelling of each word is then shown in the spaces below.

¹Joe and Terri live in Philadelphia. ²The <u>too</u> of them have been married for thirteen years. ³They met after Terri had an operation on her knee. ⁴While she was recovering, she had <u>too</u> ride in a special bus for people with disabilities. ⁵Because he has a spinal-cord injury, Joe used that bus <u>two</u>. ⁶It was <u>their</u> on the bus that they began getting acquainted. ⁷You never know where <u>your</u> going to meet someone special!

1. _The meaning is "the number 2," which is spelled_ two. _____ .

2. _The spelling before a verb (here,_ to ride_) is always_ to. _____

3. _The meaning is "also," which is spelled_ too. _____

4. _The meaning is "at that place," which is spelled_ there. _____

5. _The meaning is "you are," which is spelled_ you're. _(The apostrophe takes the place of the missing_ a _in_ you are.) _____

Check Your Understanding

Underline the **five** mistakes in homonyms. Then write the correct spellings of the words in the five spaces provided.

¹Now Joe and Terri have a lift for Joe's wheelchair in <u>there</u> own van. ²<u>It's</u> gas pedal and brake have been changed so that Joe can operate them by hand. ³Joe and Terri both work downtown. ⁴In this picture, <u>their</u> about to head on <u>there</u> way home. ⁵Joe is using the lift to get into the van. ⁶He'll then drive <u>too</u> a corner near Terri's office and pick her up.

1. _____their_____   2. _____Its_____

3. _____they're_____   4. _____their_____   5. _____to_____

Other Common Homonyms

brake	— slow or stop	**know**	— to understand
break	— to cause to come apart	**no**	— the opposite of *yes*
hear	— take in by ear	**right**	— correct
here	— in this place	**write**	— to form letters and words
hole	— an empty spot	**whose**	— belonging to whom
whole	— complete	**who's**	— contraction of *who is* or *who has*

Homonyms: PRACTICE 1

In the passages below, underline the correct word in the ten sets of parentheses.

¹Terri works as a receptionist in a law office. ²When *(your, you're)* answering the phone, *(writing, righting)* messages, sorting mail, and talking to visitors all at once, you need to keep both hands free. ³That's why Terri is wearing a telephone headset. ⁴She may have several phone conversations going at once. ⁵Sometimes it isn't easy remembering *(who's, whose)* on which line!

¹Joe works *(here, hear)*, in a mental-health clinic. ²He is a counselor. ³His job is to help people with *(their, there, they're)* problems. ⁴When clients first come in for counseling, they are often nervous. ⁵They don't *(know, no)* what to expect. ⁶Joe tries hard to make his clients feel comfortable. ⁷He believes that when *(you're, your)* a counselor, you should treat *(you're, your)* clients with respect.

¹Are you a "people person"? ²Or do you enjoy spending time alone? ³These are *(two, to, too)* questions to consider as you think about what kind of work you might like to do. ⁴Look around and ask yourself if *(their, there, they're)* are certain jobs that fit your personality and other ones that you wouldn't like at all.

Six More Homonyms

knew	—	past tense of *know*	**threw**	—	past tense of *throw*
new	—	opposite of old	**through**	—	into and out of; finished
peace	—	absence of war; quiet	**wear**	—	to have on (clothing)
piece	—	a part of something	**where**	—	in what place
plain	—	not fancy; obvious	**weather**	—	outside conditions
plane	—	airplane	**whether**	—	if

Homonyms: PRACTICE 2

For each sentence, underline the correct word in parentheses.

1. There is only one *(write, right)* answer to a math problem.

2. No child will be able to *(break, brake)* this toy.

3. We drove *(through, threw)* the entire state in only three hours.

4. Everyone wants *(piece, peace)* on Earth.

5. I forgot *(where, wear)* I stored the Christmas presents.

6. Are you going to order a half or a *(hole, whole)* barbecued chicken?

7. The *(weather, whether)* in England is rainy much of the time.

8. Ray and Coral, who just got married, want all *(new, knew)* furniture in their house.

9. People who cannot *(hear, here)* often communicate by American Sign Language.

10. The sign in the bus said, "*(There, They're, Their)* is no excuse for domestic violence."

Homonyms: PRACTICE 3

In the passage below, underline the correct word in each set of parentheses. **Ten** corrections are needed.

[1]Being able to read well helps a person take better care of his or her home and family. [2]Someone (_whose_, who's) reading skills aren't strong can easily be taken advantage of. [3]For instance, a stack of mail has just come (_to_, too, two) Joe and Terri's house. [4]The mail contains advertisements, letters from friends, and bills (to, _too_, two). [5](_Here_, Hear), Joe has settled down (wear, _where_) he can look (threw, _through_) the bills carefully. [6]Because he reads well, he will quickly notice if something doesn't look (_right_, write). [7]When Joe has finished reviewing the bills, he will have (piece, _peace_) of mind, knowing that they are correct. [8]A poor reader might not be able to tell (weather, _whether_) a bill is accurate or not. [9]Most companies are not out to cheat customers. [10]But they do make errors—sometimes just (_plain_, plane) old mistakes in addition—and customers need to protect themselves.

Name _____ Section _____ Date _____

Homonyms: TEST 1

Cross out the **two** homonym mistakes in each sentence. Then write the correct words in the spaces provided.

NOTE To help you review some of the homonyms in the chapter, definitions are given in four of the sentences.

It's

your

1. ~~Its~~ not too late to change ~~you're~~ mind.

It is not too late to change the mind *that belongs to you.*

brakes

whether

2. Russ ~~breaks~~ at every intersection, ~~weather~~ there is a stop sign or not.

Russ *stops* at every intersection, *if* there is a stop sign or not.

write

whole

3. Chen showed me how to ~~right~~ my ~~hole~~ name in Chinese characters.

Chen showed me how to *form the letters of* my *complete* name.

know

there

4. Before we visited friends in Montreal, I didn't ~~no~~ that French and English are both spoken ~~their~~.

I didn't *understand* that French and English are both spoken *in that place.*

peace

right

5. My uncle is one of those people who give you no ~~piece~~ and quiet until you agree that he is ~~write~~.

whose

their

6. Farm turkeys, ~~who's~~ bodies are big and fat, have lost ~~there~~ ability to fly.

too

plane

7. Because ~~to~~ many flights were scheduled to leave at the same time, our ~~plain~~ had to sit waiting on the runway for over an hour.

break

who's

8. If you ~~brake~~ your promises, ~~whose~~ going to accept your word in the future?

hear

no

9. I ~~here~~ you remembered to bring canned soup on your camping trip, but ~~know~~ can opener.

knew

threw

10. No one ~~new~~ who ~~through~~ the soda can onto the basketball court while the game was in progress.

Name _____ Section _____ Date _____

Score: (Number right) _____ x 10 = _____%

Homonyms: TEST 2

Cross out the **two** homonym mistakes in each sentence. Then write the correct words in the spaces provided.

where
you're

1. The words on the tombstone read, "I'd rather be ~~wear~~ ~~your~~ standing."

whole
they're

2. In the ~~hole~~ world, there are only a few hundred Siberian tigers. In fact, ~~their~~ almost extinct.

There
break

3. ~~Their~~ is a custom at a Jewish wedding for the groom to step on a glass and ~~brake~~ it.

weather
two

4. In really cold ~~whether~~, Jeremy always wears ~~to~~ pairs of socks.

it's
to

5. The doctor says ~~its~~ going to take at least six weeks for Jenna's sprained foot ~~too~~ heal.

new
its

6. Please place each of these ~~knew~~ books in ~~it's~~ proper place on the shelves.

know
their

7. Many young people don't ~~no~~ where ~~there~~ ancestors came from.

know
Who's

8. The test was full of silly questions I didn't ~~no~~ how to answer, such as "~~Whose~~ buried in Grant's Tomb?"

threw
plain

9. My wasteful sister ~~through~~ out a pepperoni pizza because she prefers ~~plane~~ pizza.

know
right

10. If fortunetellers really ~~no~~ the future, why aren't they all lottery winners? They should be able to choose the ~~write~~ numbers.

Name _____ Section _____ Date _____

Score: (Number right) _____ x 10 = _____ %

Homonyms: TEST 3

The passage below contains **ten** errors in homonyms. Find these errors and cross them out. Then write the correct words in the spaces provided.

¹Amelia Earhart was famous during her lifetime for being a daring pilot. ²After her death—or at least, after what was probably her death—she became even more famous, as the center of a mystery. ³As a young woman, Earhart earned her pilot's license and became something of a wanderer. ⁴When she flew across the Atlantic Ocean with too men in 1928, the unusual trip made headlines. ⁵In 1937, Earhart began her boldest trip yet. ⁶With a navigator named Fred Noonan to assist her, she set out to fly around the world. ⁷Their plain took off from Miami, Florida, in June. ⁸They flew to New Guinea, wear they stopped to rest and make repairs before taking off for an island in the Pacific on July 1. ⁹But on that date, Earhart's radio messages stopped. ¹⁰The aircraft and it's crew had disappeared.

¹¹Earhart may have simply run out of fuel over the Pacific. ¹²Or perhaps unexpected bad whether caused the airplane to brake up into pieces. ¹³But another theory says that Earhart was murdered. ¹⁴In 1937, Japan was building strong military defenses on some Pacific islands. ¹⁵Some historians believe that Earhart was forced down by Japanese troops who were afraid that she had spotted there secret military buildup. ¹⁶After all these years, no one knows who's theory is write. ¹⁷Threw the years since, many have searched for the missing aircraft, but no sign of it has been found. ¹⁸And Amelia Earhart remains one of the most famous pilots in the world.

1. two _____

2. plane _____

3. where _____

4. its _____

5. weather _____

6. break _____

7. their _____

8. whose _____

9. right _____

10. Through _____

Name _____   Section _____   Date _____

Score: (Number right) _____ x 10 = _____%

Homonyms: TEST 4

In each group below, **one** sentence uses homonyms correctly. Write the letter of that sentence in the space provided.

_____*a*_____   **1. a.** It's easy to see from your face that you're very tired.
            b. Its easy to see from your face that you're very tired.
            c. It's easy to see from your face that your very tired.

_____*b*_____   **2. a.** It isn't right to break you're promise.
            b. It isn't right to break your promise.
            c. It isn't write to break your promise.

_____*c*_____   **3. a.** Does anyone no why this empty box is sitting hear?
            b. Does anyone know why this empty box is sitting hear?
            c. Does anyone know why this empty box is sitting here?

_____*c*_____   **4. a.** Surely your not going to eat that whole cake all by yourself.
            b. Surely your not going to eat that hole cake all by yourself.
            c. Surely you're not going to eat that whole cake all by yourself.

_____*a*_____   **5. a.** Maura and Julie are so different that it's difficult to believe that they're sisters.
            b. Maura and Julie are so different that its difficult to believe that their sisters.
            c. Maura and Julie are so different that it's difficult to believe that there sisters.

_____*c*_____   **6. a.** Since beginning his karate class, Brian claims he can brake a stack of two bricks with his bare hand.
            b. Since beginning his karate class, Brian claims he can break a stack of too bricks with his bare hand.
            c. Since beginning his karate class, Brian claims he can break a stack of two bricks with his bare hand.

_____*b*_____   **7. a.** Its impossible to cancel the party—the guests are already on they're way.
            b. It's impossible to cancel the party—the guests are already on their way.
            c. Its impossible to cancel the party—the guests are already on their way.

_____*c*_____   **8. a.** You're cat is going to break its leg if it jumps down from that tall tree.
            b. Your cat is going to break it's leg if it jumps down from that tall tree.
            c. Your cat is going to break its leg if it jumps down from that tall tree.

_____*b*_____   **9. a.** The water is so cold that it's hard to breathe when your in it.
            b. The water is so cold that it's hard to breathe when you're in it.
            c. The water is so cold that its hard to breathe when you're in it.

_____*c*_____   **10. a.** If they're is life on other planets, it's probably very different from life on Earth.
            b. If there is life on other planets, its probably very different from life on Earth.
            c. If there is life on other planets, it's probably very different from life on Earth.

Name _____ Section _____ Date _____

Score: (Number right) _____ x 10 = _____%

Homonyms: TEST 5

In each group below, **one** sentence uses homonyms correctly. Write the letter of that sentence in the space provided.

_c_   **1. a.** Now that Mrs. Ringwald is in the hospital, no one nos whose going to teach her class.
      b. Now that Mrs. Ringwald is in the hospital, no one knows whose going to teach her class.
      c. Now that Mrs. Ringwald is in the hospital, no one knows who's going to teach her class.

_a_   **2. a.** Here in Detroit, many people earn their living in the automobile industry.
      b. Hear in Detroit, many people earn their living in the automobile industry.
      c. Hear in Detroit, many people earn they're living in the automobile industry.

_c_   **3. a.** Excuse me, but you're radio is playing too loudly for the other passengers.
      b. Excuse me, but your radio is playing to loudly for the other passengers.
      c. Excuse me, but your radio is playing too loudly for the other passengers.

_a_   **4. a.** Too many people write unsigned letters to the newspaper.
      b. To many people right unsigned letters to the newspaper.
      c. Two many people write unsigned letters to the newspaper.

_c_   **5. a.** To brake the habit of smoking takes a whole lot of willpower.
      b. To break the habit of smoking takes a hole lot of willpower.
      c. To break the habit of smoking takes a whole lot of willpower.

_c_   **6. a.** You're wasting to much time worrying about things you can't control.
      b. Your wasting to much time worrying about things you can't control.
      c. You're wasting too much time worrying about things you can't control.

_a_   **7. a.** After two weeks, the lost cat returned, thin and dirty and without its collar.
      b. After too weeks, the lost cat returned, thin and dirty and without it's collar.
      c. After to weeks, the lost cat returned, thin and dirty and without its collar.

_b_   **8. a.** Unfortunately, it's easy to take you're family and friends for granted.
      b. Unfortunately, it's easy to take your family and friends for granted.
      c. Unfortunately, its easy to take your family and friends for granted.

_b_   **9. a.** Their are too many empty storefronts in the downtown area.
      b. There are too many empty storefronts in the downtown area.
      c. They're are two many empty storefronts in the downtown area.

_a_   **10. a.** Where will the party be held if the weather turns bad?
      b. Wear will the party be held if the whether turns bad?
      c. Where will the party be held if the whether turns bad?

⑬ Capital Letters

Basics about Capital Letters

Here are six main uses of capital letters:

1 THE FIRST WORD IN A SENTENCE OR DIRECT QUOTATION

- The ice-cream man said, "Try a frozen banana bar. They're delicious."

2 THE WORD "I" AND PEOPLE'S NAMES

- Because I was the first caller in the radio contest, I won two backstage passes to the Jennifer Lopez concert. My friend Maria Santana went with me.

3 NAMES OF SPECIFIC PLACES, INSTITUTIONS, AND LANGUAGES

- Janice, who lives in Boston and works as a lab technician at Newton Hospital, grew up on a farm in Kokomo, Indiana.

- The signs in the airport terminal were written in Spanish, English, and Japanese.

4 PRODUCT NAMES

Capitalize the brand name of a product, but not the kind of product it is.

- Every morning Ben has Tropicana orange juice and Total cereal with milk.

5 CALENDAR ITEMS

Capitalize the names of days of the week, months, and holidays.

- At first, Thanksgiving was celebrated on the last Thursday in November, but it was changed to the fourth Thursday of the month.

6 TITLES

Capitalize the titles of books, TV or stage shows, songs, magazines, movies, articles, poems, stories, papers, and so on.

- Sitting in the waiting room, Dennis nervously paged through issues of *Newsweek* and *People* magazines.

- Gwen wrote a paper titled "Portrayal of Women in Rap Music Videos" that was based on videos shown on MTV.

NOTE The words *the, of, a, an, and,* and other little, unstressed words are not capitalized when they appear in the middle of a title. That is why *of* and *in* are not capitalized in "Portrayal of Women in Rap Music Videos."

Understanding Capital Letters

Notice how capital letters are used in the following passage about Mark Wilson, a Philadelphia high-school student.

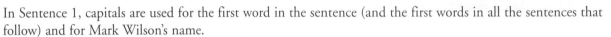

¹This is Mark Wilson. ²Mark is a sophomore at Furness High School in Philadelphia. ³Mark lives with his family on Algard Street on the other side of Philadelphia. ⁴"To get to school," Mark says, "I take two buses and a train. ⁵The trip lasts an hour and a half." ⁶Today is a Sunday in March, so Mark gets to stay home and relax. ⁷Mark travels so far to school because he is determined to be the best that he can be, no matter what the obstacles are.

In Sentence 1, capitals are used for the first word in the sentence (and the first words in all the sentences that follow) and for Mark Wilson's name.
In Sentences 2 and 3, capitals are used for specific institutions (Furness High School) and places (Algard Street, Philadelphia).
In Sentences 4 and 5, capitals are used for Mark's name and the word "I."
In Sentence 6, capitals are used for calendar items: a day of the week (Sunday) and a month (March).

Check Your Understanding

The following passage contains **five** errors in capitalization. Underline those words, and then write them, properly capitalized, in the spaces that follow.

¹Mark decided to attend <u>furness</u> in order to enroll in the school's law enforcement program. ²He is interested in a career in federal law enforcement. ³<u>because</u> of that interest, Mark says, "I also took part in a summer 'boot camp' program held at a military base in <u>willow</u> Grove, Pennsylvania." ⁴There, Mark learned about military life, military history, and military discipline. ⁵He has taken part in other special programs, too. ⁶For four days last <u>february</u>, he attended an academic enrichment program at <u>dartmouth</u> College in New Hampshire.

1.   Furness
2.   Because
3.   Willow
4.   February
5.   Dartmouth

Capital Letters: PRACTICE 1

Each of the short passages that follow contains **five** errors in capitalization. Underline the words that need capitalizing. Then write these words correctly in the spaces provided.

¹Mark has always been a young man who thinks for himself. ²<u>peer</u> pressure doesn't influence him. ³He says, "<u>most</u> kids care too much about what other kids think. ⁴You've got to be your own person." ⁵His parents have encouraged him to aim high. ⁶They want Mark and his younger brother <u>kenny</u> involved in school and extra-curricular activities. ⁷"I didn't finish high school myself," says Mark's dad. ⁸"Now <u>i</u> work in a furniture warehouse over in <u>kensington</u>. ⁹I've taken Mark in to work so he can see what it's like to work your tail off in 100-degree heat. ¹⁰He knows that doing well in school is the key to getting a job where he uses his head, not his back."

1. __Peer__

2. __Most__

3. __Kenny__

4. __I__

5. __Kensington__

¹Although he works hard in school and out of it, Mark is in most ways a typical teenager. ²<u>on</u> this <u>sunday</u>, when he was in the kitchen with his mom, the photographer told him to act natural. ³In response, he put out his hand and asked, "<u>can i</u> have some money?" ⁴Do you think he wants some new <u>nike</u> sneakers?

6. __On__

7. __Sunday__

8. __Can__

9. __I__

10. __Nike__

Capital Letters: PRACTICE 2

Underline the **two** words that need capitalizing in each sentence. Then write these words correctly in the spaces provided.

1. Our brother's usual breakfast of <u>pepsi</u> and <u>doritos</u> makes me shake my head.

   <u>Pepsi</u>   <u>Doritos</u>

2. In <u>december</u> 2001, the city of <u>buffalo</u> received almost seven feet of snow.

   <u>December</u>   <u>Buffalo</u>

3. <u>my</u> parents asked, "<u>why</u> did you get in so late last night?"

   <u>My</u>   <u>Why</u>

4. On next <u>monday</u>, which is <u>christmas</u>, most local stores will be closed.

   <u>Monday</u>   <u>Christmas</u>

5. Few people recognize the name of Chester <u>arthur</u>, who was the twenty-first president of the United <u>states</u>.

   <u>Arthur</u>   <u>States</u>

6. Before <u>thanksgiving</u>, our church always delivers turkeys and cases of <u>progresso</u> soup to poor families.

   <u>Thanksgiving</u>   <u>Progresso</u>

7. Norm's "dream car" for some day is a <u>lexus</u>, but meanwhile he drives an old <u>chevrolet</u> station wagon.

   <u>Lexus</u>   <u>Chevrolet</u>

8. Every <u>january</u>, our grandparents travel to <u>florida</u> for a winter vacation.

   <u>January</u>   <u>Florida</u>

9. When you get to <u>penn avenue</u>, you will find a lot of fast-food restaurants.

   <u>Penn</u>   <u>Avenue</u>

10. A recent issue of *newsweek* magazine described the most popular movies of the last ten years, including *gladiator*.

    <u>Newsweek</u>   <u>Gladiator</u>

Capital Letters: PRACTICE 3

Each of the short passages that follow contains **five** errors in capitalization. Underline the words that need capitalizing. Then write these words correctly in the spaces provided.

¹It's rare to find Mark without a book. ²He began reading a lot as a way to pass the time during his long trip to school. ³The first books he remembers really liking were a series of novels by W.E.B. Griffin. ⁴The novels, which take place within the philadelphia police department, include such titles as *men at war* and *Honor Bound*. ⁵After Mark worked his way through that series, his english teacher recommended some historical fiction. ⁶Mark also likes biographies, and he is pictured here reading a biography of John Wanamaker, the founder of a famous department store. ⁷It's nice to spend a lazy sunday afternoon just lying on the couch with a good book.

1.   Philadelphia
2.   Men
3.   War
4.   English
5.   Sunday

¹One of the reasons Mark wants to do well in school is that he knows his younger brother Kenny is watching him. ²Kenny notices Mark's efforts, and he tells a visitor, "don't be a fool. stay in school." ³He adds, "Mark and I are alike in some ways. ⁴We both play the trumpet." ⁵He asks Mark, "Would you rather go to Dartmouth College or temple university here in Philadelphia?" ⁶Kenny is only in fifth grade, but he's learned that people have to plan ahead to get the things that they want. ⁷But on this beautiful march day, all he really wants is to go skating with his friends.

6.   Don't
7.   Stay
8.   Temple
9.   University
10.   March

Name _____   Section _____   Date _____

Score: (Number right) _____ x 10 = _____ %

Capital Letters: TEST 1

Underline the **two** words that need to be capitalized in each sentence. Then write the words correctly in the spaces provided.

NOTE   To help you master capitalization, explanations are given for the first four sentences.

1. Last summer, my mother and i visited my aunt in New orleans.
    Capitalize the word *I* and the names of specific places.
    _____I_____   _____Orleans_____

2. The car salesman said, "here's a used buick you folks might be interested in."
    Capitalize the first word of a direct quotation and the brand name of a car.
    _____Here's_____   _____Buick_____

3. Every wednesday after school, Cara goes to chinese-language school.
    Capitalize the days of the week and the names of foreign languages.
    _____Wednesday_____   _____Chinese_____

4. The november issue of *prevention* magazine had an article you could use for your report.
    Capitalize the months of the year and the titles of magazines, but not the word *magazine*.
    _____November_____   _____Prevention_____

5. My grandfather's real name is henrik, but when he left norway, he started calling himself Hank.
    _____Henrik_____   _____Norway_____

6. When i was a little girl, I thought that cheerios grew on a cereal bush.
    _____I_____   _____Cheerios_____

7. Being located right on Lake michigan makes chicago a very windy city.
    _____Michigan_____   _____Chicago_____

8. Every other july, the members of the baker family get together for a big reunion.
    _____July_____   _____Baker_____

9. To celebrate my birthday next thursday, my family is taking me out to my favorite vietnamese restaurant.
    _____Thursday_____   _____Vietnamese_____

10. At least once a year, my cousin james and I make popcorn, sit down, and watch the movie *The Wizard of oz*.
    _____James_____   _____Oz_____

Name _____ Section _____ Date _____

Score: (Number right) _____ x 10 = _____ %

Capital Letters: TEST 2

Underline the **two** words that need to be capitalized in each sentence. Then write the words correctly in the spaces provided.

1. The friends argued over whether to get pizza from domino's or Pizza hut.

    _____Domino's_____   _____Hut_____

2. Every day in may, our local kroger supermarket is giving away a $100 gift certificate.

    _____May_____   _____Kroger_____

3. The disc jockey said, "be the ninth caller and win a trip to beautiful bermuda!"

    _____Be_____   _____Bermuda_____

4. Next term in english class, we'll be reading *The great Gatsby*.

    _____English_____   _____Great_____

5. Members of the high-school marching band are selling giant hershey bars to raise funds for their trip to hawaii.

    _____Hershey_____   _____Hawaii_____

6. This issue of *glamour* magazine has an article called "Look Like a million Dollars for Ten Bucks."

    _____Glamour_____   _____Million_____

7. This year, the month of february will contain a friday the thirteenth.

    _____February_____   _____Friday_____

8. Our favorite roller coaster is in an amusement park called Cedar point in sandusky, Ohio.

    _____Point_____   _____Sandusky_____

9. everybody in my mother's family speaks greek as well as English.

    _____Everybody_____   _____Greek_____

10. At the computer store on washington Boulevard, there are great prices on macintosh computers.

    _____Washington_____   _____Macintosh_____

Name _____   Section _____   Date _____

Capital Letters: TEST 3

Underline the **two** words that require capital letters in each short passage below. Then write these words (with capital letters) in the spaces provided.

1. Last <u>may</u>, my grandmother visited <u>colorado</u>. She bought a beautiful shawl there and claims she has never been cold since.

    _____May_____   _____Colorado_____

2. Because Randall has an evening class on <u>thursdays</u>, he often stays on campus for dinner. He usually carries some <u>ritz</u> peanut-butter crackers to eat before class.

    _____Thursdays_____   _____Ritz_____

3. A sleek black sports car with tinted windows came to a sudden stop on <u>spruce</u> <u>street</u>. A woman and her large sheepdog then came out of a pet store and hopped into the back seat.

    _____Spruce_____   _____Street_____

4. The best <u>christmas</u> gift I ever got was a <u>monopoly</u> set. The family played that game on and off for the next ten years.

    _____Christmas_____   _____Monopoly_____

5. During a break in our <u>english</u> class, I asked Reba why she was moving out of her apartment. She replied, "<u>my</u> neighbors in the apartment above me are as quiet as mice—mice in combat boots, that is."

    _____English_____   _____My_____

Name _____ Section _____ Date _____

Score: (Number right) _____ x 10 = _____ %

Capital Letters: TEST 4

In each group below, **one** sentence uses capital letters correctly. Write the letter of that sentence in the space provided.

_c_ **1. a.** Before moving into the house, lynn scrubbed the floors with lysol.
  b. Before moving into the house, Lynn scrubbed the floors with lysol.
  c. Before moving into the house, Lynn scrubbed the floors with Lysol.

_b_ **2. a.** Ellen's dinner was a Roast Beef Sandwich from Arby's and a Salad from Wendy's.
  b. Ellen's dinner was a roast beef sandwich from Arby's and a salad from Wendy's.
  c. Ellen's dinner was a roast beef Sandwich from Arby's and a Salad from Wendy's.

_a_ **3. a.** Our hostess asked, "Have you ever visited Nashville before?"
  b. Our hostess asked, "have you ever visited Nashville before?"
  c. Our hostess asked, "have You ever visited Nashville before?"

_c_ **4. a.** My little niece often watches her videotape of *Beauty and the beast.*
  b. My little niece often watches her videotape of *Beauty and The Beast.*
  c. My little niece often watches her videotape of *Beauty and the Beast.*

_b_ **5. a.** Brian foolishly complained to the police officer, "But sir, i never stop at that Stop Sign."
  b. Brian foolishly complained to the police officer, "But sir, I never stop at that stop sign."
  c. Brian foolishly complained to the police officer, "but sir, I never stop at that stop sign."

_a_ **6. a.** On the last Friday in May, Ross Hospital stopped admitting emergency patients.
  b. On the last friday in may, Ross hospital stopped admitting emergency patients.
  c. On the last Friday in May, ross hospital stopped admitting emergency patients.

_c_ **7. a.** On Memorial day and the Fourth of july, our dog howls when she hears the fireworks.
  b. On Memorial day and the fourth of July, our dog howls when she hears the fireworks.
  c. On Memorial Day and the Fourth of July, our dog howls when she hears the fireworks.

_a_ **8. a.** Grandpa heated up some Log Cabin syrup to pour over his Eggo waffles.
  b. Grandpa heated up some Log Cabin Syrup to pour over his Eggo Waffles.
  c. Grandpa heated up some Log cabin syrup to pour over his Eggo waffles.

_b_ **9. a.** When I visited Mexico, I had a chance to practice my spanish.
  b. When I visited Mexico, I had a chance to practice my Spanish.
  c. When I visited mexico, I had a chance to practice my Spanish.

_c_ **10. a.** On Monday, I must have a paper titled "Hate Crimes" ready for my english class.
  b. On Monday, I must have a paper titled "Hate crimes" ready for my english class.
  c. On Monday, I must have a paper titled "Hate Crimes" ready for my English class.

Name _____   Section _____   Date _____

Score (Number right)_____ x 10 = _____ %

Capital Letters: TEST 5

In each group below, **one** sentence uses capital letters correctly. Write the letter of that sentence in the space provided.

_____c_____ **1. a.** The man at the door said, "Can I interest you in a subscription to *time* magazine?"
  b. The man at the door said, "can I interest you in a subscription to *Time* magazine?"
  c. The man at the door said, "Can I interest you in a subscription to *Time* magazine?"

_____a_____ **2. a.** The teacher asked us to write a paper titled "The Dangers of Television."
  b. The teacher asked us to write a paper titled "The Dangers Of Television."
  c. The teacher asked us to write a paper titled "The dangers of television."

_____a_____ **3. a.** A tractor-trailer loaded with chemicals flipped over at the corner of Oak and Cherry.
  b. A Tractor-Trailer loaded with chemicals flipped over at the corner of Oak and Cherry.
  c. A tractor-trailer loaded with chemicals flipped over at the corner of oak and cherry.

_____c_____ **4. a.** On sunday, Trina cut her visa card in half to try to stop her impulse buying.
  b. On Sunday, trina cut her visa card in half to try to stop her impulse buying.
  c. On Sunday, Trina cut her Visa card in half to try to stop her impulse buying.

_____c_____ **5. a.** For years, the slogan for Timex Watches was "It takes a licking and keeps on ticking."
  b. For years, the slogan for Timex watches was "it takes a licking and keeps on ticking."
  c. For years, the slogan for Timex watches was "It takes a licking and keeps on ticking."

_____b_____ **6. a.** My friend Pedro is taking two classes at blackstone Community College.
  b. My friend Pedro is taking two classes at Blackstone Community College.
  c. My friend pedro is taking two classes at Blackstone community college.

_____b_____ **7. a.** A woman rushed into the restaurant, asking, "has anyone found a Canon camera?"
  b. A woman rushed into the restaurant, asking, "Has anyone found a Canon camera?"
  c. A woman rushed into the restaurant, asking, "Has anyone found a Canon Camera?"

_____a_____ **8. a.** I'm looking forward to the Thursday night marathon of old *I Love Lucy* episodes.
  b. I'm looking forward to the Thursday night marathon of old *I love lucy* episodes.
  c. I'm looking forward to the thursday night marathon of old *I love Lucy* episodes

_____c_____ **9. a.** Kendra is taking language courses at rider college. She plans to become a high-school Spanish teacher.
  b. Kendra is taking language courses at Rider college. She plans to become a high-school spanish teacher.
  c. Kendra is taking language courses at Rider College. She plans to become a high-school Spanish teacher.

_____c_____ **10. a.** My brother, a physical therapist, has worked at grandview hospital since september.
  b. My brother, a physical therapist, has worked at grandview Hospital since september.
  c. My brother, a physical therapist, has worked at Grandview Hospital since September.

14 Parallelism

Basics about Parallelism

Two or more equal ideas should be expressed in **parallel**, or matching, form. The absence of parallelism is jarring and awkward to read. Parallelism will help your words flow smoothly and clearly. Here's an example:

Not parallel   The new restaurant has fresh food, reasonable prices, and service that is fast.

The first two features of the restaurant—*fresh food* and *reasonable prices*—are described in parallel form. In each case, we get a descriptive word followed by the word being described:

fresh food, reasonable prices

But with the last feature, we get the word being described first and then a descriptive word:

service that is fast

To achieve parallelism, the nonparallel item must have the same form as the first two:

Parallel   The new restaurant has fresh food, reasonable prices, and **fast service**.

Here are some additional examples of problems with parallelism and explanations of how to correct them:

Not parallel   The children were arguing in the lobby, talked during the movie, and complained on the ride home.

Talked and *complained* are similar in form. But *were arguing* is not. It must be changed so that it has the same form as the other two.

Parallel   The children **argued** in the lobby, talked during the movie, and complained on the ride home.

Not parallel   Our neighbors spend a lot of time shopping, visiting friends, and they go to the movies.

The sentence lists a series of activities. *Shopping* and *visiting* both end in *-ing*. To be parallel, *they go to the movies* must be revised to include an *-ing* word.

Parallel   Our neighbors spend a lot of time shopping, visiting friends, and **going to the movies**.

Not parallel   My aunt is selfish, impatient, and she is not a kind person.

To be parallel, *she is not a kind person* should have a form that matches *selfish* and *impatient*.

Parallel   My aunt is selfish, impatient, and **unkind.**

Not parallel   Every morning I have to feed the dog and bringing in the mail.

Feed the dog and *bringing in the mail* are not parallel. For parallelism, both must be in the same form.

Parallel   Every morning I have to feed the dog and **bring in the mail.**

Understanding Parallelism

See if you can underline the **three** errors in parallelism in the following passage. Then look at the corrections below.

¹This is Jasmin Santana. ²In this picture, Jasmin is laughing, answering the telephone, and <u>she works at the computer</u>. ³It is typical for Jasmin to be doing several things at once. ⁴She is a full-time employee and a full-time student as well. ⁵Jasmin has to be very organized, efficient, and <u>with discipline</u> to get everything done. ⁶Sometimes she is discouraged by how busy she is. ⁷But she knows she will feel pride, happiness, and <u>relieved</u> when she earns her college degree.

1. <u>working at the computer.</u>
2. <u>disciplined</u>
3. <u>relief</u>

Check Your Understanding

Underline the **three** mistakes in parallelism in the following passage. Then write the correct forms in the spaces provided.

¹Jasmin works for an organization called Philadelphia Futures. ²Philadelphia Futures helps motivated high-school students in many ways. ³The organization matches them with mentors and teaches them good study skills. ⁴Jasmin is the Philadelphia Futures receptionist. ⁵She spends a lot of time answering the phone, <u>the typing of letters</u>, and greeting visitors. ⁶But she also works directly with the students in the program. ⁷She provides them with information, encouragement, and <u>she is their friend</u>. ⁸In this picture, Jasmin is shown with Virgen on the left, Julio in the middle, and <u>on the right is Kimberly</u>.

1. <u>typing letters</u>
2. <u>friendship.</u>
3 <u>Kimberly on the right.</u>

Parallelism: PRACTICE 1

Each of the short passages below contains errors in parallelism. Underline the errors. Then correct them in the spaces provided.

¹When she lived at home, Jasmin loved her grandmother's cooking. ²But now she lives on her own, and she doesn't have much time to prepare meals. ³After work, she usually makes a sandwich, heats up some soup, or she might scramble some eggs. ⁴Then she's off to campus, where she spends the evening listening to a lecture, she takes notes, and asking questions. ⁵But sometimes she has to take a break. ⁶"I call Grandma and say, 'I am so stressed out!'" Jasmin says. ⁷"And she says, 'Come over, and I'll cook for you.' ⁸I go over and she feeds me, babies me, and is talking Spanish to me. ⁹That always makes me feel better."

1. __scrambles some eggs__
2. __taking notes__
3. __talks Spanish to me__

¹Jasmin moved into her own apartment when she was just 17. ²She could have lived at home and saved money, time, and making a lot of effort. ³But back in her neighborhood, she was too distracted by friends who didn't understand why college was so important to her. ⁴They wanted her to hang out, party, and having fun. ⁵Jasmin likes to have fun, too, but doing well in school is more important to her. ⁶Sometimes living alone is boring, depressing, and it makes her feel lonely. ⁷Other times she loves feeling independent, grown-up, and having a sense of responsibility. ⁸Even when she feels lonely, she is sure her decision will pay off in the end.

4. __effort__
5. __have fun__
6. __lonely__
7. __responsible__

¹When she gets home after a long night of classes, Jasmin reviews her notes, reads her next day's assignments, and is studying for any upcoming tests. ²She often falls asleep over her textbooks. ³It's hard to find time to clean her apartment, shop for groceries, and the doing of laundry. ⁴She sometimes envies other students who work only part-time or don't have to work at all. ⁵She sees them attending class during the day and go out with their friends when they want to. ⁶"I'd like to have more time for a social life," she admits, "but that's not my top priority right now."

8. __studies for any upcoming tests__
9. __do laundry__
10. __going out__

Parallelism: PRACTICE 2

The part of each sentence that needs revising is *italicized*. On the line, rewrite this part to make it match the other item(s) listed.

1. My little brother would play video games night and day if it weren't for eating and *to have to sleep.*

   having to sleep [OR sleeping]

2. Amos chose a bouquet of white roses, red carnations, and *tulips that were yellow.*

   yellow tulips

3. Smoking and *to spit* are both prohibited on the subway.

   spitting

4. These apples are not only small but also *have a sour taste.*

   sour

5. It is easier to wash dishes every day than *letting them pile up* for a week.

   [to] let them pile up

6. In a foreign country, a visitor is overwhelmed with strange sounds, *smells that surprise*, and unusual sights.

   surprising smells

7. Laura usually either braids her hair or *is putting it up in a French twist.*

   puts it up in a French twist

8. Detective stories, popular music, and *sports that are on television* are the things that my grandparents enjoy most.

   television sports [OR televised sports]

9. For lunch we were given limp bologna sandwiches, *peanut-butter crackers that were stale*, and warm sugary punch.

   stale peanut-butter crackers

10. Many runaways are lured to the city by the bright lights, *activity going on constantly*, and empty promises.

    constant activity

Parallelism: PRACTICE 3

The passage below contains **five** errors in parallelism. Underline the errors. Then correct them in the spaces provided.

¹In spite of her difficult schedule, Jasmin is smiling, focused, and she stays positive. ²She keeps her goals in mind. ³Those goals are to do well in college and getting admitted to law school. ⁴She wants to earn her law degree, become a judge, and working to help the Latino community. ⁵"I see so many people around me get in trouble, go to jail, and giving up on themselves," she says. ⁶"As a judge, I'll be in a position to see that people get the help they need."

⁷Jasmin is grateful for the support of her family as she works to achieve her dreams. ⁸"My mom and my aunts are my best friends. ⁹And Grandma is terrific. ¹⁰She'd like to see me settling down, get married, and having kids, but if going to school is what makes me happy, she respects that, too."

1. ___positive_____

2. ___[to] get admitted to law school_____

3. ___work to help the Latino community_____

4. ___give up on themselves_____

5. ___getting married_____

Name _____ Section _____ Date _____

Score: (Number right) _____ x 10 = _____%

Parallelism: TEST 1

The part of each sentence that needs revising is *italicized*. On the line, rewrite this part to make it match the other item(s) listed.

NOTE To help you master parallelism, explanations are given for the first three sentences.

1. Nina has a high fever and *a throat that is sore.*

A throat that is sore must be changed to the same form as *a high fever.*

a sore throat

2. On a busy highway, traveling too slow is almost as bad as *to drive* too fast.

To drive must be changed to the same form as *traveling.*

driving

3. Humming computers, beeping fax machines, and *the ring of telephones* are part of almost every modern office.

The ring of telephones must have the same form as *humming computers* and *beeping fax machines.*

ringing telephones

4. These grapes are big, sweet, and *full of juice.*

juicy

5. To love your family, your work, and *giving love to your friends*—this is happiness.

your friends

6. Tonight's menu includes *chicken that is roasted,* baked potatoes, and steamed broccoli.

roast [OR roasted] chicken

7. I never thought I'd miss my sister's shrill laughter and *jokes that are stupid,* but I do.

stupid jokes

8. All dumbbell Donald asks of a girlfriend is that she adore him, *the lending of money,* and center her entire life around him.

lend him money

9. My New Year's resolutions were to stop talking so much, *losing weight,* and to do more reading.

to lose weight

10. The diner at the table next to me made choking noises, *was turning red,* and pointed to his throat.

turned red

Name _____ Section _____ Date _____

Parallelism: TEST 2

The part of each sentence that needs revising is *italicized*. On the line, rewrite this part to make it match the other item(s) listed.

1. Golden retriever puppies are adorable, with big eyes, soft fur, and *expressions of sweetness.*

   sweet expressions
   _____

2. Long hours, *pay that was low*, and unpleasant coworkers are the reasons I left my job.

   low pay
   _____

3. Our hostess told us to help ourselves to the buffet and *we could get drinks* in the kitchen.

   [to] get drinks
   _____

4. The sick boy's mother gave him some aspirin, tucked him in bed, and *was pouring* him a cup of tea.

   poured
   _____

5. The house we wanted to buy had a big backyard, sunny rooms, and *a kitchen that was modern.*

   a modern kitchen
   _____

6. My uncle usually wears loud ties, *shoes that are scuffed*, and wrinkled shirts.

   scuffed shoes
   _____

7. The speaker had sweaty hands, an upset stomach, and *a voice that was nervous.*

   a nervous voice
   _____

8. For exercise, I either play basketball at the gym or *the riding of a bike* in the park.

   ride a bike
   _____

9. Our neighbors include a dress designer, *a person who teaches second grade*, and a car salesperson.

   a second-grade teacher
   _____

10. Without warning, the sky got dark, a wind sprang up, and *there was a drop in the temperature.*

    the temperature dropped
    _____

Name _____ Section _____ Date _____

Score: (Number right) _____ x 10 = _____ %

Parallelism: TEST 3

There are **ten** problems with parallelism in the following selection. Cross out each error in parallelism, and write the correction above the line.

¹The novel *Les Miserables* was written in the 1800s by French author Victor Hugo. ²It tells

the story of Jean Valjean. ³Poor and ~~being full of hunger~~ [hungry], Valjean stole a loaf of bread one day.

⁴He was arrested and ~~receiving~~ [received] a sentence of five years as a slave in a galley ship. ⁵His attempts

to escape added years to his sentence. ⁶In the end, Valjean served nineteen years for stealing

the bread. ⁷He left prison bitter, vengeful, and ~~full of anger~~ [angry]. ⁸But a surprising event changed

Valjean's mind and ~~was softening~~ [softened] his heart.

⁹Valjean could find nothing to eat and no place ~~for sleeping~~ [to sleep] because everyone was afraid of

him. ¹⁰Finally, he stormed angrily into the house of a bishop. ¹¹He demanded a scrap of food

and ~~was asking~~ [asked] for permission to sleep in the stable. ¹²To Valjean's surprise, the bishop

welcomed him kindly and ~~in a warm fashion~~ [warmly]. ¹³He ate dinner with Valjean and then led him to

a comfortable bedroom.

¹⁴During the night, Valjean sneaked out of bed and ~~was stealing~~ [stole] the knives and forks from

the dining room. ¹⁵In the morning, soldiers brought him and the silverware to the bishop's

door. ¹⁶The bishop greeted him as a friend and ~~was responding~~ [responded], "I am glad you took the

silverware I gave you." ¹⁷Convinced that Valjean was innocent, the soldiers went away. ¹⁸Valjean

spent the rest of his life helping people, sharing with them, and ~~he showed~~ [showing] them the

kindness the bishop had shown him.

Name _____ Section _____ Date _____

Score (Number right)_____ x 10 = _____ %

Parallelism: TEST 4

In each group below, **one** sentence uses parallelism correctly. Write the letter of that sentence in the space provided.

___b___ **1. a.** My older brother and the only sister I have are coming to my graduation.
      b. My older brother and my only sister are coming to my graduation.
      c. My older brother and the only sister of mine are coming to my graduation.

___a___ **2. a.** On hot days I close the windows, turn on the fans, and complain a lot.
      b. On hot days I close the windows, turn on the fans, and am complaining a lot.
      c. On hot days I close the windows, turning on the fans, and complain a lot.

___b___ **3. a.** Our manager requires us to smile constantly, to speak in a cheerful way, and to move quickly.
      b. Our manager requires us to smile constantly, to speak cheerfully, and to move quickly.
      c. Our manager requires us to smile constantly, to speak in a cheerful way, and to be moving quickly.

___a___ **4. a.** Grass like velvet and flowers like jewels make the park a beautiful place to visit.
      b. Grass like velvet and jewel-like flowers make the park a beautiful place to visit.
      c. Grass like velvet and flowers that look like jewels make the park a beautiful place to visit.

___c___ **5. a.** By the end of the hike, many of us complained of blistered feet, backs that ached, or skinned knees.
      b. By the end of the hike, many of us complained of feet that were blistered, aching backs, or skinned knees.
      c. By the end of the hike, many of us complained of blistered feet, aching backs, or skinned knees.

___c___ **6. a.** Writing a research paper and science test studying are my tasks for the weekend.
      b. Writing a research paper and to study for a science test are my tasks for the weekend.
      c. Writing a research paper and studying for a science test are my tasks for the weekend.

___a___ **7. a.** Which do you appreciate more: something given or something earned?
      b. Which do you appreciate more: something that is given to you or something earned?
      c. Which do you appreciate more: something given or something that you earn?

___a___ **8. a.** Students who make sacrifices to be in school are often the most focused, serious, and motivated.
      b. Students who make sacrifices to be in school are often the most focused, serious, and having motivation.
      c. Students who make sacrifices to be in school are often the most focused, they are serious, and motivated.

___a___ **9. a.** Watching movies, eating pizza, and playing country music are Lenny's ideas of a good time.
      b. Watching movies, to eat pizza, and playing country music are Lenny's ideas of a good time.
      c. Watching movies, eating pizza, and the playing of country music are Lenny's ideas of a good time.

___c___ **10. a.** When Marco returned home from the dance, he was frustrated, angry, and feeling depression.
      b. When Marco returned home from the dance, he was frustrated, there was anger, and he felt depressed.
      c. When Marco returned home from the dance, he was frustrated, angry, and depressed.

Parallelism: TEST 5

In each group below, one sentence uses parallelism correctly. Write the letter of that sentence in the space provided.

_c_   **1. a.** Peeling paint and windows that were broken made the old house look sad.
         b. Peeling paint and the breaking of windows made the old house look sad.
         c. Peeling paint and broken windows made the old house look sad.

_b_   **2. a.** The loud voices, air that has smoke in it, and stale smells in the room all made me want to leave quickly.
         b. The loud voices, smoky air, and stale smells in the room all made me want to leave quickly.
         c. Voices that were loud, smoky air, and stale smells in the room all made me want to leave quickly.

_c_   **3. a.** Fran sucked in her stomach, stopped breathing, and was trying to pull the zipper up.
         b. Fran sucked in her stomach, was not breathing, and tried to pull the zipper up.
         c. Fran sucked in her stomach, stopped breathing, and tried to pull the zipper up.

_c_   **4. a.** The book, with its tattered pages and cover that was missing, had been read many times.
         b. The book, with its tattered pages and that had a cover missing, had been read many times.
         c. The book, with its tattered pages and missing cover, had been read many times.

_a_   **5. a.** Students from lower-income families often have to hold jobs, go to school, and take care of children all at the same time.
         b. Students from lower-income families often have to hold jobs, go to school, and caring for children all at the same time.
         c. Students from lower-income families often have to hold jobs, going to school, and take care of children all at the same time.

_b_   **6. a.** The movie featured terrible acting, excessive violence, and plot twists that were ridiculous.
         b. The movie featured terrible acting, excessive violence, and ridiculous plot twists.
         c. The movie featured terrible acting, violence to excess, and ridiculous plot twists.

_a_   **7. a.** Attending class regularly and taking notes carefully are real keys to success in school.
         b. Attending class regularly and to take notes carefully are real keys to success in school.
         c. To attend class regularly and taking notes carefully are real keys to success in school.

_b_   **8. a.** The babysitter's nails, long and red, heavy eye makeup, and jangling jewelry all frightened the twins.
         b. The babysitter's long red nails, heavy eye makeup, and jangling jewelry all frightened the twins.
         c. The babysitter's long red nails, eye makeup that was heavy, and jangling jewelry all frightened the twins.

_b_   **9. a.** The driving rain turned the park into a swamp and the highway was a river.
         b. The driving rain turned the park into a swamp and the highway into a river.
         c. The driving rain turned the park into a swamp and made a river of the highway.

_a_   **10. a.** I know not how others may feel, but as for me, give me liberty or give me death.
         b. I know not how others may feel, but as for me, give me liberty or else I would prefer to die.
         c. I know not how others may feel, but as for me, liberty or give me death.

PART TWO   Extending the Skills

PART TWO
Extending the Skills

PREVIEW

Part Two presents some topics not included in Part One:

15 Preparing a Paper   169

16 Punctuation Marks   171

17 Pronoun Forms   178

18 Pronoun Problems   187

19 Adjectives and Adverbs   197

20 Misplaced and Dangling Modifiers   207

21 Word Choice   214

22 Numbers and Abbreviations   220

It also includes additional information about many of the topics presented in Part One:

23 More about Subjects and Verbs   225

24 More about Subject-Verb Agreement   235

25 More about Verbs   242

26 Even More about Verbs   253

27 More about Run-Ons and Comma Splices   261

28 More about Commas   265

29 More about Apostrophes   271

30 More about Quotation Marks   277

31 More about Homonyms   282

32 More about Capital Letters   289

15 Preparing a Paper

Basics about Preparing a Paper

Here are important guidelines for preparing a paper.

THE TITLE

Most of your school papers will begin with a title. The title of a paper prepared on a computer should be about an inch and a half from the top of the page. The title of a handwritten paper should be on the top line of the first page. For example, here are the title and the opening part of a paper about the author's brother.

	A Shy Brother
	My older brother is the shyest person I know. Whenever there
	are more than two people in a group, he will stop talking. He has
	never raised his hand to answer a question in class...

Use the above correctly written example to identify each of the following statements as either true (**T**) or false (**F**).

___F___ **1.** The title should be set off in quotation marks.

___F___ **2.** The title should have a period after it.

___T___ **3.** The title should be capitalized.

___T___ **4.** The title should be centered on the page.

___T___ **5.** A line should be skipped between the title and the first sentence.

You should have answered "False" for the first two items and "True" for the last three. Here is a checklist for how to handle a title:

● Type the title about an inch and a half below the top of the first page. For handwritten papers, put the title on the top line of the first page.

● Center the title.

● Do not use quotation marks around the title or put a period after the title.

● Capitalize each word in the title. (The only exceptions are small words such as *a, the, and, of, in,* and *for* in the middle of a title.)

● Skip a line between the title and the first sentence of the paper.

169

INDENTING THE FIRST LINE

The first line of a paragraph should be **indented**—that is, set in—about one-half inch from the left-hand margin. (Note the indentation of the first line of the paper about the shy brother.) Do not indent the other sentences in a paragraph.

MARGINS

Leave enough margin on all four sides of a paper to avoid a crowded look. The standard margins on a typed paper are about an inch and a half on the top and sides of the paper and an inch on the right and at the bottom.

OTHER GUIDELINES

1 Use full-sized paper (8 1/2 by 11 inches).

2 Write or type on only one side of the paper.

3 Ideally, type your paper using double-spacing. If you are writing by hand, do the following:
   - Use blue or black ink—never pencil.
   - Use wide-lined paper, or write on every other line of narrow-lined paper.
   - Write letters and punctuation marks as clearly as you can, taking care to distinguish between small and capital letters.

4 If your teacher so requests, include a cover page on which you put your name, the date, the title, and the section number of your course.

● Practice

What **five** corrections are needed in the student paper shown below? Explain the corrections needed in the five numbered spaces below.

	Family meetings
	My family has found various ways to get along well. One way is having
	family meetings. We meet twice a month to discuss and handle our
	problems before they get out of hand. This has saved the members of
	my family a great deal of aggravation. For instance, when my brother . . .

1. The title should be centered.

2. The second word of the title needs to be capitalized.

3. A line should be skipped after the title.

4. The paragraph's first line should be indented.

5. A margin is needed on the right side.

(16) Punctuation Marks

Eight Types of Punctuation Marks

This chapter first describes three marks of punctuation that are used to end a sentence: the period (.), the question mark (?), and the exclamation point (!). The chapter then describes five additional marks of punctuation: the colon (:), semicolon (;), hyphen (-), dash (—), and parentheses ( ).

THE PERIOD (.)

Use a **period** at the end of a statement, a mild command, or an indirect question.

- The children jumped over all the rain puddles.
  (A statement)
- Hand me the red pen.
  (A mild command)
- I wonder if there will be a surprise quiz today.
  (An indirect question)

THE QUESTION MARK (?)

Use a **question mark** after a sentence that asks a question.

- Are you ready for the test?
- How did the car get scratched?
- "Can I have your phone number?" Susanne asked Phil.

Indirect questions tell the reader about questions, rather than asking them directly. They end with periods, not question marks.

- The teacher asked if we were ready for the test.
- I wonder how the car got scratched.
- Susanne asked Phil if she could have his phone number.

THE EXCLAMATION POINT (!)

Use an **exclamation point** after a word or statement that expresses extreme emotion or that gives a strong command.

- Help!
- Wow!
- I just got a huge raise!
- Cut that out!

Note Exclamation points lose their power if they are used too frequently. Use them only when you wish to emphasize strong emotion.

● Practice 1

Place a period, question mark, or exclamation point at the end of each of the following sentences.

Example   Will we see each other again **?**

1. Our family car has trouble starting on cold or wet mornings**.**
2. What classes are you taking this semester**?**
3. Watch out for that barbed wire**!**
4. Please fill out an application, and then take a seat**.**
5. May I use your computer**?**
6. Iced tea was first served at the 1904 World's Fair**.**
7. That speeding car is going to hit us**!**
8. My brother asked if he could use my computer**.**
9. Do you think it's going to rain**?**
10. Bicycles, which don't pollute, may be the world's best method of transportation**.**

THE COLON (:)

The **colon** directs attention to what follows. It has three main uses:

1 Use a colon to introduce a list.

- On her first day of vacation, Carrie did three things**:** she watched a funny movie, took a long nap, and ate at her favorite restaurant.

2 Use a colon to introduce a long or a formal quotation.

- The autobiography of Arthur Ashe begins with the following Biblical quotation**:** "Since we are surrounded by so great a cloud of witnesses, let us lay aside every weight, and the sin which so easily ensnares us, and let us run with endurance the race that is set before us."

3 Use a colon to introduce an explanation.

- Bert suddenly canceled his evening plans for a simple reason**:** his car was out of gas.

The use of a colon in the opening of a letter is explained on page 267.

● Practice 2

Add **one** colon to each sentence.

1. This dessert requires only three ingredients**:** graham crackers, marshmallows, and chocolate chips.
2. The book *Anna Karenina* begins with this famous observation**:** "Happy families are all alike; every unhappy family is unhappy in its own way."
3. By the end of her first date with Bill, Julie was positive of one thing**:** there would never be a second.
4. James left the carnival loaded down with treats**:** cotton candy, stuffed toys, balloons, and three live goldfish.
5. Instead of the anger he expected, Darryl felt only one emotion when his son was brought home by the police**:** great relief.

THE SEMICOLON (;)

A **semicolon** indicates that the reader should pause. It has three main uses:

1 Use a semicolon to join two complete thoughts that are closely related, but are not connected by a joining word (such as *and, but,* or *so*).

- Our cat knocked over a can of Coca-Cola; the soda foamed over the white carpet.

2 Use a semicolon to join two closely related complete thoughts with a transitional word or word group (such as *afterwards, however, instead, therefore,* and *on the other hand*). Follow the transitional word or word group with a comma.

- LeQuita began school without knowing any English; nevertheless, she will graduate at the top of her class.

The use of a semicolon to join two complete thoughts is explained in "More about Run-Ons and Comma Splices" on pages 261–262.

3 Use semicolons to separate items in a series when the items themselves contain commas.

- Driving down Sunset Strip, we passed La Boutique, which sells women's clothing; The Friendly Cafe, which serves twenty different kinds of coffee; and Pet Palace, which sells snakes, parrots, and spiders.

● Practice 3

Add one or more semicolons to each sentence.

1. Many hopeful actors move to Hollywood; most leave disappointed.

2. We went to the airport to pick up my cousin; however, her flight had been canceled.

3. Winners in the dog show were Lady Luck, a German shepherd; Skipper's Delight, a golden retriever; and Nana, a miniature poodle.

4. The emergency room was crowded; everyone looked worried.

5. Hank thought the glass contained lemonade; instead, he drank pure lemon juice.

THE HYPHEN (-)

Hyphens are used within a word or between two words. Following are three main uses of hyphens:

1 Use a hyphen to divide a word at the end of a line of writing.

- The lawyer stood up, put on her jacket, shoved a bundle of papers into her brief-case, and hurried to court.

Note   Here are rules for dividing a word at the end of a line:

   a Never divide a word which has only one syllable.

   b Divide words only between syllables.

   c Never divide a word in a way that leaves only one or two letters alone on a line.

   d When dividing a word that already contains a hyphen, divide where the hyphen is.

2 Use a hyphen to join two or more words that act together to describe a noun that follows them.

- The sports car swerved around the slow-moving truck.

3 Put a hyphen in any number from twenty-one to ninety-nine and in a fraction that is written out, such as one-fourth or two-thirds.

Note Words made up of two or more words are sometimes hyphenated (for example, *baby-sit* and *fine-tune*). There is no clear rule to cover such cases, so when you're unsure about whether or not to hyphenate such words, check your dictionary.

Practice 4

Add a hyphen to each sentence.

1. Polls show that two̭thirds of the voters would support higher taxes.

2. You've handed in a very welḽwritten story.

3. That angry̭looking boss actually has a sweet personality.

4. Although Trudy turned thirty last month, she tells everyone she's twenty̭eight.

5. José was telling me about a beautiful greeṋeyed girl he saw on the subway.

THE DASH (—)

While the hyphen is used within or between individual words, the **dash** is used between parts of a sentence. Following are three common uses of the dash:

1 Dashes may be used to set off and emphasize interrupting material. Use them when you wish to give special attention to words that interrupt the flow of the sentence.

- Everyone in that family—including the teenagers—has a weight problem.

2 Use a dash to signal the end of a list of items.

- Family support, prayer, and hope—these are what got Grady through all those months in recovery.

3 A dash may be used to introduce a final element—a list of items, an explanation, or a dramatic point.

- Anne's refrigerator was packed with food for the party—trays of cold cuts, bottles of pickles, loaves of bread, and several pitchers of lemonade.
- Ravi hurriedly left work in the middle of the day—his wife was having labor pains.
- My wallet was found in a trash can—minus its cash.

Note As mentioned above, the colon can also be used to introduce a list or an explanation. A colon tends to add more formality and less drama to a sentence than a dash.

When typing, form a dash with two hyphens, leaving no space between them; do not leave spaces before or after the dash.

● Practice 5

Add **one** or **two** dashes, as needed, to each sentence.

1. Several papers important papers are missing from my desk.

2. A year after their divorce, Oscar and Ruby did something surprising they got married again.

3. Delicious food, wonderful service, and low prices that's all I ask in a restaurant.

4. The maple tree in our front yard it had been standing there for sixty years blew down last night.

5. Harold walked into the room wearing an odd outfit an elegant tuxedo, a rose in his buttonhole, and cheap rubber sandals.

PARENTHESES ( )

Here are two common uses of **parentheses**:

1 Use parentheses to set off material that interrupts the flow of a sentence. While dashes are used to emphasize interrupting material, parentheses are generally used for material you do not wish to emphasize.

   ● Aunt Fern (who arrived two hours late) brought the biggest gift.

2 Place parentheses around numbers that introduce items in a list within a sentence.

   ● Ron's work for the evening is as follows: (1) finish a history paper, (2) read a chapter in the science text, and (3) wash a load of laundry.

● Practice 6

Add **one** set of parentheses to each sentence.

1. The tree by our front door (a sycamore) is home to a family of robins.

2. My mother (whose maiden name is Wojcik) was born in a small town in Poland.

3. The Twice Around Resale Shop (it's at Fifth and Maple) has wonderful clothing bargains.

4. To perform this magic trick, you need (1) a styrofoam cup, (2) a rubber band, and (3) two feet of thread.

5. Harvey Whitman and Erica Whitman (they're not related) will conduct a seminar on leadership for company managers.

Name ______________________________ Section ______________ Date ______________

Score: (Number right) ________ x 10 = ____________%

Punctuation Marks: TEST 1

Place a period (.), question mark (?), or exclamation point (!) at the end of each of the following sentences.

1. The moon is about 239,000 miles from Earth.
2. Are you ready for the test?
3. That's a great white shark heading toward the swimmers!
4. I wonder if this water is safe to drink.
5. I'm so happy right now I could fly!
6. I can't figure out how to turn on this computer.
7. Would you like some help with that suitcase?
8. Your choices for breakfast are scrambled eggs, pancakes, or cereal.
9. That man is pointing a gun at us!
10. Did you take any notes in the class?

Name _____ Section _____ Date _____

Score: (Number right) _____ x 10 = _____%

Punctuation Marks: TEST 2

Each of the following sentences needs one of the kinds of punctuation marks in the box. In the space provided, write the letter of the mark needed. Then add that mark to the sentence.

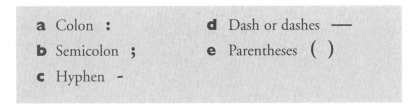

a Colon **:**   **d** Dash or dashes ——

b Semicolon **;**   **e** Parentheses **( )**

c Hyphen **-**

_____ *d* _____ **1.** Horrible acting, laughable dialogue, and a ridiculous plot if you like these things, you'll love this movie.

_____ *b* _____ **2.** The soup simmered all morning its delicious aroma filled the house.

_____ *c* _____ **3.** The story of Ferdinand is about a fierce looking bull who loves flowers.

_____ *a* _____ **4.** Groucho Marx had this to say about people, dogs, and reading "Outside of a dog, a book is a man's best friend. Inside a dog it's too dark to read."

_____ *b* _____ **5.** The beach was clean and inviting the water was cool and blue.

_____ *a* _____ **6.** There will be auditions tomorrow for three parts in the play the father, the mother, and the twelve-year-old daughter.

_____ *c* _____ **7.** My usually soft spoken brother began to shout angrily.

_____ *d* _____ **8.** Before I waded into the pond, I noticed someone else was already there a baby alligator.

_____ *e* _____ **9.** My grandfather actually, he's my great-grandfather will be visiting us over the holidays.

_____ *a* _____ **10.** Eleanor Roosevelt wrote this about courage "You gain strength, courage and confidence by every experience in which you really stop to look fear in the face. You are able to say to yourself, 'I lived through this horror. I can take the next thing that comes along.'"

⑰ Pronoun Forms

Basics about Pronouns

A **pronoun** is a word that can be used in place of a noun.

- Mel scrubbed the potatoes. Then **he** peeled some carrots.

  In the second sentence above, the word *he* is a pronoun that is used in place of the noun *Mel*.

For more information on pronouns, see "Parts of Speech," pages 326–328.

This chapter explains how to choose the correct pronoun to use in a sentence. It covers the following four areas:

1 Personal pronouns as subjects, objects, and possessives

2 Pronouns with *and* or *or*

3 Pronouns in comparisons

4 *Who* and *whom*

PERSONAL PRONOUNS AS SUBJECTS, OBJECTS, AND POSSESSIVES

Pronouns have different forms, or cases, depending on their use in a sentence. As explained below, they may serve as **subjects**, **objects**, or **possessives**.

Subject Pronouns

Subject pronouns act as the subjects of verbs. Here are the subject forms of personal pronouns:

	First Person	Second Person	Third Person
Singular	I	you	he, she, it
Plural	we	you	they

- **I** have an itch.

  I is the subject of the verb *have*.

- **She** always remembers her nieces' birthdays.

  She is the subject of the verb *remembers*.

- **They** agreed to the deal and shook hands.

  They is the subject of the verbs *agreed* and *shook*.

Object Pronouns

Object pronouns act as the objects of verbs or of prepositions. Here is a list of the object forms of personal pronouns:

	First Person	Second Person	Third Person
Singular	me	you	him, her, it
Plural	us	you	them

When a pronoun receives the action of a verb, an object pronoun should be used.

- Clara pinched **him**.

    Him receives the action of the verb *pinched*. *Him* tells who was pinched.

- Jeff is addicted to Coca-Cola. He drinks **it** for breakfast.

    It receives the action of the verb *drinks*. *It* tells what Jeff drinks for breakfast.

When a pronoun is the object of a preposition, an object pronoun should be used. Prepositions are words such as *to, for, with*, and *from*. (A longer list of prepositions is on page 29.)

- My sister tossed the car keys to **me**.

    Me is the object of the preposition *to*.

- Because it was her husband's birthday, Flo knitted a tie for **him**.

    Him is the object of the preposition *for*.

When the preposition *to* or *for* is understood, an object pronoun must still be used.

- My sister tossed **me** the car keys.

    The preposition *to* is implied before the pronoun *me*.

- Flo knitted **him** a tie.

    The preposition *for* is implied before the pronoun *him*.

Possessive Pronouns

Possessive pronouns show that something is owned, or possessed. Here are possessive forms of personal pronouns:

	First Person	Second Person	Third Person
Singular	my, mine	your, yours	his, her, hers, its
Plural	our, ours	your, yours	their, theirs

- If Lucille needs a sweater, she can borrow **mine**.
  Mine means *the sweater belonging to me*.

- The house lost most of **its** roof during the tornado.
  Its roof means *the roof belonging to the house*.

- Roger and Emily saw many of **their** friends at the party.
  Their friends means *the friends belonging to Roger and Emily*.

NOTE Possessive pronouns never contain an apostrophe.

- During the last storm, our apple tree lost all of **its** blossoms (not "it's blossoms").

● Practice 1

Each sentence contains one pronoun. Underline each pronoun. Then, in the space in the margin, identify the pronoun by writing **S** for a subject pronoun, **O** for an object pronoun, and **P** for a possessive pronoun. The first item is done for you as an example.

   O   **1.** The concert gave <u>me</u> a headache.

   P   **2.** <u>Your</u> father is very friendly.

   S   **3.** <u>They</u> once lived in Texas.

   O   **4.** Read the letter out loud to <u>us</u>.

   S   **5.** Apparently <u>she</u> is somebody famous.

   P   **6.** The door on <u>my</u> closet has a broken hinge.

   O   **7.** A stone almost hit <u>me</u> in the eye.

   O   **8.** Stu gave <u>them</u> nothing but trouble.

   S   **9.** <u>I</u> often forget to bring a calculator to math class.

   P   **10.** Next Friday, <u>our</u> brother will be twenty-eight.

● Practice 2

Fill in each blank with the appropriate pronoun in the margin. Before making your choice, decide if you need a subject, an object, or a possessive pronoun.

her, she 1. Over the summer, Melba changed ___her___ hair color, job, and boyfriend.

Me, I 2. ___I___ will treat you to lunch today.

our, us 3. Over the last ten years, twenty-three foster children have lived with ___us___.

your, you 4. You should iron ___your___ shirt before going to the job interview.

we, us 5. Will you join ___us___ at the movies Friday night?

They, Them 6. ___They___ cannot find an apartment they like in this neighorhood.

I, me 7. Richard must give ___me___ a ride to school tomorrow.

him, his 8. When he died at the age of ninety-six, Grandpa still had all of ___his___ teeth.

he, him 9. Jill spotted her son on the playground and brought ___him___ a sandwich.

We, Us 10. ___We___ held a family meeting to decide how to split up household chores.

PRONOUNS WITH *AND* AND *OR*

Deciding which pronoun to use may become confusing when there are two subjects or two objects joined by *and* or *or*. However, the rules remain the same: Use a subject pronoun for the subject of a verb; use an object pronoun for the object of a verb or preposition.

- My brother and **I** loved *The Wizard of Oz* books.
  I is a subject of the verb loved. Brother is also a subject of loved.

- Our parents often read to my brother and **me**.
  Me is an object of the preposition to. Brother is also an object of to.

You can figure out which pronoun to use by mentally leaving out the other word that goes with *and* or *or*. For instance, in the first example above, omitting the words *my brother and* makes it clear that *I* is the correct pronoun to use: . . . **I** loved *The Wizard of Oz* books. (You would never say "**Me** loved *The Wizard of Oz* books.")

Try mentally omitting words in the following sentences. Then fill in each blank with the correct pronoun in parentheses.

- The prom was so long ago, I can't remember all of the details. Either Gene or *(I, me)* ___I___ drove. Furthermore, I can't remember whether Katie Davis went with him or *(I, me)* ___me___.

The correct choice for the first blank becomes clear when the words "Either Gene or" are omitted: *I drove. I* is a subject of the verb *drove*.

　　The correct choice for the second blank becomes clear when the words "him or" are omitted: *I can't remember whether Katie Davis went with . . . me. Me* is an object of the preposition *with.*

Practice 3

In each sentence, a choice of a subject or an object pronoun is given in parentheses. In the blank space, write the correct pronoun.

1. Is that package addressed to my brother or *(I, me)* __me__ ?

2. According to Jess, either *(he, him)* __he__ or his roommate will fix the broken window.

3. The piano is too heavy for Kate and *(she, her)* __her__ to move on their own.

4. Robbie and *(he, him)* __he__ first met when they were in the fourth grade.

5. That strong coffee kept Dad and *(we, us)* __us__ awake for hours.

6. My mother heard that the new position of floor manager will go either to her coworker Ken or *(she, her)* __her__ .

7. For many years, *(we, us)* __we__ and Dale have sat next to each other at football games.

8. In the books about the Hardy boys, *(they, them)* __they__ and their detective father work together to solve mysteries.

9. Mark and *(I, me)* __I__ had been arguing loudly when our teacher walked into the room.

10. She simply frowned at Mark and *(I, me)* __me__ and left.

PRONOUNS IN COMPARISONS

When pronouns are used in comparisons, they often follow the word *than* or *as*.

- My best friend, Matt, is a better athlete than **I**.
- Rhonda's behavior puzzled you as much as **me**.

Words are often omitted in comparisons to avoid repetition. To see whether you should use a subject or an object pronoun, mentally fill in the missing words. In the first sentence above, *I* is the subject of the understood verb *am*:

- My best friend, Matt, is a better athlete than **I** [am].

In the second sentence, *me* is the object of the verb *puzzled*. That verb is understood, but not stated, in the second part of the comparison:

- Rhonda's behavior puzzled you as much as [it puzzled] me.

Now try to fill in the correct pronouns in the following comparisons:

- Brad was my first crush. I never adored anyone as much as *(he, him)* __him__ .
- I had never met anyone as playful and kind as *(he, him)* __he__ .

In the first blank above, you should have written the object form of the pronoun, *him*: *I never adored anyone as much as [I adored] him*. *Him* is the object of the verb *adored*, which is missing but understood in the sentence.

In the second blank above, you should have written the subject form of the pronoun, *he*: *I had never met anyone as playful and kind as he [was]*. *He* is the subject of the understood verb *was*.

● **Practice 4**

In each sentence, a choice of a subject or an object pronoun is given in parentheses. In the blank space, write the correct pronoun.

1. Della has been in the choir longer than *(we, us)* ___we___.

2. Our argument bothers you as much as *(I, me)* ___me___.

3. Omar told his teammates he runs faster than *(they, them)* ___they___.

4. My little brother is five inches taller than *(I, me)* ___I___.

5. The math final worries me more than *(she, her)* ___her___; she is hardly studying for it.

6. We don't give parties as often as *(them, they)* ___they___.

7. As a child, I had a pet collie; there was no relative I loved as much as *(he, him)* ___him___.

8. My family and our friends all caught the flu, but we weren't as sick as *(they, them)* ___they___.

9. Julius bats the ball farther than his sister, but she runs the bases faster than *(he, him)* ___he___.

10. That buzzing noise in the lamp annoys Dad more than *(we, us)* ___us___; he has to leave the room.

WHO AND WHOM

Who is a subject pronoun; *whom* is an object pronoun.

● The person **who** owns the expensive car won't let anybody else park it.
    Who owns the expensive car is a dependent word group. *Who* is the subject of the verb *owns.*

● The babysitter **whom** they trust cannot work tonight.
    Whom they trust is a dependent word group. *Whom* is the object of the verb *trust.* The subject of *trust* is *they.*

As a general rule, to know whether to use *who* or *whom*, find the first verb after *who* or *whom*. Decide whether that verb already has a subject. If it doesn't have a subject, use the subject pronoun *who*. If it does have a subject, use the object pronoun *whom*.

See if you can fill in the right pronoun in the following sentences.

● The arrested person is a man *(who, whom)* ___whom___ my sister once dated.

● The man and woman *(who, whom)* ___who___ live next door argue constantly.

In the first sentence above, look at the verb *dated.* Does it have a subject? Yes, the subject is *sister.* Therefore the object pronoun *whom* is the correct choice: *The arrested person is a man whom my sister once dated. Whom* is the object of the verb *dated.*

In the second sentence above, look at the verb *live.* Does it have a subject? No. Therefore the subject pronoun *who* is the correct choice: *The man and woman who live next door argue constantly. Who* is the subject of the verb *live.*

Note In informal speech and writing, *who* is often substituted for *whom*:

● The babysitter who they trust cannot work tonight.

In formal writing, however, *whom* is generally used. In the practices and tests in this chapter, use the formal approach.

● **Practice 5**

In each blank space, write the correct choice of pronoun.

1. The company hired a secretary *(who, whom)* _____who_____ can speak Spanish.

2. Ron's first boss was a man *(who, whom)* _____whom_____ he could not please.

3. I admire a man *(who, whom)* _____who_____ cries at movies.

4. Chester Arthur is a President *(who, whom)* _____whom_____ few Americans remember.

5. Students *(who, whom)* _____who_____ cheated on the test were suspended.

WHO AND WHOM IN QUESTIONS

In questions, *who* is a subject pronoun, and *whom* is an object pronoun. You can often decide whether to use *who* or *whom* in a question in the same way you decide whether to use *who* or *whom* in a statement.

● **Who** should go?

The verb after *who* is *should go*, which does not have another subject. Therefore use the subject form of the pronoun, *who*.

● **Whom** should I send?

I is the subject of the verb *should send*, so use the object form of the pronoun, *whom*.

● **Practice 6**

Fill in each blank with either *who* or *whom*.

1. *(Who, Whom)* _____Who_____ will do the dishes tonight?

2. *(Who, Whom)* _____Whom_____ were you expecting?

3. *(Who, Whom)* _____Who_____ woke up in the middle of the night?

4. *(Who, Whom)* _____Who_____ is making all that racket?

5. *(Who, Whom)* _____Whom_____ did you just call on the phone?

Name _____ Section _____ Date _____

Score: (Number right) _____ x 10 = _____%

Pronoun Forms: TEST 1

Fill in each blank with the appropriate pronoun from the margin.

She, Her   **1.** _____She_____ got the highest grade on the mid-term test.

they, their   **2.** The twins had braces on _____their_____ teeth for three years.

we, us   **3.** We are sure that getting married is the right thing for _____us_____.

they, them   **4.** Since my aunt and uncle enjoy basketball more than I do, I gave the tickets to _____them_____.

I, me   **5.** She and _____I_____ have been friends since we were little children.

he, him   **6.** I don't know whether to believe you or _____him_____.

she, her   **7.** Hector and his sister both speak some Spanish, but Hector is more fluent than _____she_____.

he, him   **8.** We enjoyed no teacher as much as _____him_____; he was always interesting.

who, whom   **9.** Our mayor is a former nun _____who_____ decided to enter politics.

who, whom   **10.** The principal is a young man _____who_____ has earned the community's respect.

Name _____   Section _____ Date _____

Pronoun Forms: TEST 2

Fill in each blank with the appropriate pronoun from the margin.

we, us   **1.** You are welcome to drive to the meeting with _____us_____.

they, their   **2.** All of my blue jeans have holes in _____their_____ knees.

I, me   **3.** My mother changes her mind more frequently than _____I_____.

who, whom   **4.** The man _____whom_____ the car hit is my uncle.

we, us   **5.** Next weekend, you and _____we_____ should go to a movie together.

I, me   **6.** My dog and _____I_____ often hike in the woods for hours at a time.

she, her   **7.** Sarah's boss said there was no employee he valued as much as _____her_____.

he, him   **8.** Does that red sports car belong to his parents or _____him_____?

who, whom   **9.** The mechanic _____who_____ usually works on our car is on vacation.

he, him   **10.** When the captain's boat capsized, _____he_____ and his crew had a
                 dangerous adventure.

18 Pronoun Problems

Three Common Pronoun Problems

This chapter explains three common problems with pronouns:

1 Pronoun shifts in number   A pronoun must agree in number with the noun it refers to.

> *Incorrect*   Each of my sisters has **their** own room.
>
> *Correct*   Each of my sisters has **her** own room.

2 Pronoun shifts in person   Pronouns must be consistent in person. Unnecessary shifts in person (for example, from *I* to *one*) confuse readers.

> *Incorrect*   **One's** patience runs thin when I am faced with a slow-moving line at the bank.
>
> *Correct*   **My** patience runs thin when I am faced with a slow-moving line at the bank.

3 Unclear pronoun reference   A pronoun must clearly refer to the noun it stands for.

> *Incorrect*   Michael gave Arnie **his** car keys. (Does *his* refer to Michael or Arnie?)
>
> *Correct*   Michael gave **his** car keys to Arnie.

PRONOUN SHIFTS IN NUMBER

A pronoun must agree in number with the noun it refers to, which is called the pronoun's **antecedent**. Singular nouns require singular pronouns; plural nouns require plural pronouns.

In the following examples, pronouns are printed in **boldface type**; the antecedents are printed in *italic* type.

- The dying *tree* lost all **its** leaves.
  The antecedent *tree* is singular, so the pronoun must be singular: *its*.

- When *Vic* was in the Army, **his** little brother wrote to **him** almost every day.
  The antecedent *Vic* is singular, so the pronouns must be singular: *his* and *him*.

- Do the *neighbors* know that **their** dog is loose?
  The antecedent *neighbors* is plural, so the pronoun must be plural: *their*.

- *Sarah and Greg* act like newlyweds, but **they** have been married for years.
  The antecedent *Sarah and Greg* is plural, so the pronoun must be plural: *they*.

● Practice 1

In each blank space, write the noun or nouns that the given pronoun refers to.

Example   The ridges on our fingertips have a function. They help fingers to grasp things.

They refers to _____ridges_____.

1. The photographer realized she had run out of film.

    She refers to _____photographer_____.

2. The cat hid its kittens in the hayloft.

    Its refers to _____cat_____.

3. Kate and Barry don't get along with their stepfather.

    Their refers to _____Kate and Barry_____.

4. Martin never drinks coffee in the evening. It keeps him awake all night.

    It refers to _____coffee_____.

5. Nora is a year older than her brother, but they are both in sixth grade.

    They refers to _____Nora and her brother_____.

● Practice 2

In the spaces provided for each sentence, write **(a)** the pronoun used and **(b)** the noun or nouns that the pronoun refers to.

1. The movie started late, and it was badly out of focus.

    The pronoun _____it_____ refers to _____movie_____.

2. Marlene buys most of her clothing at thrift shops.

    The pronoun _____her_____ refers to _____Marlene_____.

3. As the horse neared the finish line, his energy ran out.

    The pronoun _____his_____ refers to _____horse_____.

4. A man was at the door a minute ago, but now he is gone.

    The pronoun _____he_____ refers to _____man_____.

5. Carla and Vicki are twins, but they don't look alike.

    The pronoun _____they_____ refers to _____Carla and Vicki_____.

Indefinite Pronouns

Most pronouns refer to one or more particular persons or things. However, **indefinite pronouns** do not refer to particular persons or things. The following indefinite pronouns are always singular:

anybody	either	neither	one
anyone	everybody	no one	somebody
anything	everyone	nobody	someone
each	everything	nothing	something

- *Something* has left **its** muddy footprints on the hood of the car.

- *One* of my sisters has lost **her** job.

- *Everybody* is entitled to change **his** or **her** mind.

    The indefinite pronouns *something, one*, and *everybody* are singular. The personal pronouns that refer to them must also be singular: *its, his* or *her*.

Note on Gender Agreement   Choose a pronoun that agrees in gender with the noun it refers to. Because *one of my sisters* is clearly feminine, use *her*. But *everybody* includes males and females, so use *his* or *her*. If *his* or *her* seems awkward in a sentence, try rewriting the sentence with a plural subject:

- People are entitled to change **their** minds.

The following indefinite pronouns are always plural:

both	many	several
few	other	

- *Both* of my brothers worked **their** way through college.

    Both, the subject of this sentence, is plural, so the plural pronoun *their* is used.

The following indefinite pronouns are singular or plural, depending on their context:

all	more	none
any	most	some

- *Some* of the pie is fine, but its crust is burnt.

    Some here refers to one thing—the pie, so the singular pronoun *its* is used.

- *Some* of the students forgot their books.

    Some here refers to several students, so the plural pronoun *their* is used.

● **Practice 3**

In the spaces provided for each sentence, write **(a)** the pronoun or pronouns needed and **(b)** the word that the pronoun or pronouns refer to.

Example Neither of the boys has had *(his/their)* measles shot yet.

The pronoun needed is ___his___. The word it refers to is ___neither___.

1. Everything in the office has *(its/their)* own place.

   The pronoun needed is ___its___. The word it refers to is ___everything___.

2. Neither of my uncles has ever smoked in *(his/their)* life.

   The pronoun needed is ___his___. The word it refers to is ___neither___.

3. Many restaurants in town post *(its/their)* menus in the window.

   The pronoun needed is ___their___. The word it refers to is ___restaurants___.

4. Don't eat any of those grapes until you've washed *(it/them)*.

   The pronoun needed is ___them___. The word it refers to is ___grapes___.

5. Is anyone brave enough to read *(their/his or her)* essay aloud to the class?

   The pronoun needed is ___his or her___. The word it refers to is ___anyone___.

6. Both of the girls invited *(her mother/their mothers)* to the mother-daughter luncheon.

   The pronoun needed is ___their___. The word it refers to is ___both___.

7. Everybody loses *(their/his or her)* temper occasionally.

   The pronoun needed is ___his or her___. The word it refers to is ___everybody___.

8. Nobody can enter that plant without *(their/his or her)* security badge.

   The pronoun needed is ___his or her___. The word it refers to is ___nobody___.

9. Most of the room has been painted, and *(it is/they are)* almost dry.

   The pronoun needed is ___it is___. The word it refers to is ___room___.

10. Most of the invitations have been addressed, but *(it still needs/they still need)* to be stamped.

    The pronoun needed is ___they___. The word it refers to is ___invitations___.

A Note on Collective Nouns

A **collective noun** refers to a group of persons or things considered to be a unit. Collective nouns are usually singular. Following are some examples.

audience	committee	group	quartet
band	couple	herd	society
class	family	jury	team

● The *class* started late, and **it** ended early.
   Class refers to a single unit, so the singular pronoun *it* is used.

However, if a collective noun refers to the individual members of the group, a plural pronoun is used.

● The *class* handed in **their** essays before vacation.

Many writers feel it is awkward to use a collective noun as a plural. They prefer to revise the sentence.

● The class *members* handed in **their** essays before vacation.

PRONOUN SHIFTS IN PERSON

A pronoun that refers to the person who is speaking is called a **first-person pronoun**. Examples of first-person pronouns are *I, me,* and *our.* A pronoun that refers to someone being spoken to, such as *you*, is a **second-person pronoun**. And a pronoun that refers to another person or thing, such as *he, she*, or *it*, is a **third-person pronoun**.

Following are the personal pronouns in first-, second-, and third-person groupings:

	First Person	Second Person	Third Person
Singular	I, me, my, mine	you, your, yours	he, him, his; she, her, hers; it, its
Plural	we, us, our, ours	you, your, yours	they, them, their, theirs

When a writer makes unnecessary shifts in person, the writing may become less clear. The sentences below, for example, show some needless shifts in person. (The words that show the shifts are **boldfaced**.)

● The worst thing about **my** not writing letters is that **you** never get any back.
   The writer begins with the first-person pronoun *my*, but then shifts to the second-person pronoun *you*.

● Though **we** like most of **our** neighbors, there are a few **you** can't get along with.
   The writer begins with the first-person pronouns *we* and *our*, but then shifts to the second-person pronoun *you*.

These sentences can be improved by eliminating the shifts in person:

● The worst thing about **my** not writing letters is that **I** never get any back.

● Though **we** like most of **our** neighbors, there are a few **we** can't get along with.

● Practice 4

Write the correct pronoun in each space provided.

they, we   **1.** Whenever students are under a great deal of stress, ___*they*___ often stop studying.

one, you   **2.** If you want to do well in this course, ___*you*___ should plan on doing all the assignments on time.

you, me   **3.** When I took a summer job as a waitress, I was surprised at how rude some customers were to ___*me*___.

we, you   **4.** It's hard for us to pay for health insurance, but ___*we*___ don't dare go without it.

you, I   **5.** When ___*I*___ drive on the highway, I get disgusted at the amount of trash I see.

I, you   **6.** Although I like visiting my Aunt Rita, ___*I*___ always feel as if my visit has disrupted her life.

we, you   **7.** When we answer the telephone at work, ___*we*___ are supposed to say the company name.

I, one   **8.** I would like to go to a school where ___*I*___ can meet many people who are different from me.

you, they   **9.** Dog owners should put tags on their dogs in case ___*they*___ lose their pets.

we, they   **10.** People often take a first-aid course so that ___*they*___ can learn how to help choking and heart-attack victims.

UNCLEAR PRONOUN REFERENCE

A pronoun must refer clearly to its antecedent—the word it stands for. If it is unclear which word a pronoun refers to, the sentence will be confusing. As shown below, some pronouns are unclear because they have two possible antecedents. Others are unclear because they have no antecedent.

Two Possible Antecedents

A pronoun's reference will not be clear if there are two possible antecedents.

● Eva told her mother that she had received a postcard from Alaska.
  Who received the postcard, Eva or her mother?

● I wrote a to-do list with my purple pen, and now I can't find it.
  What can't the writer find, the list or the pen?

An unclear sentence with two antecedents can sometimes be corrected by using the speaker's exact words.

● Eva told her mother, "**I** received (or: "**You** received) a postcard from Alaska."

For an explanation of how to use quotation marks, see pages 127–136 in "Quotation Marks."

In some cases, the best solution is to replace the pronoun with the word it was meant to refer to.

● I wrote a to-do list with my purple pen, and now I can't find **the list** (*or:* **the pen**).

No Antecedent

A pronoun's reference will not be clear if there is no antecedent.

● I just received our cable TV bill. **They** said the Disney Channel is providing a free preview next month.

Who said there's a free preview? We don't know because *they* has no word to refer to.

● My older brother is a chemist, but **that** doesn't interest me.

What doesn't interest the writer? The pronoun *that* doesn't refer to any word in the sentence.

To correct an unclear reference in which a pronoun has no antecedent, replace the pronoun with the word or words it is meant to refer to.

● I just received our cable TV bill. **The cable company** said the Disney Channel is providing a free preview next month.

● My older brother is a chemist, but **chemistry** doesn't interest me.

● Practice 5

In each sentence below, underline the correct word or words in parentheses.

1. At a local deli, (they / *the owners*) provide each table with a free bowl of pickles.

2. Joan said the cordless phone is under the red pillow, but I can't find (it / *the phone*).

3. Rita asked Paula (*if she could help with the dishes.* / , "*Can I help with the dishes?*")

4. In a letter from Publisher's Clearing House, (they / *the contest organizers*) all but promise that I have already won ten million dollars.

5. When my cousins arrived at the picnic with the homemade pies, (*my cousins* / they) were very welcome.

● **Practice 6**

Revise each sentence to eliminate the unclear pronoun reference.

Wording of revisions may vary.

1. When Nick questioned the repairman, he became very upset.

When Nick questioned the repairman, the repairman became very upset.

_____

2. My parents are expert horseshoe players, but I've never become any good at it.

My parents are expert horseshoe players, but I've never become any good

at horseshoes.

3. Mary Alice told her sister that her boyfriend was moving to another state.

Mary Alice told her sister, "My boyfriend is moving to another state."

[OR "Your boyfriend is moving to another state."]

4. I bought a stationary bicycle that has a timer, but I never use it.

I bought a stationary bicycle that has a timer, but I never use the timer.

[OR I never use the bicycle.]

5. I went to the hardware store for 100-watt light bulbs, but they didn't have any.

I went to the hardware store for 100-watt light bulbs, but the clerks didn't

have any.

Name _____ Section _____ Date _____

Score: (Number right) _____ x 10 = _____ %

Pronoun Problems: TEST 1

A. In each blank space, write the pronoun that agrees in number with the word or words it refers to.

its, their **1.** The school has asbestos in many of _____*its*_____ classrooms.

her, their **2.** My mother and her sister often share _____*their*_____ clothing and jewelry.

his or her, their **3.** No one in the class remembered _____*his or her*_____ textbook.

her, their **4.** Neither of the little girls wants to share _____*her*_____ toys.

B. For each sentence, cross out the pronoun that makes a shift in person. Then, in the space provided, write a pronoun that corrects the shift in person.

_____*us*_____ **5.** We work at a store where the owners don't provide ~~you~~ with any health insurance.

_____*I*_____ **6.** I wanted to see the movie star, but ~~one~~ couldn't get past her security guard.

_____*their*_____ **7.** Members of that gang said they feel the gang is like ~~your~~ family.

C. In each sentence below, choose the correct word or words and write them in the space provided.

8. Lonnie stopped at the post office and asked ____*a postal worker*____ to hold his mail while he was on vacation.
  a. a postal worker
  b. them

9. Carrie told Linda _*, "You got four phone calls this afternoon."*_____

_____

  a. that she had gotten four phone calls that afternoon.
  b. , "You got four phone calls this afternoon."

10. Andrea could be a cafeteria server again next semester, but she really hates _____
  _*working in the cafeteria.*_____
  a. it.
  b. working in the cafeteria.

Name _____   Section _____   Date _____

Pronoun Problems: TEST 2

A. In each blank space, write the pronoun that agrees in number with the word or words it refers to.

his, their   **1.** Each of my brothers has _____his_____ own television.

its, their   **2.** Some of the businesses in town have a day-care center for the children of _____their_____ employees.

her, their   **3.** One of the hens has laid _____her_____ egg on an old blanket in the shed.

his or her, their **4.** Everybody in our apartment building was told to lock _____his or her_____ door in the evening.

B. For each sentence, cross out the pronoun that makes a shift in person. Then, in the space provided, write a pronoun that corrects the shift in person.

_____me_____   **5.** The constant ringing of my telephone often drives ~~one~~ crazy.

_____they_____   **6.** If people want something from the kitchen, ~~you~~ have to go and get it.

he (or she)   **7.** The newspaper carrier didn't realize that ~~you~~ would have to deliver papers at 5 a.m.

C. In each sentence below, choose the correct word or words and write them in the space provided.

8. Jeanine is a devoted user of coupons at the supermarket, but I can't find the time for _____
collecting coupons _____
   a. it.
   b. collecting coupons.

9. Ian told his father _____, "You're late for your doctor's appointment." _____

_____
   a. he was late for his doctor's appointment.
   b. , "You're late for your doctor's appointment."

10. In this letter from the bank, _____the customer service manager says_____
my account is overdrawn.
   a. the customer service manager says
   b. they say

⑲ Adjectives and Adverbs

Basics about Adjectives and Adverbs

This chapter explains the following:

1 How to identify adjectives and adverbs

- The **circular** *(adjective)* house is **unusual** *(adjective).*
- The **extremely** *(adverb)* small boy climbed the rope **very** *(adverb)* **quickly** *(adverb).*

2 How to use adjectives and adverbs in comparisons

- I'm a **worse** cook than my brother, but our sister is the **worst** cook in the family.

3 How to use two troublesome pairs: *good* and *well, bad* and *badly*

- I can usually work **well** and do a **good** job even when I don't feel **well**.
- In addition to his **bad** attitude, the outfielder has been playing **badly**.

4 How to avoid double negatives

Incorrect   I can't hardly wait for summer vacation.
Correct   I can hardly wait for summer vacation.

IDENTIFYING ADJECTIVES AND ADVERBS

Adjectives

An **adjective** describes a noun or pronoun. It generally answers such questions as "What kind of? Which one? How many?"

An adjective may come before the noun or pronoun it describes.

- The **weary** hikers shuffled down the **dusty** road.

  The adjective *weary* describes the noun *hikers*; it tells what kind of hikers. The adjective *dusty* describes the noun *road*; it tells what kind of road.

- The **green** car has **two** antennas.

  The adjective *green* tells which car has the antennas. The adjective *two* tells how many antennas there are.

- Don't go to the **new** movie at the mall unless you want a **good** nap.

  The adjective *new* tells which movie; the adjective *good* tells what kind of nap.

An adjective that describes the subject of a sentence may also come after a linking verb (such as *be, is, seem,* and *were*).

- That dog's skin is **wrinkled** and **dry**.

  The adjectives *wrinkled* and *dry* describe the subject, *skin*. They follow the linking verb *is*.

For more information on linking verbs, see "Subjects and Verbs," pages 27–36.

● Practice 1

Complete each sentence with an appropriate adjective. Then underline the noun or pronoun that the adjective describes.   *Answers will vary.*

Examples   My _____favorite_____ sweater had shrunk in the wash.

The school principal was _____strict_____.

1. This _____rainy_____ weather really bothers me.

2. I'm in the mood for a(n) _____action_____ movie.

3. I've never read such a(n) _____depressing_____ book.

4. A(n) _____selfish_____ person makes a poor boss.

5. My aunt has an unusually _____soft_____ voice.

6. The dance at school last night was _____terrific_____.

7. My _____favorite_____ pants are at the cleaners.

8. It's too bad that you are so _____shy_____.

9. _____Rose_____ bushes are growing in front of the house.

10. Sylvia wrote her sister a(n) _____angry_____ letter.

Adverbs

An **adverb** is a word that describes a verb, an adjective, or another adverb. Many adverbs end in *-ly*. Adverbs generally answer such questions as "How? When? Where? How much?"

● The chef **carefully** spread raspberry frosting over the cake.

The adverb *carefully* describes the verb *spread*. *Carefully* tells how the chef spread the frosting.

● The robber stood **there**.

The adverb *there* describes the verb *stood*. *There* (meaning "in that place") tells where the robber stood.

● Ann was **extremely** embarrassed when she stumbled on stage.

The adverb *extremely* describes the adjective *embarrassed*. It tells how much Ann was embarrassed.

● That lamp shines **very brightly**.

The adverb *very* describes the adverb *brightly*. *Very* tells how *brightly* the lamp shines. The adverb *brightly* describes the verb *shines*; it tells how the lamp shines.

Adverbs with Action Verbs

Be careful to use an adverb—not an adjective—with an action verb. Compare the following:

Incorrect	Correct
The boss slept sound at his desk. *Sound* is an adjective.	The boss slept **soundly** at his desk.
The graduates marched proud. *Proud* is an adjective.	The graduates marched **proudly**.
The batter swung wild at all the pitches. *Wild* is an adjective.	The batter swung **wildly** at all the pitches.

● Practice 2

Complete each sentence with the adverb form of the adjective in the margin. (Change each adjective in the margin to an adverb by adding *-ly*.)

Example   *quick*   Sandra read the book too _____quickly_____.

bright   **1.** The soap bubbles glistened _____brightly_____ in the midday sun.

helpless   **2.** The family watched _____helplessly_____ as their house burned.

hurried   **3.** The two teachers spoke _____hurriedly_____ between classes.

shy   **4.** The little girl peeked _____shyly_____ at her new neighbor.

honest   **5.** A good businessperson deals _____honestly_____ with everyone.

quiet   **6.** The old woman hummed _____quietly_____ as she did her shopping.

longing   **7.** The cat stared _____longingly_____ at the leftover tuna casserole.

frequent   **8.** Cable TV channels _____frequently_____ show the same movie ten or more times in one month.

kind   **9.** Our neighbor _____kindly_____ offered to feed our pets while we were gone.

serious   **10.** Many teenagers complain that their parents don't take them _____seriously_____.

● Practice 3

Complete each sentence correctly with either the adverb or adjective in the margin.

rapid, rapidly   **1.** Felipe spoke _____rapidly_____ in Spanish to his grandfather.

rapid, rapidly   **2.** Their _____rapid_____ conversation was difficult for me to follow.

quiet, quietly   **3.** The frog sat _____quietly_____ on a lily pad.

patient, patiently   **4.** The mother is _____patient_____ with her youngster.

patient, patiently   **5.** Ravi waited _____patiently_____ for the elevator to arrive.

willing, willingly   **6.** How many of you are _____willing_____ to sell tickets for the play?

prompt, promptly   **7.** The invitation asks for a _____prompt_____ response.

rapid, rapidly   **8.** The helicopter descended _____rapidly_____ toward the hospital.

cheerful, cheerfully   **9.** Olga smiled _____cheerfully_____ at the customer.

cheerful, cheerfully   **10.** Her _____cheerful_____ smile warmed the room.

USING ADJECTIVES AND ADVERBS IN COMPARISONS
Comparing Two Things

In general, to compare two things, add *-er* to adjectives and adverbs of one syllable.

● Grilling food is **faster** than roasting.
  The adjective *faster* is used to compare two methods: grilling and roasting.

● My mother works **longer** each day than my father.
  The adverb *longer* is used to compare how long two people work each day.

For longer adjectives and adverbs, do not add *-er*. Instead, add the word *more* when comparing two things.

● My dog is **more intelligent** than my cat.
  The words *more intelligent* describe the subject *dog*; they are being used to compare two things, the dog and the cat.

● Marie sings **more sweetly** than I do.
  The words *more sweetly* describe the verb *sings*; they compare the ways two people sing.

● Practice 4

Write in the correct form of the word in the margin by adding either *-er* or *more*.

Examples   *thin*   Kate is _____thinner_____ than her twin sister.

carefully I prefer to ride with Dan. He drives _____more carefully_____ than you.

full   **1.** This bag of potato chips is _____fuller_____ than that one.

affectionate   **2.** My dog is _____more affectionate_____ than my boyfriend.

gray   **3.** This shirt looks _____grayer_____ than it did before I washed it.

neat   **4.** The inside of my car is _____*neater*_____ than the inside of my apartment.

annoying   **5.** There are few sounds _____*more annoying*_____ than fingernails scratching a board.

Comparing Three Things

In general, to compare three or more things, add *-est* to adjectives and adverbs of one syllable.

● Grilling food is faster than roasting, but microwaving is **fastest** of all.

   The adjective *fastest* is used to compare three methods: grilling, roasting, and microwaving. It indicates that microwaving is faster than the other two.

● My mother works longer each day than my father, but in my family, I work **longest**.

   The adverb *longest* is used to compare how long three or more people work each day. It indicates that of the three, I work the most number of hours.

For longer adjectives and adverbs, do not add *-est*. Instead, add the word *most* when comparing three or more things.

● My dog is more intelligent than my cat, but my parrot is the **most intelligent** pet I have ever had.

   Most intelligent is used to compare three animals. It shows which one is the smartest.

● Among the couples I know, my brother and sister-in-law are the **most happily** married of all.

   Most happily is used to compare how happy many married couples are. It indicates that my brother and sister-in-law are more happily married than any of the other couples I know.

● Practice 5

Write in the correct form of the word in the margin by adding either *-est* or *most*.

Examples   *cold*   The _____*coldest*_____ it ever gets around here is about zero degrees Fahrenheit.

   delightful   The _____*most delightful*_____ play of the year is now at the Morgan Theater.

young   **1.** Eliza is the _____*youngest*_____ of eight children.

important   **2.** The _____*most important*_____ thing in Julia's life is clothes.

fresh   **3.** The Metro Mart has the _____*freshest*_____ vegetables in town.

artistic   **4.** Of the eighteen students in my class, Juan is the _____*most artistic*_____.

difficult   **5.** My brother enjoys playing the _____*most difficult*_____ video games he can find.

Notes about Comparisons

1   Do not use both an *-er* ending and *more*, or an *-est* ending and *most*.

Incorrect   My uncle's hair is more curlier than my aunt's.

Correct   My uncle's hair is **curlier** than my aunt's.

2   Certain short adjectives and adverbs have irregular forms:

	Comparing two	Comparing three or more
bad, badly	worse	worst
good, well	better	best
little	less	least
much, many	more	most

- The grape cough syrup tastes **better** than the orange syrup, but the lemon cough drops taste the **best**.

- Sid is doing **badly** in speech class, but I'm doing even **worse**.

● Practice 6

Cross out the incorrect word or words of comparison in each of the following sentences. Then write the correction on the line provided.

Example   _____*easier*_____   The test was ~~more easier~~ than I expected.

_____*worst*_____   **1.** That was the ~~baddest~~ accident I've ever seen.

_____*better*_____   **2.** It is ~~gooder~~ to try and fail than not to try at all.

_____*older*_____   **3.** My mother is ~~more older~~ than my father.

_____*less*_____   **4.** I use ~~littler~~ oil in my cooking than I used to.

_____*sweeter*_____   **5.** This grapefruit is actually ~~more sweeter~~ than that orange.

_____*least*_____   **6.** This year we had the ~~most little~~ rain we've had in years.

_____*most beautiful*_____   **7.** I think the peacock is the ~~most beautifulest~~ of all birds.

_____*worse*_____   **8.** The macaroni salad tastes ~~worser~~ than the potato salad.

_____*most*_____   **9.** Cheap Charlie's is the ~~more~~ expensive of all the variety stores in town.

_____*less*_____   **10.** I'm on a diet, so put ~~more little~~ mayonnaise on my sandwich than usual.

USING TWO TROUBLESOME PAIRS:
GOOD **AND** *WELL*, *BAD* **AND** *BADLY*

Good is an adjective that often means "enjoyable," "talented," or "positive."

- I had a **good** day.
- Sue is a **good** skier.
- Think **good** thoughts.

As an adverb, *well* often means "skillfully" or "successfully."

- Sue skis **well**.
- The schedule worked **well**.
- Pedro interacts **well** with others.

As an adjective, *well* means "healthy."

- The patient is **well** once again.

Bad is an adjective. *Badly* is an adverb.

- I look **bad**.

  Bad is an adjective that comes after the linking verb *look*. It describes the appearance of the subject of the sentence, *I*.

- I need sleep **badly**.

  Badly is an adverb that describes the verb *need*. It explains how much the sleep is needed.

● Practice 7

Complete the sentence with the correct word in the margin.

good, well **1.** Ike hums really _____well_____.

good, well **2.** Did you have a _____good_____ day at school?

bad, badly **3.** I need a haircut _____badly_____.

bad, badly **4.** My mother has a really _____bad_____ headache.

good, well **5.** No student did very _____well_____ on the math test.

bad, badly **6.** Luckily, no one was _____badly_____ hurt in the accident.

good, well **7.** This machine bakes bread very _____well_____.

bad, badly **8.** After a week on a liquids-only diet, Ben looks really ___bad___.

good, well **9.** Keep taking the antibiotic until it's gone, even if you think you are completely _____well_____.

good, well **10.** Working in a nursing home was a _____good_____ experience for me.

AVOIDING DOUBLE NEGATIVES

In standard English, it is incorrect to express a negative idea by pairing one negative with another. Common negative words include *not, nothing, never, nowhere, nobody,* and *neither.* To correct a double negative, either eliminate one of the negative words or replace a negative with a positive word.

Incorrect	I **shouldn't** go **nowhere** this weekend.
Correct	I **should** go **nowhere** this weekend.
Correct	I **shouldn't** go **anywhere** this weekend.

Shouldn't means *should not,* so the first sentence above contains two negatives: *not* and *nowhere.* In the first correct sentence, *not* has been eliminated. In the second correct sentence, *nowhere* has been replaced with a positive word.

The words *hardly, scarcely,* and *barely* are also negatives. They should not be paired with other negatives such as *never* and *not.* Correct a double negative containing *hardly, scarcely,* or *barely* by eliminating the other negative word.

Incorrect	I **couldn't scarcely** recognize you.
Correct	I **could scarcely** recognize you.

● Practice 8

Correct the double negative in each sentence by crossing out one of the negative words and writing any additional correction above the line.   *Answers may vary.*

Example   I won't ~~never~~ go to that restaurant again.

                will

OR   I ~~won't~~ never go to that restaurant again.

     ever

1. Don't ~~never~~ stick anything into an electrical outlet.

2. The two sisters ~~don't~~ scarcely speak to one another.

   will

3. I ~~won't~~ never believe a word that Vicky says.

              anything

4. Some days I feel that I can't do ~~nothing~~ right.

          anywhere

5. Ken can't go ~~nowhere~~ without running into one of his ex-girlfriends.

              can

6. It's so dark in this room that I ~~can't~~ scarcely read.

          ever

7. My neighbor shouldn't ~~never~~ have tried to fix the roof on her own.

        anything

8. Pete won't say ~~nothing~~ unless he's sure he's right.

      would

9. Nobody ~~wouldn't~~ believe what happened to me in class today.

       will

10. That salesperson ~~won't~~ never stop trying, even when a customer starts walking away.

Name _____ Section _____ Date _____

Score: (Number right) _____ x 10 = _____%

Adjectives and Adverbs: TEST 1

Cross out the adjective or adverb error in each sentence and write the correction in the space at the left.

Example ____sweeter____ This peach is ~~more sweeter~~ than candy.

____suddenly____ **1.** We braked our car ~~sudden~~ to avoid a dog.

____good____ **2.** How did you get to be so ~~well~~ in math?

____calmly____ **3.** Let's try to settle our disagreement ~~calm~~.

____faster____ **4.** To get a job as a secretary, I will have to be able to type ~~more faster~~.

____nicest____ **5.** James is the ~~most nicest~~ of all the waiters.

____well____ **6.** I feel pretty good, but the doctor says I'm not ~~good~~ yet.

____carefully____ **7.** Sam printed his name ~~careful~~ across the top of the page.

____brightly____ **8.** Although it is cold, the sun is shining ~~bright~~.

____anything____ **9.** Nobody knows ~~nothing~~ about why the manager was fired.

____better____ **10.** My sister has a ~~more good~~ chance than I do of making the team.

Name _____ Section _____ Date _____

Score: (Number right) _____ x 10 = _____%

Adjectives and Adverbs: TEST 2

Each short paragraph below contains **two** errors in adjective and/or adverb use. Find the errors and cross them out. Then write the correct form of each word or words in the space provided.

1. We eat three different kinds of cereal in my house. One teenager wants the ~~most sweetest~~ sugar-coated cereal he can find. The other doesn't like ~~nothing~~ sweet, so he eats shredded wheat instead. I eat hot oatmeal every morning.

    a. _____sweetest_____

    b. _____anything_____

2. Many people become ~~bad~~ depressed during the winter. Their mood improves ~~quick~~ when they receive natural-light therapy.

    a. _____badly_____

    b. _____quickly_____

3. I can't decide which book to read for my report. *The Old Man and the Sea* is ~~more short~~ than *The Great Gatsby*, so at first I thought I'd read that. But now that I've glanced through *Gatsby*, it seems the ~~most interesting~~ book.

    a. _____shorter_____

    b. _____more interesting_____

4. Mr. Kensington has the ~~goodest~~ sense of humor in his family. For instance, he'll say that his knee is stiff from a war injury. But if you ask him to explain, he'll tell you ~~cheerful~~ that he got old and his knee "wore out."

    a. _____best_____

    b. _____cheerfully_____

5. Nothing is ~~more good~~ on a cold day than cuddling up on the sofa with hot cocoa and a good magazine. But I've got so much studying to do lately that I ~~haven't scarcely~~ any time to read anything but textbooks.

    a. _____better_____

    b. _____have scarcely_____

㉚ Misplaced and Dangling Modifiers

Basics about Misplaced and Dangling Modifiers

This chapter explains two common modifier problems:

1 Misplaced modifiers

Incorrect The man bought a tie at the department store **with yellow and blue stripes**.

Correct The man bought **a tie with yellow and blue stripes** at the department store.

2 Dangling modifiers

Incorrect **Biting my lip**, not laughing was difficult.

Correct **Biting my lip, I found it difficult** not to laugh.

MODIFIERS

A **modifier** is one or more words that describe another word or word group. For example, the modifier below is **boldfaced**, and the word it modifies is underlined.

● My cousin has a <u>cat</u> **with all-white fur**.
  The modifier *with all-white fur* describes *cat*.

Here are a few more examples:

● The <u>woman</u> **behind the cash register** is the owner of the store.

● I have **nearly** a <u>thousand</u> baseball cards.

● He <u>printed</u> his name **neatly**.

MISPLACED MODIFIERS

A **misplaced modifier** is a modifier that is incorrectly separated from the word or words that it describes. Misplaced modifiers seem to describe words that the author did not intend them to describe. When modifiers are misplaced, the reader may misunderstand the sentence. Generally, the solution is to place the modifier as close as possible to the word or words it describes. Look at the following examples.

Misplaced modifier Sam bought a used car from a local dealer with a smoky tailpipe.

Corrected version Sam bought a used <u>car</u> **with a smoky tailpipe** from a local dealer.

In the first sentence above, the modifier *with a smoky tailpipe* is misplaced. Its unintentional meaning is that the local dealer has a smoky tailpipe. To avoid this meaning, place the modifier next to the word that it describes, *car*.

Misplaced modifier The robin built a nest at the back of our house of grass and string.

Corrected version The robin built a <u>nest</u> **of grass and string** at the back of our house.

In the first sentence above, the words *of grass and string* are misplaced. Because they are near the word *house*, the reader might think that the house is made of grass and string. To avoid this meaning, place the modifier next to the word that it describes, *nest*.

Misplaced modifier   Take the note to Mr. Henderson's office which Kim wrote.

Corrected version   Take the <u>note</u> **which Kim wrote** to Mr. Henderson's office.

In the first sentence above, the words *which Kim wrote* are misplaced. The words must be placed next to *note*, the word that they are clearly meant to describe.

Following is another example of a sentence with a misplaced modifier. See if you can correct it by putting the modifier in another place in the sentence. Write your revision on the lines below.

Misplaced modifier   I am going to New Orleans to visit my aunt on a train.

I am going on a train to New Orleans to visit my aunt.

The original version of the sentence seems to say that the speaker will visit with his aunt on the train. However, the modifier *on a train* is meant to tell how the speaker is going to New Orleans. To make that meaning clear, the modifier needs to be placed closer to the words *am going:* "I <u>am</u> going **on a train** to New Orleans to visit my aunt."

● Practice 1

Underline the misplaced words in each sentence. Then rewrite the sentence in the space provided, placing the modifier where its meaning will be clear.

1. I'm returning the shirt to the store <u>that is too small.</u>

   I'm returning the shirt that is too small to the store.

2. The plants by the lamp <u>with small purple blossoms</u> are violets.

   The plants with small purple blossoms by the lamp are violets.

3. We watched as our house burned to the ground <u>with helpless anger.</u>

   We watched with helpless anger as our house burned to the ground.

4. The woman in that boat <u>that is waving</u> is trying to tell us something.

   The woman that is waving in that boat is trying to tell us something.

5. The bracelet on Roberta's arm <u>made of gold links</u> belongs to her mother.

   The bracelet made of gold links on Roberta's arm belongs to her mother.

Certain Single-Word Modifiers

Certain single-word modifiers—such as *almost, only, nearly,* and *even*—limit the words they modify. Such single-word modifiers must generally be placed before the word they limit.

> *Misplaced modifier*   Christie almost sneezed fifteen times last evening.
>
> *Corrected version*   Christie sneezed **almost** <u>fifteen</u> times last evening.

Because the word *almost* is misplaced in the first sentence, readers might think Christie *almost sneezed fifteen times,* but in fact did not sneeze at all. To prevent this confusion, put *almost* in front of the word it modifies, *fifteen.* Then it becomes clear that Christie must have sneezed a number of times.

● Practice 2

Underline the misplaced words in each sentence. Then rewrite the sentence in the space provided, placing the modifier where its meaning will be clear.

1. Carrie <u>nearly</u> has sixty freckles on her face.

    Carrie has nearly sixty freckles on her face.
    _____

2. Suelyn <u>almost</u> cried through the whole sad movie.

    Suelyn cried through almost the whole sad movie.
    _____

3. I didn't <u>even</u> make one mistake on the midterm test.

    I didn't make even one mistake on the midterm test.
    _____

4. The terrible fall <u>nearly</u> broke every bone in the skier's body.

    The terrible fall broke nearly every bone in the skier's body.
    _____

5. By the end of the war, twenty countries were <u>almost</u> involved in the fighting.

    By the end of the war, almost twenty countries were involved in the fighting.
    _____

DANGLING MODIFIERS

You have learned that a misplaced modifier is incorrectly separated from the word or words it describes. In contrast, a **dangling modifier** has no word in the sentence to describe. Dangling modifiers usually begin a sentence. When a modifier begins a sentence, it must be followed right away by the word or words it is meant to describe. Look at this example:

> *Dangling modifier* Sitting in the dentist's chair, the sound of the drill awakened Larry's old fears.

The modifier *sitting in the dentist's chair* is followed by *the sound of the drill.* This word order suggests that the sound of the drill was sitting in the dentist's chair. Clearly, that is not what the author intended. The modifier was meant to describe the word *Larry.* Since the word *Larry* is not in the sentence (*Larry's* is a different form of the word), it is not possible to correct the dangling modifier simply by changing its position in the sentence.

Here are two common ways to correct run-ons and comma splices.

● **METHOD 1: Follow the dangling modifier with the word or words it is meant to modify.**

After the dangling modifier, write the word it is meant to describe, and then revise as necessary. Using this method, we could correct the sentence about Larry's experience at the dentist's office like this:

> *Correct version*   Sitting in the dentist's chair, **Larry found that** the sound of the drill awakened **his** old fears.

Now the modifier is no longer dangling. It is followed by the word it is meant to describe, *Larry*.

Following is another dangling modifier. How could you correct it using the method described above? Write your correction on the lines below.

> *Dangling modifier*   Depressed and disappointed, running away seemed the only thing for me to do.

Depressed and disappointed, I felt that running away was the only thing for me to do.

_____

The dangling modifier in the above sentence is *depressed and disappointed*. It is meant to describe the word *I*, but there is no *I* in the sentence. So you should have corrected the sentence by writing *I* after the opening modifier and then rewriting as necessary: "Depressed and disappointed, **I felt that** running away **was** the only thing for me to do."

● **Practice 3**

Underline the dangling modifier in each sentence. Then, on the lines provided, revise the sentence, using the first method of correction.   *Revisions may vary.*

1. Out of money, my only choice was to borrow from a friend.

    Out of money, I decided that my only choice was to borrow from a friend.

    _____

2. While jogging, a good topic for Anton's English paper occurred to him.

    While jogging, Anton thought of a good topic for his English paper.

    _____

3. Bored by the lecture, Jed's thoughts turned to dinner.

    Bored by the lecture, Jed began thinking about dinner.

    _____

4. Moving around the sun, Earth's speed is more than 66,000 miles per hour.

    Moving around the sun, Earth travels at a speed of more than 66,000 miles per hour.

    _____

5. Loudly booing and cursing, the fans' disapproval of the call was clear.

    Loudly booing and cursing, the fans clearly showed their disapproval of the call.

    _____

● **METHOD 2: Add a subject and a verb to the opening word group.**

The second method of correcting a dangling modifier is to add a subject and a verb to the opening word group, and revise as necessary. We could use this method to correct the sentence about Larry's experience at the dentist's office.

> *Dangling modifier* Sitting in the dentist's chair, the sound of the drill awakened Larry's old fears.
>
> *Correct version*   **As Larry was** sitting in the dentist's chair, the sound of the drill awakened **his** old fears.

In this revision, the subject *Larry* and the verb *was* have been added to the opening word group.

Following is the dangling modifier that you revised using the first method of correction. How could you correct it using the second method? Write your revision on the lines below.

> *Dangling modifier* Depressed and disappointed, running away seemed the only thing for me to do.

Because I was depressed and disappointed, running away seemed the only thing for
me to do.

You should have revised the sentence so that *I* and the appropriate verb are in the opening word group: "**Because I was** depressed and disappointed, running away seemed the only thing for me to do."

● **Practice 4**

Underline the dangling modifier in each sentence. Then, on the lines provided, revise the sentence, using the second method of correction.

1. While waiting for an important call, Peg's phone began making weird noises.

   While Peg was waiting for an important call, her phone began making weird noises.

2. After being shampooed, Trish was surprised by the carpet's new look.

   After the carpet was shampooed, Trish was surprised by its new look.

3. Touched by the movie, tears came to my eyes.

   Since I was touched by the movie, tears came to my eyes.

4. After eating one too many corn dogs, Stella's stomach rebelled.

   After Stella ate one too many corn dogs, her stomach rebelled.

5. Born on the Fourth of July, Rob's birthday cake was always red, white, and blue.

   Because Rob was born on the Fourth of July, his birthday cake was always red,
   white, and blue.

Name _____ Section _____ Date _____

Score: (Number right) _____ x 10 = _____%

Misplaced and Dangling Modifiers: TEST 1

In each sentence, underline the **one** misplaced or dangling modifier. (The first five sentences contain misplaced modifiers; the second five sentences contain dangling modifiers.) Then rewrite each sentence so that its intended meaning is clear. *Some revisions may vary.*

1. The customer demanded that the waiter take her order <u>rudely</u>.

   The customer rudely demanded that the waiter take her order.

2. I peeled the potatoes before I cooked them <u>with a paring knife</u>.

   I peeled the potatoes with a paring knife before I cooked them.

3. In one week, the cat <u>nearly</u> had caught every mouse in the house.

   In one week, the cat had caught nearly every mouse in the house.

4. The child playing on the jungle gym <u>with fuzzy orange hair</u> is my nephew.

   The child with fuzzy orange hair playing on the jungle gym is my nephew.

5. We discovered an Italian bakery a few miles from our house <u>that had just opened</u>.

   We discovered an Italian bakery that had just opened a few miles from our house.

6. After <u>visiting the bakery</u>, the aroma of freshly baked bread filled our car.

   After we visited the bakery, the aroma of freshly baked bread filled our car.

7. <u>Lying on the sunny beach</u>, thoughts of skin cancer began to enter my mind.

   As I lay on the sunny beach, thoughts of skin cancer began to enter my mind.

8. <u>Not meaning to be cruel</u>, George's careless remark hurt Jackie's feelings.

   Not meaning to be cruel, George hurt Jackie's feelings with his careless remark.

9. <u>Though not a fan of science fiction</u>, the new *Star Trek* movie, to my surprise, was very enjoyable.

   Though not a fan of science fiction, I found the new Star Trek movie, to my surprise,
   was very enjoyable.

10. <u>Exhausted by his first day at school</u>, Sam's eyes closed in the middle of his favorite TV show.

    Exhausted by his first day at school, Sam closed his eyes in the middle of his favorite
    TV show.

Name _____ Section _____ Date _____

Score: (Number right) _____ x 10 = _____%

Misplaced and Dangling Modifiers: TEST 2

Each group of sentences contains **one** misplaced modifier and **one** dangling modifier. Underline the two errors. Then, on the lines provided, rewrite the sentences that contain the errors so that the intended meanings are clear. *Some revisions may vary.*

1. I mailed a letter to my cousin who lives in Alaska <u>without a stamp</u>. <u>Embarrassed</u>, the post office sent it back to me a week later.

   I mailed a letter without a stamp to my cousin who lives in Alaska. I was embarrassed when the

   post office sent it back to me a week later.

2. Lin's mother answered the door, and Jim asked if he could speak to Lin <u>politely</u>. <u>Impressed with Jim's manner</u>, the answer was "Certainly. Please come in."

   Lin's mother answered the door, and Jim asked politely if he could speak to Lin. Impressed with

   Jim's manner, her mother answered, "Certainly. Please come in."

3. The thunderstorm ended, and Shannon saw the sun burst through the clouds. <u>Searching the sky</u>, a glorious rainbow appeared. It <u>nearly</u> lasted a minute and then faded from view.

   . . . As she was searching the sky, a glorious rainbow appeared. It lasted nearly a minute and

   then faded from view.

4. <u>Not meaning to embarrass you</u>, but please answer a question about your birthday present. Will you wear the sweater that I bought for you <u>ever</u>? If you won't, I could exchange it for something else.

   I don't mean to embarrass you, but please answer a question about your birthday present. Will

   you ever wear the sweater that I bought for you?

5. Most of Ms. Nichol's students were gazing blankly into space one warm spring day. In fact, Ms. Nichol noticed that two students <u>only</u> were paying attention. <u>Clapping her hands together sharply</u>, the students woke up from their daydreams.

   . . . In fact, Ms. Nichol noticed that only two students were paying attention. When she clapped

   her hands together sharply, the students woke up from their daydreams.

Basics about Word Choice

Not all writing problems involve grammar. A sentence may be grammatically correct, yet fail to communicate well because of the words that the writer has chosen. This chapter explains three common types of ineffective word choice:

1 Slang

Slang	My sister is **something else**.
Revised	My sister is a very special person.

2 Clichés

Cliché	This semester, I have **bitten off more than I can chew**.
Revised	This semester, I have taken on more work than I can manage.

3 Wordiness

Wordy	It is **absolutely essential and necessary** that you borrow some folding chairs for the party.
Revised	It is essential that you borrow some folding chairs for the party.

SLANG

Slang expressions are lively and fun to use, but they should be avoided in formal writing. One problem with slang is that it's not always understood by all readers. Slang used by members of a particular group (such as teenagers or science-fiction fans) may be unfamiliar to people outside of the group. Also, slang tends to change rapidly. What was *cool* for one generation is *awesome* for another. Finally, slang is by nature informal. So while it adds color to our everyday speech, it is generally out of place in writing for school or work. Use slang only when you have a specific purpose in mind, such as being humorous or communicating the flavor of an informal conversation.

Slang	After a bummer of a movie, we pigged out on a pizza.
Revised	After a **disappointing** movie, we **devoured** a pizza.

● Practice 1

Revisions may vary.

Rewrite the slang expression (printed in *italic type*) in each sentence.

1. Tiffany did not *have a clue* about what was being taught in her science class.

   <u>understand</u>

2. When my parents see my final grades, I will be *dead meat*.

   <u>in trouble</u>

3. Everyone was *grossed out* when the cat brought home a dead rat.
   <u>disgusted</u>

4. Exhausted by their trip, the twins *sacked out* as soon as they got home.
   <u>fell asleep</u>

5. Freddie is really *in la-la land* if he thinks he can make a living as a juggler.
   <u>unrealistic</u>

CLICHÉS

A cliché is an expression that was once lively and colorful. However, because it has been used too often, it has become dull and boring. Try to use fresh wording in place of predictable expressions. Following are a few of the clichés to avoid in your writing:

Common Clichés

avoid like the plague	last but not least	sick and tired
better late than never	light as a feather	sigh of relief
bored to tears	make ends meet	time and time again
easy as pie	pie in the sky	tried and true
in the nick of time	pretty as a picture	under the weather
in this day and age	sad but true	without a doubt

> *Cliché*   Our new family doctor is as sharp as a tack.
> *Revised*   Our new family doctor is **very insightful**.

● Practice 2

Revisions may vary.

Rewrite the cliché *(printed in italic type)* in each sentence.

1. Although the box was *light as a feather*, Jeremy refused to carry it.
   <u>extremely light</u>

2. *In this day and age*, teenagers face many temptations.
   <u>Today</u>

3. Smoking cigarettes is *playing with fire*.
   <u>very risky</u>

4. On the first day of summer vacation, I felt *free as a bird*.
   <u>carefree</u>

5. Luke must really have been hungry because he *chowed down* three burgers at dinner.
   <u>ate</u>

WORDINESS

Some writers think that using more words than necessary makes their writing sound important. Actually, wordiness just annoys and confuses your reader. Try to edit your writing carefully.

First of all, remove words that mean the same as other words in the sentence, as in the following example.

Wordy   Though huge in size and blood red in color, the cartoon monster had a sweet personality.

Revised   Though **huge** and **blood red**, the cartoon monster had a sweet personality.

Huge refers to size, so the words *in size* can be removed with no loss of meaning. *Red* is a color, so the words *in color* are also unnecessary. Following is another example of wordiness resulting from repetition. The author has said the same thing twice.

Wordy   Scott finally made up his mind and decided to look for a new job.

Revised   Scott finally **decided** to look for a new job.

Secondly, avoid puffed-up phrases that can be expressed in a word or two instead.

Wordy   Due to the fact that the printer was out of paper, Renee went to a store for the purpose of buying some.

Revised   **Because** the printer was out of paper, Renee went to a store **to buy** some.

In general, work to express your thoughts in the fewest words possible that are still complete and clear. Notice, for example, how easily the wordy expressions in the box below can be replaced by one or two words. The wordy expressions in the box on the next page can be made concise by eliminating repetitive words.

Wordy Expression	Concise Replacement
a large number of	many
at an earlier point in time	before
at this point in time	now
be in possession of	have
due to the fact that	because
during the time that	while
each and every day	daily
in order to	to
in the event that	if
in the near future	soon
in this day and time	today
made the decision to	decided

> **Examples of Wordiness due to Repetition**
>
> few ~~in number~~   listened ~~with his ears~~
>
> green ~~in color~~   punched ~~with his fist~~
>
> postponed ~~until later~~   ~~the feeling of~~ sadness
>
> small ~~in size~~   ~~hurriedly~~ rushed
>
> the first paragraph ~~at the beginning~~ of the chapter

See if you can revise the following wordy sentence by

1 replacing one group of words and

2 eliminating two unnecessary words.

- Owing to the fact that I was depressed, I postponed my guitar lesson until later.

  Because I was depressed, I postponed my guitar lesson.

  _____

The wordy expression *owing to the fact that* can be replaced by the single word *because* or *since*. The words *until later* can be eliminated with no loss of meaning. Here's a concise version of the wordy sentence: "Because I was depressed, I postponed my guitar lesson."

● Practice 3

Underline the **one** example of wordiness in each sentence that follows. Then rewrite the sentence as clearly and concisely as possible.

Corrections may vary.

Example   I suddenly realized that my date was not going to show up <u>and had stood me up.</u>

I suddenly realized that my date was not going to show up.

1. <u>Due to the fact that</u> Lionel won the lottery, he won't be coming to work today.

   Because Lionel won the lottery, he won't be coming to work today.

   _____

2. My sister <u>went ahead and made the decision</u> to take a job in Maryland.

   My sister decided to take a job in Maryland.

   _____

3. Jeff hid his extra house key and now has forgotten <u>the location where it is.</u>

   Jeff hid his extra house key and now has forgotten where it is.

   _____

4. I do not know <u>at this point in time</u> if I will be going to this school next year.

   I do not know if I will be going to this school next year.

   _____

5. Daily exercise <u>every day of the week</u> gives my mother more energy.

   Daily exercise gives my mother more energy.

   _____

Name _____   Section _____ Date _____

Score: (Number right) _____ x 10 = _____%

Word Choice: TEST 1   *Revisions may vary.*

A. Each sentence below contains **one** example of slang or clichés. Underline the error and then rewrite it, using more effective language.

    1. All morning I have been as <u>nervous as a long-tailed cat in a room full of rocking chairs.</u>

          extremely nervous _____

    2. Maddie was <u>slow as molasses</u> getting ready for school this morning.

          very slow _____

    3. After our first science lab, I felt totally <u>clueless.</u>

          confused _____

    4. Public interest in the upcoming election seems <u>dead as a doornail.</u>

          to have died out _____

    5. Dad <u>freaked out</u> when I got home at 3 a.m.

          lost his temper _____

B. Underline the **one** example of wordiness in each sentence that follows. Then rewrite the sentence as concisely as possible.

    6. We were glad to hear the test had been postponed <u>until a later date.</u>

          We were glad to hear the test had been postponed. _____

    7. Because <u>of the fact that</u> it was raining, we canceled our trip.

          Because it was raining, we canceled our trip. _____

    8. Please call me <u>at the point in time</u> when you are ready to go.

          Please call me when you are ready to go. _____

    9. The store opens at 10 a.m. <u>in the morning.</u>

          The store opens at 10 a.m. _____

   10. Reba forgot her jacket and had to return <u>back again</u> to her house for it.

          Reba forgot her jacket and had to return to her house for it. _____

Name _____ Section _____ Date _____

Score: (Number right) _____ x 10 = _____%

Word Choice: TEST 2

Revisions may vary.

Each item below contains **two** examples of ineffective word choice: slang, clichés, or wordiness. Underline the errors. Then rewrite each underlined part as clearly and concisely as possible.

1. In the event that I get the part-time job, I will heave a sigh of relief.

   a. ___If___

   b. ___be relieved___

2. Thirty-seven students signed up for the creative-writing class, but only twenty-four could be accepted. The other thirteen were really bummed out. They asked the teacher to consider opening a second section of the class, but he gave them the cold shoulder.

   a. ___disappointed___

   b. ___ignored them___

3. Wally assembled the big circular track for his son's model train. Then he connected the cars, hooking them up together. Finally, he threw the switch and watched the train glide around the track. He was as pleased as punch that it all worked perfectly.

   a. ___connected the cars___

   b. ___very pleased___

4. The microwave oven I bought from your store is a loser. Although I have followed the manufacturer's instructions, the oven has never worked properly. I expect you to replace the oven in the very near future. If that is not possible, please return my money.

   a. ___defective___

   b. ___very soon___

5. The movie I saw last night was advertised as a comedy, but I didn't laugh once. Instead, it completely weirded me out. It showed married people who hated one another and parents who shouted at their children. Why do people in this day and age think it is funny for people to mistreat one another?

   a. ___made me feel uneasy___

   b. ___today___

(22) Numbers and Abbreviations

Basics about Numbers and Abbreviations

This chapter explains the following:

1 **When to write out numbers (*one, two*) and when to use numerals (*1, 2*)**

2 **When to use abbreviations and which ones to use**

NUMBERS

Here are guidelines to follow when using numbers.

1 **Spell out any number that can be written in one or two words. Otherwise, use numerals.**

   ● When my grandmother turned **sixty-nine**, she went on a **fifteen**-day trip across **nine**
states.

   ● The mail carrier delivered **512** pieces of mail today.

   Note When written out, numbers twenty-one through ninety-nine are hyphenated.

2 **Spell out any number that begins a sentence.**

   ● **Eight hundred and seventy-one** dollars was found in the briefcase.

   To avoid writing out a long number, you can rewrite the sentence:

   ● The briefcase contained **$871**.

3 **If one or more numbers in a series need to be written as numerals, write all the numbers as numerals.**

   ● The movie theater sold **137** tickets to a horror movie, **64** to a comedy, and **17** to a romance.

4 **Use numerals to write the following.**

   a **Dates**

      ● My grandfather was born on July **4, 1949**.

   b **Times of the day**

      ● The last guest left at **1:45** a.m.

      But when the word *o'clock* is used, the time is spelled out:

      ● I got home at **six o'clock**.

      Also spell out the numbers when describing amounts of time:

      ● Marian worked **fifty** hours last week.

   c **Addresses**

      ● The bookstore is located at **1216** North **48th** Street.

   d **Percentages**

      ● Nearly **70** percent of the class volunteered for the experiment.

e Pages and sections of a book
- Jeff read pages **40–97** of the novel, which includes chapters **2** and **3**.

f Exact amounts of money that include change
- My restaurant bill was **$8.49**.

g Scores
- The Sacramento Kings beat the Los Angeles Lakers **94–90**.
- People with an IQ between **20** and **35** are considered severely retarded.

5 When writing numerals, use commas to indicate thousands.
- Angie has **1,243** pennies in a jar.
- The number that comes after **999,999** is **1,000,000**.

BUT Do not use commas in telephone numbers (1-800-555-1234), zip codes (08043), street numbers (3244 Oak Street), social security numbers (372-45-0985), or years (2004).

● Practice 1

Cross out the **one** number mistake in each sentence. Then write the correction in the space provided.

_50_ **1.** No wonder these cookies cost $5.25—they're ~~fifty~~ percent butter!

two **2.** The pro football player wore a gold earring and ~~2~~ diamond rings.

seven **3.** By ~~7~~ o'clock, the temperature had dipped below freezing.

_2001_ **4.** Nelson began working at his present job in ~~two thousand and one~~.

_40_ **5.** For next week, please read pages 1–~~forty~~ in Chapter 1.

Twenty-six **6.** ~~26~~ students helped out at the homeless shelter at 31 South Lake Street.

_2:45_ **7.** Last night I woke up at midnight and didn't fall asleep again until ~~two forty-five~~.

ten **8.** Did you know that an official baseball weighs about five ounces and a regulation basketball hoop is ~~10~~ feet above the floor?

_50_ **9.** For their wedding, the couple invited 260 people, 210 of the bride's friends and relatives and ~~fifty~~ of the groom's.

_2,456_ **10.** In the mayoral election, the winner received ~~two thousand four hundred and fifty-six~~ more votes than her nearest opponent.

ABBREVIATIONS

Abbreviations can save you time when taking notes. However, you should avoid abbreviations in papers you write for classes. The following are among the few that are acceptable in formal writing.

1   Titles that are used before and after people's names
- **Ms.** Glenda Oaks
- **Dr.** Huang
- Keith Rodham, **Sr.**

2   Initials in a person's name
- Daphne **A.** Miller
- **T.** Martin Sawyer

3   Time and date references
- The exam ended at 4:45 **p.m.**
- Cleopatra lived from about 69 to 30 **B.C.**

4   Organizations, agencies, technical words, countries, or corporations known by their initials. They are usually written in all capital letters and without periods.
- YMCA
- FBI
- VCR
- AIDS
- USA
- NBC

● Practice 2

Cross out the **one** abbreviation mistake in each sentence. Then write the correction in the space provided.

century	**1.** Buddhism was founded in the sixth ~~cent.~~ B.C. by Buddha.
Philadelphia	**2.** Dr. Diamond works for the YMCA in ~~Phila.~~
Canada	**3.** Mr. Ostrow emigrated from Russia to ~~Can.~~ in 1995.
Monday	**4.** On ~~Mon.~~, I have an appointment at IBM with Ms. Janice Grant.
Kansas	**5.** Dwight D. Eisenhower was born in Abilene, ~~Kan.~~, in 1890.
William	**6.** My brother ~~Wm.~~ tried to get his VCR to record a show at 5:30 p.m.
retired	**7.** When my grandfather ~~retd.~~, he volunteered to work with a local AIDS group.
number	**8.** In 1970, the FBI expanded the ~~nmbr.~~ of criminals on its most-wanted list from ten to sixteen.
California	**9.** My cousin is getting married at 9:30 a.m. on the beach in Santa Cruz, ~~Calif.~~
college	**10.** According to an NBC reporter, many of today's ~~coll.~~ students drink in binges.

Name _____ Section _____ Date _____

Score: (Number right) _____ x 10 = _____%

Numbers and Abbreviations: TEST 1

Cross out the one number or abbreviation mistake in each of the following sentences. Then write the correction on the line provided.

One hundred and two   **1.** ~~102~~ patients visited Dr. Jamison's clinic today.

_____three_____   **2.** I wrote ~~3~~ protest letters to CBS when my favorite show was canceled.

_____university_____   **3.** That ~~univ.~~ has 143 professors and 894 students.

_____population_____   **4.** Davenport, Iowa, has a ~~pop.~~ of over 100,000.

_____hospital_____   **5.** The ~~hosp.~~ has treated eighteen patients with AIDS.

___superintendent___   **6.** Mr. Pidora has been ~~supt.~~ of schools for the past nine years.

_____eight_____   **7.** We finally reached the outskirts of New York City at ~~8~~ o'clock.

_____13_____   **8.** Only ~~thirteen~~ percent of the customers preferred the new brand of cereal.

_____$1,220_____   **9.** The IRS says my aunt owes ~~one thousand, two hundred and twenty dollars~~ in back taxes.

_____sandwich_____   **10.** I got up at 2:30 a.m. and made myself a tuna ~~sand.~~ on rye.

Name _____ Section _____ Date _____

Score: (Number right) _____ x 10 = _____%

Numbers and Abbreviations: TEST 2

Cross out the one number or abbreviation mistake in each of the following sentences. Then write the correction on the line provided.

_____five_____ **1.** Ms. Bradley begins her day at 5 o'clock.

_____January_____ **2.** An officer of the NAACP will speak on campus in ~~Jan.~~

_____thirty_____ **3.** Shelly watched a program on PBS for ~~30~~ minutes before going to work.

_____reference_____ **4.** I listed Dr. Keenan as a ~~ref.~~ on my résumé.

_____80_____ **5.** The vendors sold ~~eighty~~ soft pretzels, 145 soft drinks, and 106 hot dogs.

_____Francisco_____ **6.** While in San ~~Fran.~~, we were part of a six-car accident on the Golden Gate Bridge.

_____America_____ **7.** The twenty-seven students in Mrs. Greene's class are learning about South ~~Amer.~~

_____Boulevard_____ **8.** The YWCA on Waverly ~~Blvd.~~ is having an open house in two weeks.

_____$1.50_____ **9.** Since the meal was about ten dollars, the tip should be at least ~~one dollar and fifty cents.~~

_____11_____ **10.** On September ~~eleven~~, 2001, terrorists attacked the World Trade Center and the Pentagon.

㉓ More about Subjects and Verbs

More about Subjects

THE SUBJECT AND DESCRIPTIVE WORDS

A subject is often accompanied by one or more words that describe it. See if you can find the subjects of the following sentences and the words that describe them.

- A very large truck stalled on the bridge.
- Some tomatoes are yellow.
- Two young boys were playing catch in the alley.

In the first sentence, *truck* is the subject. The words *a*, *very*, and *large* describe the word *truck*. In the second sentence, *tomatoes* is the subject, and *some* describes it. In the third sentence, the subject is *boys*; the words describing that subject are *two* and *young*.

For more information on descriptive words (also known as adjectives and adverbs), see "Adjectives and Adverbs," pages 197–206, and "Parts of Speech," pages 332–334.

● Practice 1

Add an appropriate word to each blank. The word that you insert will be the subject of the sentence. It will tell who or what the sentence is about. *Answers will vary.*

1. A _____burglar_____ crept through the dark house.

2. Only three _____apples_____ are left in the refrigerator.

3. The _____lizard_____ swam across the river.

4. David's gold _____chains_____ glittered in the sunlight.

5. _____Fran_____ reminded me to eat some lunch.

6. Several _____kittens_____ were crowded into the small cage.

7. _____Julie_____ ate the raspberries right from the box.

8. _____English_____ is my favorite school subject.

9. Without a sound, a _____hawk_____ grabbed the field mouse by the neck.

10. My mother never went to college. _____She_____ has always felt bad about that.

THE SUBJECT AND PREPOSITIONAL PHRASES

The subject of a sentence is never part of a prepositional phrase. As explained on page 29, a **prepositional phrase** is a group of words that begins with a preposition (a word like *in, from, of,* or *with*) and ends with a noun or pronoun (the object of the preposition). Following are some common prepositions:

about	before	down	like	to
above	behind	during	of	toward
across	below	except	off	under
after	beneath	for	on	up
among	beside	from	over	with
around	between	in	since	without
at	by	into	through	

Here are a few examples of prepositional phrases:

- in the house
- of the world
- from the bakery
- with your permission

Now look at the sentence below. What is the subject? Write your answer here: _____ bunch _____

- A bunch of green grapes fell onto the supermarket floor.

    The answer is *bunch*, but many people would be tempted to choose *grapes*. In this case, however, *grapes* is part of the prepositional phrase *of green grapes*, so it cannot be the subject.

As you look for the subject of a sentence, it may help to cross out the prepositional phrases. For example, look at the following sentences. In each sentence, find the prepositions and cross out the prepositional phrases. Then underline the subject. After finding each subject, read the explanation that follows.

- The sick man, ~~with shaking hands~~, poured the pills ~~from the brown bottle.~~

    The prepositions are *with* and *from*. Cross out *with shaking hands* and *from the brown bottle*, and you are left with the sentence *The sick man poured the pills.* Ask yourself, "Who poured the pills?" The answer, *man*, is the subject of the sentence.

- A student ~~in the class~~ fell asleep ~~during the long lecture.~~

    In and *during* are prepositions. You should have crossed out the prepositional phrases *in the class* and *during the long lecture.* When you do this, you are left with the sentence *A student fell asleep.* Ask yourself, "Who fell asleep?" The answer, *student*, is the subject of the sentence.

For more information on prepositions, see "Parts of Speech," pages 331–332.

● Practice 2

Cross out the **one** prepositional phrase in each sentence. Then underline the subject of the sentence.

Example The pack ~~of cookies~~ disappeared quickly.

1. The blueberries ~~in this pie~~ are bitter.

2. ~~On weekends~~, Troy works overtime.

3. The woman ~~with a pierced nose~~ is my hairdresser.

4. Leaves ~~from our neighbor's tree~~ covered our lawn.

5. ~~During the school play~~, the lead actress lost her voice.

6. Some ~~of the roof shingles~~ are loose.

7. ~~Like her father,~~ Abby adores baseball.

8. The dust ~~under your bed~~ contains tiny creatures.

9. One ~~of my best friends~~ is a computer programmer.

10. ~~From my bedroom window,~~ I can watch my neighbor's TV.

A Note on Singular and Plural Subjects

In addition to finding subjects, you should note whether a subject is **singular** (one) or **plural** (more than one). Most plural subjects simply end in *s*:

Singular	The **car** in front of us is speeding.
Plural	The **cars** in front of us are speeding.

Some plural subjects are irregular:

Singular	The **child** was crying.
Plural	The **children** were crying.

A **compound subject** is two or more subjects connected by a joining word such as *and*. Compound subjects are usually plural.

Compound	The **car** and the **truck** in front of us are speeding.

For more information on compound subjects, see "Subject-Verb Agreement," pages 47–56.

● **Practice 3**

Underline the subject or subjects of each sentence. Then in the space on the left, write **S** if the subject is singular and **P** if the subject is plural.

Example   __P__   <u>Love</u> and <u>hate</u> are closely related emotions.

__P__   **1.** The <u>leaves</u> on our new house plant are turning yellow.

__P__   **2.** <u>Books</u> are often my best companions.

__S__   **3.** The <u>noise</u> of the fireworks frightens the baby.

__P__   **4.** The <u>guitarist</u> and <u>drum player</u> do not like one another.

__S__   **5.** The <u>aroma</u> of barbecued ribs tempts almost everyone.

__P__   **6.** Three <u>men</u> in my family are named Michael.

__S__   **7.** This <u>envelope</u> has a postmark from Chicago.

__P__   **8.** Our <u>oven</u> and <u>refrigerator</u> are both out of order right now.

__S__   **9.** A <u>deck</u> of cards is useful for many different games.

__P__   **10.** Every summer, <u>tourists</u> and <u>mosquitoes</u> descend on the Florida coast.

More about Verbs

Every complete sentence contains a verb. In general, as explained briefly on page 27, there are two types of verbs: **action verbs** and **linking verbs**.

FINDING ACTION VERBS

See if you can double-underline the action verb in the following two sentences. Then read the explanations.

● The moon <u><u>disappeared</u></u> behind the clouds.
● The impatient customer <u><u>tapped</u></u> her fingers on the counter.

In looking for the verb in the first sentence, you can eliminate the prepositional phrase *behind the clouds*. That leaves the words *the moon disappeared*. The *moon* is what did something, so it is the subject of the sentence. What did the moon do? It *disappeared*. So *disappeared* is the action verb.

In the second sentence, you can also eliminate a prepositional phrase: *on the counter*. That leaves *The impatient customer tapped her fingers*. The subject is *customer*—that's who did something. What did the customer do? She *tapped*. So *tapped* is the action verb in that sentence.

Just as a sentence can contain a compound subject, a sentence can contain a **compound verb**: two or more verbs that have the same subject or subjects. For example, here's another version of one of the sentences above:

● The impatient customer tapped her fingers on the counter and cleared her throat.

In this version, the customer did two things: *tapped* (her fingers) and *cleared* (her throat). Therefore, the subject *customer* has a compound verb: *tapped* and *cleared*.

In case you have trouble finding the verb of a sentence, here is one other way to identify a verb: Try putting a pronoun such as *I, you, he, she, it,* or *they* in front of the word you suspect is a verb. If the word is a verb, the resulting sentence will make sense. Notice, for instance, that for the sentences on the previous page, *it disappeared* and *she tapped* make sense.

● Practice 4

Double-underline the action verb or verbs in each sentence. You may find it helpful to first identify and underline the subject and to cross out any prepositional phrases.

1. Members of the audience applauded loudly.

2. Before the party, I took a short nap.

3. Without warning, the can of red paint slid off the ladder.

4. Wesley tripped on the steps.

5. The huge tree on the front lawn shades our front porch in the afternoon.

6. Aunt Lois opened the package and gasped in delight.

7. A German shepherd waited patiently for his owner to return.

8. The angry bull snorted loudly and charged at the red blanket.

9. Without a word, Paul raced out of the house and into the front yard.

10. By 7 a.m., impatient shoppers were gathering at the front entrance of the mall for a special sale.

LINKING VERBS

Linking verbs do not show action. **Linking verbs** join (or link) the subject to one or more words that describe the subject. Look at the following examples.

● Before the race, the runners were anxious.

The subject of this sentence is *runners.* The sentence has no action verb—the runners did not **do** anything. Instead, the verb *were* links the subject to a word that describes it: *anxious.* (*Before the race* is a prepositional phrase, and so it cannot contain the subject or the verb.)

● Cara's boyfriend is a good mechanic.

The subject of this sentence is *boyfriend.* The linking verb *is* joins that subject with words that describe it: *a good mechanic.*

Most linking verbs are forms of the verb *be.* Here are forms of *be*, which is the most used verb in the English language:	am	were	had been
	is	will be	will have been
	are	have been	
	was	has been	

Here are other common words that can be linking verbs.	appear	feel	seem	sound
	become	look	smell	taste

Now see if you can double-underline the linking verbs in the following two sentences.

- George <u><u>looks</u></u> uncomfortable in a suit and tie.
- Sometimes anger <u><u>is</u></u> a healthy emotion.

If you underlined *looks* in the first sentence, you were right. *Looks* links the subject, *George*, to words that describe him: *uncomfortable in a suit and tie.*

If you underlined *is* in the second sentence, you were right. *Is* links the subject, *anger*, to words that describe it: *a healthy emotion.*

● Practice 5

Double-underline the **one** word that is a linking verb in each sentence. You may find it helpful to first identify and underline the subject and to cross out any prepositional phrases.

1. That <u>nurse</u> <u><u>was</u></u> kind.
2. The <u>kitchen</u> <u><u>smells</u></u> spicy.
3. <u>Trisha</u> and <u>I</u> <u><u>are</u></u> roommates.
4. <u>Velvet</u> <u><u>feels</u></u> soft and silky.
5. The chocolate <u>cookies</u> <u><u>taste</u></u> salty and dry.
6. ~~After jogging~~, <u>I</u> <u><u>am</u></u> always hungry.
7. Those <u>dishes</u> ~~from the dishwasher~~ still <u><u>look</u></u> dirty.
8. ~~Since his divorce~~, <u>Nate</u> <u><u>seems</u></u> unhappy.
9. The <u>cashier</u> ~~at our supermarket~~ <u><u>is</u></u> a student ~~at Jefferson High School.~~
10. ~~During the hot, dry summer~~, the <u>farmers</u> <u><u>were</u></u> uneasy ~~about their crops.~~

MAIN VERBS AND HELPING VERBS

Most of the verbs you have looked at so far have been just one word—*wrote, drifted, is, look,* and so on. But many verbs consist of a main verb plus one or more **helping verbs**.
Look at the following two sentences and explanations.

- My sister is joining a book club.

Sister is the subject of this sentence. She is the person who is doing something. What is she doing? She *is joining* (a book club). In this sentence, *is* is a helping verb, and *joining* is the main verb.

Joining by itself would not make sense as a verb. It would be incorrect to say, "My sister joining a book club." Words that end in *-ing* cannot be the verb of a sentence unless they are accompanied by a helping verb.

- Mikey should have given his dog a bath before the pet contest.

In this sentence, *Mikey* is the subject. What should he have done? He *should have given* (his dog a bath). *Should* and *have* are helping verbs. The last verb in the word group, *given*, is the main verb.

Given by itself could not be the verb. It would not be correct to say, "Mikey given his dog a bath . . ."

The helping verbs are listed in the box below.

Forms of *be*:	be, am, is, are, was, were, being, been
Forms of *have*:	have, has, had
Forms of *do*:	do, does, did
Special verbs:	can, could, may, might, must, ought (to), shall, should, will, would
	These special verbs are also known as ***modals***.

The **modals**, unlike the other helping verbs, do not change form to indicate tense. In other words, they do not take such endings as *-ed, -s,* and *-ing*. After the modals, always use the basic form of a verb, the form in which a verb is listed in the dictionary (*go, see, work*, and so on).

- You *can* turn in the paper tomorrow.
- We *should* visit Dee in the hospital.

Now see if you can underline the main verbs and the helping verbs in the following two sentences. Then read the explanations.

- Gwen <u>has visited</u> the learning skills lab.
- I <u>will be running</u> in the school's five-mile race.

In the first sentence, *Gwen* is the subject. She is the one who has done something. To find the verb, we can ask, "What did Gwen do?" The answer is *has visited. Has* is the helping verb, and *visited* is the main verb.

In the second sentence, *I* is the subject. What will that subject be doing? He or she *will be running.* So in this sentence, *will* and *be* are helping verbs, and *running* is the main verb.

● Practice 6

Fill in the blanks under each sentence.

1. As usual, my brother was complaining about his homework.

   Helping verb(s): _____was_____   *Main verb:* _____complaining_____

2. The students will decorate the classroom for the teacher's surprise party.

   Helping verb(s): _____will_____   *Main verb:* _____decorate_____

3. The dental appointment should take about an hour.

   Helping verb(s): _____should_____   *Main verb:* _____take_____

4. Surprisingly, I do enjoy learning grammar.

   Helping verb(s): _____do_____   *Main verb:* _____enjoy_____

5. Margaret has planted parsley and other herbs in her backyard.

   Helping verb(s): _____has_____   *Main verb:* _____planted_____

6. You should have called your mother on her birthday.

   Helping verb(s): _____should have_____   *Main verb:* _____called_____

7. The video-game machine will accept only quarters.

   Helping verb(s): _____will_____ *Main verb:* _____accept_____

8. That drunk driver could have killed Aunt Esther.

   Helping verb(s): ____could have____ *Main verb:* _____killed_____

9. My girlfriend must have forgotten our date this evening.

   Helping verb(s): ____must have____ *Main verb:* ____forgotten____

10. The star basketball player at our college might have injured himself seriously.

    Helping verb(s): ____might have____ *Main verb:* _____injured_____

WORDS THAT ARE NOT VERBS

Here is some added information that will help when you look for verbs in a sentence.

1   The verb of a sentence never begins with the word *to*.

   ● The instructor **agreed** to provide ten minutes for study before the quiz.

     Although *provide* is a verb, *to provide* cannot be the verb of a sentence. The verb of this sentence is *agreed*.

2   Certain words—such as *always, just, never, not,* and *only*—may appear between the main verb and the helping verb. Such words are **adverbs**. They describe the verb, but they are never part of it.

   ● Our canary **does** not **sing** in front of visitors.

   ● We **will** never **eat** at that restaurant again.

   ● You **should** always **wear** your seat belt in a moving vehicle.

   For more information on adverbs, see "Adjectives and Adverbs," pages 197–206, and "Parts of Speech," pages 333–334.

● Practice 7

In the space provided, write the complete verb in each sentence.

1. My uncle is not wearing his toupee anymore.

   Complete verb: _____is wearing_____

2. The children hurried to finish their art projects by the end of the class.

   Complete verb: _____hurried_____

3. The noodles should not be boiled more than seven minutes.

   Complete verb: ____should be boiled____

4. The teacher has promised to return the papers by Friday.

   Complete verb: ____has promised____

5. Reba will always love her ex-husband.

   Complete verb: _____will love_____

Name _____ Section _____ Date _____

Score: (Number right) _____ x 5 = _____%

More about Subjects and Verbs: TEST 1

For each sentence, cross out any prepositional phrases. Then, on the lines provided, write the subject(s) and verb(s), including any helping verb(s).

1. The coffee ~~from the leaking pot~~ stained the carpet.

   Subject(s): _____ coffee _____   *Verb(s):* _____ stained _____

2. My cousins ~~in Louisiana~~ formed a gospel music group.

   Subject(s): _____ cousins _____   *Verb(s):* _____ formed _____

3. ~~At exactly noon,~~ my summer vacation will begin.

   Subject(s): _____ vacation _____   *Verb(s):* _____ will begin _____

4. A warm sweatshirt ~~with a hood~~ feels good ~~on a chilly day.~~

   Subject(s): _____ sweatshirt _____   *Verb(s):* _____ feels _____

5. The source ~~of heating and cooling for the house~~ is a heat pump.

   Subject(s): _____ source _____   *Verb(s):* _____ is _____

6. The cardboard boxes ~~by the river~~ are home ~~to several people.~~

   Subject(s): _____ boxes _____   *Verb(s):* _____ are _____

7. ~~For my little brother and sister,~~ happiness is a McDonald's restaurant.

   Subject(s): _____ happiness _____   *Verb(s):* _____ is _____

8. Retrievers and sheepdogs do not bite very often.

   Subject(s): ___ Retrievers . . . sheepdogs ___   *Verb(s):* _____ do . . . bite _____

9. The rug-cleaning people should have been here ~~by now.~~

   Subject(s): _____ people _____   *Verb(s):* ___ should have been ___

10. ~~After work,~~ Dena and I ate dinner and studied ~~at her apartment.~~

    Subject(s): _____ Dena . . . I _____   *Verb(s):* ___ ate . . . studied ___

Name _____ Section _____ Date _____

Score: (Number right) _____ x 5 = _____%

More about Subjects and Verbs: TEST 2

In each of the ten sentences in this paragraph, cross out any prepositional phrases. Then, underline all the subjects once and the verbs twice. Remember to include any helping verb(s) and also all parts of compound subjects and verbs.

[1]Sharks, ~~with their pointed snouts and fearsome teeth~~, terrify most people.

[2]However, ~~of the 375 or so different types of sharks~~, few have attacked people. [3]Most sharks will attack only when ~~in danger~~. [4]The great white shark is one ~~of the most dangerous sharks to humans~~. [5]Many people know and fear this shark ~~from its role in the movie Jaws~~. [6]It can grow ~~to over twenty feet in length~~. [7]The coloring ~~of the great white shark~~ is a camouflage ~~in the water~~. [8]The color ~~of its belly~~ is white. [9]~~From underneath~~, the white belly blends ~~with the bright sky overhead~~. [10]Seals, smaller fish, and people often do not see the great white shark ~~in time~~.

24   More about Subject-Verb Agreement

You have already reviewed (on pages 47–56) two situations that affect subject-verb agreement:

1   **Words between the subject and the verb**

2   **Compound subjects**

This section will cover five other situations that affect subject-verb agreement:

3   **Verb coming before the subject**

4   **More about compound subjects**

5   **Collective nouns**

6   **Indefinite pronoun subjects**

7   **Relative pronoun subjects:** *who, which, that*

VERB COMING BEFORE THE SUBJECT

The verb follows the subject in most sentences:

- *Hector* **passed** the course.
- A *rabbit* **lives** in my backyard.
- The *plane* **roared** overhead.

However, in some sentences, the verb comes *before* the subject. To make the subject and verb agree in such cases, look for the subject after the verb. Then decide if the verb should be singular or plural. Sentences in which the verb comes first include questions.

- What **was** your *score* on the test?

  The verb *was* is singular. It agrees with the singular subject *score*. *On the test* is a prepositional phrase. The subject of a sentence is never in a prepositional phrase. (See page 226.)

The verb also comes first in sentences that begin with such words as *there is* or *here are*.

- There **are** *ants* in the sugar jar.

  The verb of this sentence is the plural verb *are*, so the subject should be plural as well. You can find the subject by asking, "What are in the sugar jar?" The answer, *ants*, is the subject.

- Here **is** the *menu*.

  The subject of this sentence is *menu*, which needs a singular verb.

The verb may also come before the subject in sentences that begin with a prepositional phrase.

- On that shelf **are** the *reports* for this year.

  The sentence begins with the prepositional phrase *on that shelf*, which is followed by the plural verb *are*. You can find the subject by asking, "What are on that shelf?" The answer is the subject of the sentence: *reports*. The subject and verb agree—they are both plural.

Here's another helpful way to find the subject when the verb comes first: Try to rearrange the sentence so that the subject comes first. The subject may be easier to find when the sentence is in the normal order. For the sentences on the previous page, you would then get:

● Your *score* on the test **was** what?

● *Ants* **are** in the sugar jar.

● The *menu* **is** here.

● The *reports* for this year **are** on that shelf.

● Practice 1

Underline the subject of each sentence. Then, in the space provided, write the form of the verb that agrees with the subject. (If you have trouble finding the subject, try crossing out any prepositional phrases.)

is, are   **1.** Here _____are_____ some messages ~~for you~~.

is, are   **2.** What _____is_____ your middle name?

stands, stand   **3.** ~~Beside the stream~~ _____stands_____ a low wooden fence.

grows, grow   **4.** ~~In that little garden~~ _____grow_____ twenty herbs.

was, were   **5.** There _____were_____ black clouds ~~in the sky~~ this morning.

is, are   **6.** Where _____is_____ the box ~~for these crayons~~?

lies, lie   **7.** ~~On the table in the dining room~~ _____lies_____ a letter for you.

is, are   **8.** There _____are_____ good reasons to hire older workers.

is, are   **9.** Why _____is_____ Jamie sitting outside ~~in the car~~?

rests, rest   **10.** ~~On the bench outside of the mall~~ _____rest_____ two tired shoppers.

MORE ABOUT COMPOUND SUBJECTS

As explained on page 47, a **compound subject** is made up of two nouns connected by a joining word. Subjects joined by *and* generally take a plural verb.

However, when a compound subject is connected by *or, nor, either . . . or,* or *neither . . . nor,* the verb must agree with the part of the subject that is closer to it.

● My *aunts* or my *mother* usually **hosts** our family gatherings.

The singular noun *mother* is closer to the verb, so the singular verb *hosts* is used.

● Either *he* or *his parents* were home that night.

● Either *his parents* or *he* was home that night.

In the first sentence, the plural noun *parents* is closer to the verb, so the verb is plural. In the second sentence, the singular noun *he* is closer to the verb, so the verb must be singular.

● Neither the *teacher* nor the *students* **are** to blame for the shortage of textbooks.

The plural noun *students* is closer to the verb, so the verb is plural.

● **Practice 2**

In each sentence, underline the compound subject. Then, in the space provided, write the correct form of the verb in the margin.

smells, smell   **1.** Either the trash <u>can</u> or your <u>socks</u> _____smell_____ horrible.

tastes, taste   **2.** Neither the <u>fish</u> nor the <u>vegetables</u> _____taste_____ fresh in this restaurant.

donates, donate **3.** Her <u>sisters</u> or <u>she</u> usually _____donates_____ a cake or cookies to the community bake sale.

seems, seem   **4.** Neither <u>Polly</u> nor her <u>brothers</u> _____seem_____ surprised by their parents' announcement.

washes, wash   **5.** "On Father's Day," Don said, "either the <u>children</u> or my <u>wife</u> _____washes_____ the family car."

COLLECTIVE NOUNS

A **collective noun** refers to a group of persons or things that are thought of as one unit. Collective nouns are usually considered singular. Following are some examples.

● The **family** *lives* on Russell Avenue.

   Family refers to a single unit, so the singular verb *lives* is used. However, if a collective noun refers to the individual members of the group, a plural verb is used.

● The **family** *are* Republicans, Democrats, and Independents.

   Since one unit cannot have three different political views, *family* in this sentence clearly refers to the individual members of the group, so the plural verb *are* is used. To emphasize the individuals, some writers would use a subject that is clearly plural:

● The **members** of the family *are* Republicans, Democrats, and Independents.

● **Practice 3**

In each sentence, underline the subject and decide if it needs a singular or plural verb. Then fill in the correct form of the verb in the margin.

is, are   **1.** The <u>jury</u> _____is_____ going to announce its verdict this morning.

has, have   **2.** The <u>faculty</u> _has_ chosen one book for everyone in the school to read.

is, are   **3.** This noisy <u>audience</u> _____is_____ spoiling the movie for me.

takes, take   **4.** The <u>couple</u> _____take_____ separate vacations: she likes to hike, and he likes to lie on the beach.

marches, march **5.** Every year, the <u>band</u> _____marches_____ in the town's Thanksgiving parade.

INDEFINITE PRONOUN SUBJECTS

Indefinite pronouns are pronouns that do not refer to a specific person or thing. The ones in the box below are always singular:

anybody	either	neither	one
anyone	everybody	no one	somebody
anything	everyone	nobody	someone
each	everything	nothing	something

In the following sentences, the subjects are singular indefinite pronouns. Each of the verbs is therefore also singular.

- *Each* of the puppies **is** cute in its own way.
- *Neither* of the boys **wants** to walk the dog.
- Despite the rules, nearly *everyone* in my apartment building **owns** a pet.

Note that the indefinite pronoun *both* is always plural:

- *Both* of the puppies **are** cute in their own ways.

The definite pronoun *most* is singular or plural, depending on its context:

- *Most* of his outfit **is** white.
  Most here refers to one thing—the outfit, so the singular verb *is* is used.
- *Most* of the salespeople **are** friendly.
  Most here refers to several salespeople, so the plural verb *are* is used.

● Practice 4

Underline the subject of each sentence. Then, in the space provided, write the form of the verb that agrees with the subject.

is, are   **1.** <u>Everybody</u> at my new school _____ is _____ friendly.

feels, feel   **2.** <u>Neither</u> of those mattresses _____ feels _____ comfortable.

knows, know   **3.** <u>Nobody</u> in my family _____ knows _____ how to swim.

is, are   **4.** <u>Both</u> of my parents _____ are _____ allergic to peanuts.

has, have   **5.** <u>Most</u> of the house _____ has _____ been painted.

needs, need   **6.** <u>Each</u> of the children _____ needs _____ some attention.

seem, seems   **7.** <u>Either</u> Monday or Friday _____ seems _____ like a good day for the meeting.

goes, go   **8.** <u>Everything</u> in that box _____ goes _____ to the neighborhood garage sale.

is, are   **9.** <u>Both</u> of my best friends _____ are _____ older than I.

has, have   **10.** <u>Most</u> of the wedding invitations _____ have _____ been addressed and mailed.

RELATIVE PRONOUN SUBJECTS: *WHO, WHICH, THAT*

The relative pronouns *who, which,* and *that* are singular when they refer to a singular noun. They are plural when they refer to a plural noun.

- I met a woman *who* **is** from China.
- I met two women *who* **are** from China.

  In the first sentence above, *who* refers to the singular word *woman,* so the verb is singular too. In the second sentence, *who* refers to the plural word *women,* so the verb must be plural.

- Our car, *which* **is** only a year old, already needs a new battery.

  Which refers to *car,* a singular noun, so the singular verb *is* is used.

- My boss collects old wind-up toys *that* still **work.**

  That refers to the plural noun *toys,* so the plural verb *work* is used.

For more information on relative pronouns, see "Parts of Speech," page 328.

Practice 5

In each sentence, underline the noun that the relative pronoun refers to. Then fill in the correct form of the verb in the margin.

gives, give 1. We have planted several <u>shrubs</u>, which _____give_____ some privacy to our backyard.

gives, give 2. We have planted a <u>hedge</u>, which _____gives_____ some privacy to our backyard.

is, are 3. Rhoda dislikes all <u>foods</u> that _____are_____ good for her.

is, are 4. Rhoda dislikes all <u>food</u> that _____is_____ good for her.

was, were 5. The <u>soles</u> of my shoes, which _____were_____ covered with mud, left black footprints on the sidewalk.

was, were 6. The <u>sole</u> of my right shoe, which _____was_____ covered with mud, left black footprints on the sidewalk.

is, are 7. Lenny plays basketball with a <u>man</u> who _____is_____ twice his age.

is, are 8. Lenny plays basketball with <u>men</u> who _____are_____ twice his age.

speaks, speak 9. My niece's favorite playmate is a little <u>girl</u> who _____speaks_____ no English.

speaks, speak 10. My niece's favorite playmates are two little <u>girls</u> who _____speak_____ no English.

Name _____   Section _____ Date _____

Score: (Number right) _____ x 10 = _____%

More about Subject-Verb Agreement: TEST 1

For each sentence, fill in the correct form of the verb in the margin.

needs, need   **1.** The house or the barn _____needs_____ to be painted this year.

is, are   **2.** Also, both buildings, which _____are_____ very old, need repairs.

itches, itch   **3.** Each of these sweaters _____itches_____ .

gets, get   **4.** Our group _____gets_____ together every Friday night to play bridge.

was, were   **5.** There _____were_____ sad expressions on the students' faces.

is, are   **6.** In my English class, either a novel or short stories _____are_____ assigned every week.

hurries, hurry   **7.** Through the airport _____hurry_____ travelers from all over the world.

likes, like   **8.** My neighbors are people who _____like_____ their privacy.

is, are   **9.** Why _____are_____ the lights off?

knows, know   **10.** No one _____knows_____ how long the rain delay will continue.

Name _____   Section _____   Date _____

Score: (Number right) _____ x 10 = _____ %

More about Subject-Verb Agreement: **TEST 2**

For each sentence, fill in the correct form of the verb in the margin.

is, are   **1.** There _____are_____ three fast-food restaurants in the next block.

was, were   **2.** What _____were_____ the reasons for the workers' strike?

plays, play   **3.** Someone in the apartment upstairs _____plays_____ a guitar late at night.

is, are   **4.** Some cookies or a cake _____is_____ needed for dessert.

was, were   **5.** Among the guests _____was_____ a private detective.

has, have   **6.** The jury _____have_____ conflicting opinions.

was, were   **7.** The students and their teacher _____were_____ sitting in a circle.

is, are   **8.** There _____are_____ many hungry people in America's cities.

makes, make   **9.** The mayor is a woman who _____makes_____ things happen in our town.

was, were   **10.** Neither the children nor their father _____was_____ aware that someone was at the door.

25 More about Verbs

Verb Tenses

All verbs have various **tenses**—forms that indicate the time the sentence is referring to. This chapter explains the following about verb tenses:

1 **The four principal verb parts that are the basis for all of the tenses**

2 **The most common verb tenses in English**

Six main tenses	present, past, future present perfect, past perfect, future perfect
Three progressive tenses	present progressive, past progressive, future progressive

THE FOUR PRINCIPAL PARTS OF VERBS

Each verb tense is based on one of the four principal parts of verbs. Following are explanations of each of those verb parts.

1 **Basic Form** The basic form is the form in which verbs are listed in the dictionary. It is used for the present tense for all subjects except third-person singular subjects.

   ● I **ask** questions in class.

   Third-person singular verbs are formed by adding *-s* to the basic form.

   ● Sue **asks** questions in class.

2 **Past Tense Form** The past tense of most verbs is formed by adding *-ed* or *-d* to the basic form.

   ● We **asked** the teacher to postpone the test.

   ● I **amused** the children by doing magic tricks.

3 **Present Participle** The present participle is the *-ing* form of a verb. It is used in the progressive tenses, which you will learn about later in the chapter.

   ● Jack is **asking** the teacher something in the hallway.

   ● I am **amusing** the children while their mother does errands.

4 **Past Participle** The past participle of a verb is usually the same as its past-tense form. The past participle is the form that is used with the helping verbs *have, has,* and *had* and with *am, is, are, was,* or *were.*

   ● The teachers have **asked** us to study in groups.

   ● I was **amused** when the children asked if I could stay forever.

Here are the principal parts of three regular verbs:

Basic Form	Past Tense Form	Present Participle	Past Participle
work	worked	working	worked
smile	smiled	smiling	smiled
wonder	wondered	wondering	wondered

SIX MAIN TENSES

There are six main tenses in English. They are **present, past, future, present perfect, past perfect,** and **future perfect**.

Look at the following chart. It shows the six basic tenses of the verb *work*.

Tense	Example
Present	I **work**.
Past	I **worked**.
Future	I **will work**.
Present Perfect	I **have worked**.
Past Perfect	I **had worked**.
Future Perfect	I **will have worked**.

These tenses are explained in more detail below and on the pages that follow.

Present Tense

Verbs in the **present tense** express present action or habitual action. (A habitual action is one that is often repeated.)

- Our dog **smells** the neighbor's barbecue.

    Smells expresses a present action.

- Jay **works** as a waiter on weekends.

    Works expresses a habitual action.

The forms of present tense verbs are shown with the verb *work* in the box below. Notice the difference between the singular third-person form and the other present tense forms.

	Singular	Plural
First person	I work	we work
Second person	you work	you work
Third person	he, she, it work**s**	they work

Present tense verbs for the third-person singular end with an *s*. Here are some other sentences in the present tense with subjects that are third-person singular:

● She **reads** a book a week.

● It **takes** me a month to read a book.

● Dan **drives** an hour to school every day.

● His old car **averages** only ten miles a gallon.

Note A third-person subject is *he, she, it,* or any single person or thing other than the speaker (first person) or the person spoken to (second person).

● Practice 1

A. Fill in the present tense of *smile* for each of the following:

	Singular	Plural
First person	I ___smile___	we ___smile___
Second person	you ___smile___	you ___smile___
Third person	he, she, it ___smiles___	they ___smile___

B. Fill in each space with the present tense form of the verb shown in the margin.

drill   **1.** The dentist ___drills___ the cavity as his assistant watches.

practice   **2.** Ling ___practices___ her typing every day.

ring   **3.** Those church bells ___ring___ on the hour.

make   **4.** He suddenly ___makes___ a U-turn.

dig   **5.** Some workers ___dig___ through the stones and rubble.

trim   **6.** I ___trim___ my fingernails before playing the piano.

clean   **7.** Dinah ___cleans___ her apartment every Saturday.

tell   **8.** The nurse ___tells___ the patient to make a fist.

discover   **9.** My sister often ___discovers___ loose change in her coat pockets.

remember **10.** Children often ___remember___ the fights their parents used to have.

Past Tense

Verbs in the **past tense** express actions that took place in the past.

● Last year, Jay **worked** as a messenger.

● One day our dog **chased** a raccoon.

The past tense is usually formed by adding *-ed* or *-d* to the end of the basic form of the verb. In the above sentences, the *-ed* and *-d* endings are added to the basic forms of the verbs *work* and *chase*.

Note People sometimes drop the *-ed* or *-d* ending in their everyday speech. They then tend to omit those endings in their writing as well. For example, someone might say

● I finish the paper an hour before class.

instead of

● I **finished** the paper an hour before class.

In written English, however, the *-ed* or *-d* ending is essential.

● Practice 2

Fill in each space with the past tense form of the verb shown in the margin.

seem   **1.** The movie _____seemed_____ to end suddenly.

sail   **2.** The ship _____sailed_____ to the Bahamas last week.

wonder   **3.** Alisha _____wondered_____ where she had put her car keys.

knock   **4.** Last night someone _____knocked_____ on the door.

name   **5.** Jean _____named_____ the spotted puppy Freckles.

jump   **6.** My little brother _____jumped_____ up when I entered the room.

talk   **7.** The students _____talked_____ easily with the new instructor.

check   **8.** Bert _____checked_____ the air in his car tires before he went on vacation.

wipe   **9.** The man _____wiped_____ the lipstick off his cheek with his shirt sleeve.

play   **10.** Stan _____played_____ his guitar in a concert last summer.

Future Tense

Verbs in the **future tense** describe future actions.

● Next summer, Jay **will work** at a camp.

The future tense is formed by adding the word *will* or *shall* to the basic form of the verb.

● Practice 3

Fill in the space with the future tense form of the verb shown in the margin.

play   **1.** Stan _____will play_____ his guitar in a concert tonight.

plant   **2.** The lumberjacks _____will plant_____ new trees here next spring.

iron   **3.** I _____will iron_____ my shirt before going to the interview.

attend   **4.** Penny _____will attend_____ San Antonio Community College in the fall.

circle   **5.** The teacher _____will circle_____ any errors she finds in your paper.

Present Perfect Tense (*have* **or** *has* **+ past participle**)

The **present perfect** tense describes an action that began in the past and either has been finished or is continuing at the present time.

● I **have written** five pages of notes on the textbook chapter.

● Jay **has worked** at a number of jobs over the years.

The present perfect tense is formed by adding the correct form of the helping verb *have* to the past participle of the verb. Here are the present tense forms of *have*:

	Singular	**Plural**
First person	I have	we have
Second person	you have	you have
Third person	he, she, it has	they have

● Practice 4

Fill in each space with the present perfect tense form of the verb shown in the margin. One is done for you as an example.

pour   **1.** The hostess _____has poured_____ iced tea for most of her guests.

live   **2.** I _____have lived_____ in three different countries.

check   **3.** Because Bert will be driving a long distance, he _____has checked_____ the air in his car tires.

boil   **4.** The chef _____has boiled_____ the eggs for the salad and is now slicing them.

mix   **5.** The children _____have mixed_____ together in one box the pieces of three different puzzles.

Past Perfect Tense (*had* + past participle)

The **past perfect** tense describes an action that was completed in the past before another past action.

● Jay **had worked** as a messenger before he located a better job as a waiter.

The past perfect tense is formed by adding *had* to the past participle of a verb.

● Practice 5

Fill in the space with the past perfect tense form of the verb shown in the margin. Add *had* to the past participle of the verb. One is done for you as an example.

promise **1.** Zora _____had promised_____ to go to the meeting before she realized it was on her birthday.

struggle **2.** The man _____had struggled_____ in several part-time jobs before returning to college.

ask **3.** My sister _____had asked_____ two other men to the dance before inviting Dan.

intend **4.** I _____had intended_____ to go to the library to get material for my report, but then I realized I could use the Internet instead.

invite **5.** Hector _____had invited_____ his friends to his apartment before he knew that his roommate was ill.

Future Perfect Tense (*will have* + past participle)

The **future perfect** tense describes an action that will be completed before some time in the future.

- Jay **will have worked** at a half dozen different jobs before college graduation.

The future perfect tense is formed by adding *will have* to the past participle of a verb.

● Practice 6

Fill in the space with the future perfect tense form of the verb shown in the margin. Add *will have* to the past participle of the verb. One is done for you as an example.

complete   **1.** I _____will have completed_____ five exams by the end of finals week.

attend   **2.** By graduation day, I _____will have attended_____ five parties.

finish   **3.** You eat so slowly that I _____will have finished_____ my ice cream before you begin your spaghetti.

hire   **4.** The company _____will have hired_____ several new employees by May.

design   **5.** By the end of the summer, my mother _____will have designed_____ and sewed my sister's wedding dress.

THE PROGRESSIVE TENSES

As their names suggest, the **progressive tenses** express actions still in progress at a particular time. They are made by adding a form of the helping verb *be* to the *-ing* form of the verb, the present participle.

Present Progressive Tense (*am, are,* **or** *is* + present participle)

The **present progressive** tense expresses an action taking place at this moment or that will occur sometime in the future.

- Jay **is working** at the restaurant today.

- I **am going** to get home late tonight.

The present progressive tense is formed by adding the correct present tense form of the helping verb *be* to the *-ing* form of the verb.

Present Tense Forms of the Verb *Be*

	Singular	Plural
First person	I am	we are
Second person	you are	you are
Third person	he, she, it is	they are

● Practice 7

Below are five sentences with verbs in the present tense. Cross out each verb and change it to the present progressive in the space provided. One is done for you as an example.

1. The child ~~plays~~ with the puppy. _____is playing_____

2. The microwave ~~beeps~~ loudly. _____is beeping_____

3. The roses in the garden ~~bloom~~. _____are blooming_____

4. I ~~practice~~ my speech tonight. _____am practicing_____

5. The visitors ~~pace~~ in the hospital lobby. _____are pacing_____

Past Progressive Tense (*was* or *were* + present participle)

The **past progressive** tense expresses an action that was in progress at a certain time in the past.

● Jay **was working** yesterday.

The past progressive tense is formed by adding the correct past tense form of *be* to the *-ing* form of the verb.

Past Tense Forms of the Verb *Be*

	Singular	Plural
First person	I was	we were
Second person	you were	you were
Third person	he, she, it was	they were

● Practice 8

Below are five sentences with verbs in the past tense. Cross out each verb and change it to the past progressive in the space provided. One is done for you as an example.

1. The child ~~played~~ with the puppy. _____was playing_____

2. The microwave ~~beeped~~ loudly. _____was beeping_____

3. The roses in the garden ~~bloomed~~. _____were blooming_____

4. I ~~practiced~~ my speech last night. _____was practicing_____

5. The visitors ~~paced~~ in the hospital lobby. _____were pacing_____

Future Progressive Tense (*will be* + present participle)

The **future progressive** tense expresses an action that will be in progress at a certain time in the future.

- Jay **will be working** tomorrow.

The future progressive tense is formed by adding *will be* to the *-ing* form of the verb.

● Practice 9

Below are five sentences with verbs in the future tense. Cross out each verb and change it to the future progressive in the space provided. One is done for you as an example.

1. The child ~~will play~~ with the puppy. ___will be playing___
2. The microwave ~~will beep~~ loudly. ___will be beeping___
3. The roses in the garden ~~will bloom~~. ___will be blooming___
4. I ~~will practice~~ my speech tonight. ___will be practicing___
5. The visitors ~~will pace~~ in the hospital lobby. ___will be pacing___

A Note on *-ing* Verbs

Look at the following word groups:

- Jay working tonight.
- The visitors pacing in the hospital lobby.

The above word groups express incomplete thoughts because their verbs are incomplete. The *-ing* form of a verb cannot stand by itself as the verb of a sentence—it must be accompanied by a helping verb:

- Jay **is working** tonight.
- The visitors **were pacing** in the hospital lobby.

● Practice 10

The verb in each of the following sentences is incomplete. Correct each incomplete thought by adding *is, are, was,* or *were* in the space provided.

1. Oscar ___is___ playing the clarinet in his school band this year.
2. You ___were___ giggling in your sleep last night.
3. Even though I ___was___ sneezing and coughing, no one thought I was sick.
4. If you look down the street, you'll see that five boys ___are___ standing on the corner.
5. The customers ___were___ complaining about the long wait until a waitress offered them free cups of coffee.

A SUMMARY OF THE NINE MOST COMMON VERB TENSES

Using the regular verb *call*, the chart below illustrates the nine most common tenses in English.

The Nine Most Common Verb Tenses

Present	I **call** my grandmother Nana. My mother **calls** her Babe.
Past	A number of employees **called** in sick today.
Future	Because the flu is going around, more **will** probably **call** in sick tomorrow.
Present perfect	Rebecca **has called** the radio station at least ten times to request her favorite song.
Past perfect	No one **had called** Mitchell "Shorty" for years until he attended his grade-school reunion.
Future perfect	When you finish your first day as a telemarketer, you **will have called** forty potential customers.
Present progressive	Ken **is calling** the restaurant right now to make a reservation for dinner.
Past progressive	He **was calling** a different restaurant when I came in, but I urged him to call my favorite one.
Future progressive	Mom **will be calling** when she arrives at work and realizes she left her purse here.

Name _____   Section _____ Date _____

Score: (Number right) _____ x 10 = _____%

More about Verbs: TEST 1

A. In each space, write the **present tense** form of the verb in the margin.

Examples   *plan*   Carl _____plans_____ to enter the contest.

    attend   The students _____attend_____ a meeting on the new dress code.

soar   **1.** The hawk _____soars_____ above the cornfield.

listen   **2.** The jurors _____listen_____ to the witness.

think   **3.** Leona _____thinks_____ she passed her English exam.

B. In each space, write the **past tense** form of the verb in the margin.

Example   *promise*   My brother _____promised_____ to wash our car on Saturday.

scratch   **4.** The prisoner _____scratched_____ his initials on the cell wall.

arrive   **5.** The bus _____arrived_____ at our hotel at 7:15 a.m.

float   **6.** Five orange slices _____floated_____ on top of the red punch.

struggle   **7.** The campers _____struggled_____ through the thick underbrush near the camp.

C. In each space, write the **future tense** form of the verb in the margin.

Example   *check*   The nurse _____will check_____ your blood pressure each day.

blossom   **8.** Those trees _____will blossom_____ into fluffy white clouds.

stand   **9.** Everyone _____will stand_____ when the judge enters the courtroom.

wear   **10.** Johnny _____will wear_____ a dinosaur costume to the party.

Name _____ Section _____ Date _____

Score (Number right)_____ x 10 = _____%

More about Verbs: TEST 2

A. In each space, write the **present perfect tense** form of the verb in the margin.

Examples   *walk*   Bernice ___has walked___ over twenty miles this week.

look   I ___have looked___ all over for my glasses.

wash   **1.** The students ___have washed___ nearly seventy cars to raise money for their class trip.

learn   **2.** We ___have learned___ about the civil-rights movement in our history class this semester.

gain   **3.** Rodney ___has gained___ ten pounds in his first year of college.

notice   **4.** I ___have noticed___ changes in you since you started going to the gym.

B. In each space, write the **past perfect tense** form of the verb in the margin.

Example   *walk*   Before her heart attack, Bernice seldom ___had walked___ for exercise.

argue   **5.** Fritz ___had argued___ with a friend before the car accident.

warn   **6.** Before she left for her hair appointment, Jenna ___had warned___ us that she would soon be looking very different.

manage   **7.** Chelsea ___had managed___ to clean the entire house by the time her parents got home last evening.

C. In each space, write the **future perfect tense** form of the verb in the margin.

Example   *walk*   By the end of this month, Bernice ___will have walked___ over one-hundred miles.

work   **8.** Paco ___will have worked___ fifty-five hours by the end of the week.

interview   **9.** By the time she writes her paper, Jodi ___will have interviewed___ six nurses.

watch   **10.** By the end of the day, the children ___will have watched___ five hours of television.

26 Even More about Verbs

More about Verb Tenses

This chapter explains three other things you should know about verb tense:

1 Consistent verb tense

Inconsistent verb tense   We **parked** the car and **head** toward the movie theater.

Consistent verb tense   We **parked** the car and **headed** toward the movie theater.

2 The passive and active voices

Passive voice   I **was visited** last week by a former neighbor.

Active voice   A former neighbor **visited** me last week.

3 Nonstandard and standard verbs

Nonstandard verbs   Every week, Mandy **volunteer** at a nursing home near her apartment. She often **read** to residents there.

Standard verbs   Every week, Mandy **volunteers** at a nursing home near her apartment. She often **reads** to residents there.

CONSISTENT VERB TENSE

In your writing, avoid illogical or needless shifts in tense. For example, if you are writing a paper with the action in the past tense, don't shift suddenly to the present for no reason. Look at the examples below:

Inconsistent verb tense   In my nightmare, a hairy spider **crawled** up the side of my bed and **races** quickly onto my pillow.

There is no reason for the writer to shift suddenly from the past tense (*crawled*) to the present tense (*races*). The inconsistency can be corrected by using the same tense for both verbs:

Consistent verb tense   In my nightmare, a hairy spider **crawled** up the side of my bed and **raced** quickly onto my pillow.

● Practice 1

In each short passage, there is **one** illogical change in verb tense. Cross out the incorrect verb. Then write the correct form of that verb on the line provided.

_____crashed_____ **1.** The ice skater moved smoothly through her routine. On her last jump, however, she lost her balance and ~~crashes~~ to the ice with a thud.

_____heat_____ **2.** On many farms, machines milk the cows. The farmers then send the fresh milk to a processing plant. Workers there ~~heated~~ the milk at high temperatures. The intense heat removes bacteria.

253

<u>   picked   </u>   **3.** When Tina saw flames and smoke coming from her kitchen, she reacted quickly. She ~~picks~~ up her kitten and her purse. Then she rushed out into the fresh air.

<u>   crossed   </u>   **4.** Soldiers in the Civil War fought in bloody battles during the day. But at night, they often ~~cross~~ "enemy" lines for a friendly visit.

<u>   prepared   </u>   **5.** Melba took an inexpensive vacation this summer. She called parks and museums in the area to find out the cheapest times to visit. To save money, she ~~prepares~~ picnic lunches for her visits.

<u>   fertilizes   </u>   **6.** Tony and Lola do their gardening on weekends. While Tony digs out weeds, Lola ~~fertilized~~ plants and flowers.

<u>   delivers   </u>   **7.** Arlo works for a small greeting-card company. He writes poems for the wedding cards. Then he ~~delivered~~ the cards to the art department, where an artist sketches pictures of wedding bells or flowers.

<u>   surged   </u>   **8.** Last summer, my father went water skiing. After about five attempts, he skied around the entire lake. But when a large wave from another boat ~~surges~~ by, he flipped into the water head first.

<u>   stays   </u>   **9.** My sister complains at the drop of a hat. She often runs to her room in a rage. She ~~stayed~~ there for hours feeling sorry for herself.

<u>   disappeared   </u>   **10.** Last night, Lita went on the worst date ever. Her date, Mario, showed up an hour late. During dinner, all he talked about was himself. Then, just before the waitress brought the check, he ~~disappears~~. Lita unhappily paid the bill and took a taxi home.

THE PASSIVE AND ACTIVE VOICES

The subject of a sentence usually performs the action of the verb. In such cases, the verb is in the **active voice**. For example, look at the following sentence:

● My father **planted** the Japanese maple tree in the front yard.

The verb in this sentence is *planted*. Who performed that action? The answer is *father*, the subject of the sentence. Therefore, the verb is in the **active voice**.

Now look at this version of that sentence:

● The Japanese maple tree in the front yard **was planted** by my father.

The verb in this sentence is *was planted*. The subject of the sentence, *tree*, did not perform the action. It received the action; the tree was acted upon by the father. When the subject of a sentence is acted upon, the verb is in the **passive voice**.

Passive verbs are formed by combining a form of *to be* (*am, is, are, was, were*) with the past participle of a verb (which is usually the same as its past tense form). For example, in the sentence above, *was* plus the past participle of *plant* results in the passive verb *was planted*.

Here are some other passive verbs:

Form of *to be*	+	past participle	=	passive verb
am	+	pushed	=	am pushed
is	+	surprised	=	is surprised
was	+	delayed	=	was delayed

In general, write in the active voice. Because it expresses action, it is more energetic and effective than the passive voice. Use the passive voice when you wish to emphasize the receiver of the action or when the performer of the action is unknown.

Here are some more examples of sentences with active and passive verbs:

Active   Our landlord's son **mows** our backyard every week.
The subject of the sentence, *son*, performs the action of the sentence, *mows*.

Passive   Our backyard **is mowed** every week by our landlord's son.
The subject of the sentence—*backyard*—does not act. Instead, it is acted upon. (The passive verb is a combination of *is* plus the past participle of *mow*.)

Active   My sister **wrecked** her new car in an accident last night.
The subject of the sentence, *sister*, is the one who acted—she *wrecked* the car.

Passive   My sister's new car **was wrecked** in an accident last night.
The subject of this sentence, *car*, does not do anything. Something is done to it.

● Practice 2

Underline the verb in each sentence. Then circle the **A** in the margin if the verb is active. Circle the **P** in the margin if the verb is passive.

Example   A (P)   The car window was <u>shattered</u> by a poorly aimed baseball.

(A) P   **1.** My grandmother <u>calls</u> me almost every day.

A (P)   **2.** Rice <u>is consumed</u> every day by people all over Asia.

(A) P   **3.** Certain breeds of dog <u>bite</u> more often than others.

(A) P   **4.** The cashier <u>counted</u> the change out carefully.

A (P)   **5.** The injured man <u>was rushed</u> to the emergency room.

A (P)   **6.** The parade <u>was headed</u> by two young girls twirling batons.

(A) P   **7.** The audience <u>cheered</u> at the play's end.

A (P)   **8.** Several flights <u>were delayed</u> because of a snowstorm.

(A) P   **9.** The Yellow Pages <u>provide</u> lots of useful information.

A (P)   **10.** The words "No Trespassing" <u>were painted</u> in red letters on the fence.

Rewriting from the Passive to the Active Voice

Keep in mind that in the active voice, the subject performs the action. Here's a sentence with a passive verb. See if you can rewrite the sentence using the active voice.

Passive voice   Our roof was damaged by the storm.

Active voice   The storm damaged our roof.

In the passive version of the sentence, the subject *(roof)* was acted upon by the storm. The storm is what did the action. To write an active version of the sentence, you should have made *storm* the subject: *The storm damaged our roof.*

● Practice 3

The following sentences are written in the passive voice. For each sentence, underline the verb. Then rewrite the sentence in the active voice, changing the wording as necessary.

Example   Fruits and vegetables are painted often by artists.

Artists often paint fruits and vegetables.

1. The cat was named Leo by my brother.
   My brother named the cat Leo.

2. Soccer is played by children all over the world.
   Children all over the world play soccer.

3. The book report was prepared hastily by Sean.
   Sean prepared the book report hastily.

4. Some students were pushed around by the gym teacher.
   The gym teacher pushed around some students.

5. Shipping labels are printed quickly by the computer.
   The computer prints shipping labels quickly.

6. A nest was constructed in our mailbox by some robins.
   Some robins constructed a nest in our mailbox.

7. The alarm clock was invented by an American.
   An American invented the alarm clock.

8. The pizza restaurant was closed by the health inspector.
   The health inspector closed the pizza restaurant.

9. My telephone was used for a long-distance call by Jana without permission.
   Jana used our telephone for a long-distance call without permission.

10. Many annoying insects, such as mosquitoes, are consumed by spiders.
    Spiders consume many annoying insects, such as mosquitoes.

NONSTANDARD AND STANDARD VERBS

Nonstandard expressions such as *they ain't, we has, I be* or *he don't* are often part of successful communication among family members and friends. In both college and the working world, however, standard English is widely accepted as the norm for speaking and writing.

The chart below shows both nonstandard and standard forms of the regular verb *like*. Practice using the standard forms in your speech and writing.

	Nonstandard Forms		Standard Forms	
Present Tense	I likes	we likes	I like	we like
	you likes	you likes	you like	you like
	he, she, it like	they likes	he, she, it like**s**	they like
Past Tense	I like	we like	I like**d**	we like**d**
	you like	you like	you like**d**	you like**d**
	he, she, it like	they like	he, she, it like**d**	they like**d**

Notes

1 In standard English, always add *-s* or *-es* to a third-person singular verb in the present tense.

Nonstandard   Rex dislike his new job in Utah, and he miss his San Diego friends.

Standard   Rex **dislikes** his new job in Utah, and he **misses** his San Diego friends.

2 Always add the ending *-ed* or *-d* to a regular verb to show it is past tense.

Nonstandard   As children, Mona and her brother enjoy their piano lessons but hate practicing.

Standard   As children, Mona and her brother **enjoyed** their piano lessons but **hated** practicing.

● Practice 4

In each blank below, write the standard form of the verb in parentheses.

1. When the skinny boxer saw his huge opponent, he (*decide/decided*) _____decided_____ he was against violent sports.

2. At the family reunion last week, people (*greet/greeted*) _____greeted_____ each other with kisses.

3. Every week, Betty (*make/makes*) _____makes_____ soup from the leftovers she finds in her refrigerator.

4. The movie was so bad that everyone (*laugh/laughed*) _____laughed_____ at the "scary" parts.

5. The twins (*wish/wishes*) _____wish_____ that their parents would get back together.

6. Lester (*play/plays*) _____ plays _____ the saxophone better than anyone else I've ever heard.

7. Two nights a week, my mother and aunt (*attend/attends*) _____ attend _____ night classes.

8. Before she left on her vacation, Cindy (*water/watered*) _____ watered _____ her plants, canceled her newspaper, and ate the leftovers in her refrigerator.

9. In bed, my brother always (*pull/pulls*) _____ pulls _____ the covers over his head.

10. At high tide during yesterday's violent storm, powerful waves (*pound/pounded*) _____ pounded _____ the shore.

Name _____ Section _____ Date _____

Score: (Number right) _____ × 10 = _____%

Even More about Verbs: TEST 1

A. In each short passage, there is one illogical shift in verb tense. Cross out the incorrect verb. Then write the correct form of that verb on the line provided.

<u>   ended   </u>   **1.** The gangster movie started with a car chase, featured a half dozen gun fights, and ~~ends~~ with the death of half the characters.

<u>   worked   </u>   **2.** Josh wanted to attend college, but his parents couldn't afford to send him. So he ~~works~~ for two years after high-school graduation. With the money he saved, he attended a community college.

<u> watched </u>   **3.** Officer McFry worked the night shift last night. He patrolled the western part of the city. He also ~~watches~~ traffic at the intersection on Front Street. McFry returned home around 6:30 a.m.

<u>   play   </u>   **4.** Our service group meets at a nursing home once a month. We visit with the patients and plan fun activities for them. We sing, ~~played~~ card games, and do craft projects.

B. The following sentences are written in the passive voice. In each sentence, underline the verb. Then rewrite the sentence in the active voice, changing the wording as necessary.

5. That delicious chocolate cake <u>was baked</u> by Sidney.
    Sidney baked that delicious chocolate cake.

6. Rock music is <u>played</u> at top volume by our neighbors.
    Our neighbors play rock music at top volume.

7. The highest score on the test <u>was earned</u> by Clarita.
    Clarita earned the highest score on the test.

C. In each blank below, write the standard form of the verb in parentheses.

8. The children (*look/looked*) _____looked_____ under the sofa cushions and found eighty-three cents.

9. At home, Vicky is always in jeans, but she (*wear/wears*) _____wears_____ suits and dresses to work.

10. When he was younger, my uncle (*play/played*) _____played_____ saxophone with a dance band.

Name _____   Section _____   Date _____

Score: (Number right) _____ x 10 = _____%

Even More about Verbs: TEST 2

A.   In each short passage, there is **one** illogical shift in verb tense. Cross out the incorrect verb. Then write the correct form of that verb on the line provided.

_____sprayed_____   **1.** As we walked into the department store, a well-dressed woman from the cosmetics department approached us. Before we could protest, she ~~sprays~~ a cloud of musky-smelling perfume in our direction.

_____delivered_____   **2.** My friends worked at odd jobs this past summer. Carlos worked at a zoo, cleaning out the bird cages. Jenny worked at Pizza Hut. She ~~delivers~~ pizzas every night of the week.

_____appear_____   **3.** White flowers blossom on the apple trees every spring. Then tiny green apples ~~appeared~~. Finally, the apples turn into sweet red fruit.

_____included_____   **4.** On the first Thanksgiving, pilgrims celebrated their survival through the winter. They served many foods, but turkey was not one of them. The menu ~~includes~~ duck, goose, seafood, and eels.

B.   Each of the following sentences is written in the passive voice. Rewrite each in the active voice, changing the wording as necessary.

5. Directions to the hotel were provided by a taxi driver.

A taxi driver provided directions to the hotel. _____

6. The dinner table was always cleared by the children.

The children always cleared the dinner table. _____

7. Much air pollution is caused by cars and factories.

Cars and factories cause much air pollution. _____

C.   In each blank below, write the standard form of the verb in parentheses.

8. Before he leaves for work each morning, Duncan (*make/makes*) _____makes_____ coffee and pours it into a thermos.

9. When they were teenagers, Kate and Nellie often (*trade/traded*) _____traded_____ secrets.

10. My cat (*know/knows*) _____knows_____ which bedroom window is mine, and he scratches at it to get my attention.

More about Run-Ons and Comma Splices

You have already reviewed (on pages 87–106) the most common ways of correcting run-on sentences and comma splices:

1 Use a period and a capital letter.
2 Use a comma and a joining word.
3 Use a dependent word.

This section will describe one other method of correction:

ANOTHER METHOD OF CORRECTING A RUN-ON: USE A SEMICOLON

Run-on sentences and comma splices may be corrected by putting a **semicolon** (;) between the two complete thoughts. A semicolon is made up of a period and a comma. It is used between two closely related complete thoughts.

> *Run-on*   The fish was served with its head still on Fred quickly lost his appetite.
> *Comma splice*   The fish was served with its head still on, Fred quickly lost his appetite.
> *Correct version* The fish was served with its head still on; Fred quickly lost his appetite.

● Practice 1

Draw a line (|) between the two complete thoughts in each run-on or comma splice that follows. Then rewrite the item, using a semicolon to connect the two complete thoughts. Note the example below.

Example   The exam was not easy | there were two-hundred multiple-choice items.

> The exam was not easy; there were two-hundred multiple-choice items.

1. Dogs run in packs | cats are more solitary animals.
> Dogs run in packs; cats are more solitary animals.

2. The stack of books was too high, | it fell with a crash.
> The stack of books was too high; it fell with a crash.

3. I peered through the front-door peephole | a strange man was standing outside.
> I peered through the front-door peephole; a strange man was standing outside.

4. Steve drank the hot coffee too quickly, | the top of his mouth felt burned.
> Steve drank the hot coffee too quickly; the top of his mouth felt burned.

5. The auditorium was packed with angry people | the meeting would be an ugly one.
> The auditorium was packed with angry people; the meeting would be an ugly one.

Semicolon with a Transitional Word or Words

A semicolon is sometimes used with a transitional word (or words) and a comma to join two complete thoughts.

Run-on	The fish was served with its head still on as a result, Fred quickly lost his appetite.
Comma splice	The fish was served with its head still on, as a result, Fred quickly lost his appetite.
Correct version	The fish was served with its head still on; **as a result,** Fred quickly lost his appetite.

Below are some common transitional words that may be used when correcting a run-on or comma splice.

Common Transitional Words

afterwards	however	moreover
also	in fact	nevertheless
as a result	in addition	on the other hand
consequently	instead	otherwise
furthermore	meanwhile	therefore

● Practice 2

Draw a line between the two complete thoughts in each item. Then write out each sentence using a semicolon to connect the two thoughts.

Example   The air is very stale in the library│moreover, the lighting is poor.
    The air is very stale in the library; moreover, the lighting is poor.

1. I don't usually like desserts│however, this pumpkin pie is delicious.
   I don't usually like desserts; however, this pumpkin pie is delicious.

2. Our dog barks all the time,│as a result, the landlord has refused to renew our lease.
   Our dog barks all the time; as a result, the landlord has refused to renew our lease.

3. The house needs a new septic system,│in addition, it should have a new roof.
   The house needs a new septic system; in addition, it should have a new roof.

4. I almost never write to my brother│however, I call him several times a month.
   I almost never write to my brother; however, I call him several times a month.

5. You should eat a good breakfast│otherwise, you'll be out of energy before noon.
   You should eat a good breakfast; otherwise, you'll be out of energy before noon.

Name _____ Section _____ Date _____

More about Run-Ons and Comma Splices: TEST 1

Draw a line (|) between the two complete thoughts in each run-on or comma splice. Then rewrite each sentence using a semicolon to connect the two complete thoughts.

1. The cat slept on the windowsill|she was wrapped in warm sunlight.

   The cat slept on the windowsill; she was wrapped in warm sunlight.

2. Larry is not a good babysitter|he treats his little brother like an insect.

   Larry is not a good babysitter; he treats his little brother like an insect.

3. The wind knocked over a ladder|the ladder then broke a window.

   The wind knocked over a ladder; the ladder then broke a window.

4. We decided to leave the restaurant|the food was too expensive.

   We decided to leave the restaurant; the food was too expensive.

5. The hammer and saw began to rust,|they had been left out in the rain.

   The hammer and saw began to rust; they had been left out in the rain.

Name _____ Section _____ Date _____

Score: (Number right) _____ x 20 = _____ %

More about Run-Ons and Comma Splices: TEST 2

Draw a line (|) between the two complete thoughts in each run-on or comma splice. Then rewrite each sentence using a semicolon to connect the two complete thoughts. Note that a transitional word or phrase is part of each sentence.

1. Lorenzo is colorblind|as a result, his wife lays out his clothes every morning.

   Lorenzo is colorblind; as a result, his wife lays out his clothes every morning.

2. The weatherman predicted a sunny day|however, it is cold and cloudy.

   The weatherman predicted a sunny day; however, it is cold and cloudy.

3. The engine has cooled|therefore, you can add more water to the radiator.

   The engine has cooled; therefore, you can add more water to the radiator.

4. These raisin cookies are delicious|nevertheless, I can't eat another one.

   These raisin cookies are delicious; nevertheless, I can't eat another one.

5. The floor must be swept and mopped|in addition, the carpets must be vacuumed.

   The floor must be swept and mopped; in addition, the carpets must be vacuumed.

28 More about Commas

A comma often marks a slight pause, or break, in a sentence. These pauses or breaks occur at the point where one of the six main comma rules applies. When you read a sentence aloud, you can often hear the points where slight pauses occur.

In general, use a comma only when a comma rule applies or when a comma is otherwise needed to help a sentence read clearly.

You have already reviewed (on pages 107–116) three main uses of the comma:

1 **The comma is used to separate three or more items in a series.**

2 **The comma is used to separate introductory material from the rest of the sentence.**

3 **The comma is used between two complete thoughts connected by the joining words** *and, but,* **or** *so.* **(Or,** *nor, for,* **and** *yet* **are also joining words.)**

This chapter will consider three other uses of the comma:

4 **Around words that interrupt the flow of a sentence**

5 **For words of direct address and short expressions**

6 **In dates, addresses, and letters.**

AROUND WORDS THAT INTERRUPT THE FLOW OF A SENTENCE

Sentences sometimes contain material that interrupts the flow of thought. Such words and word groups should be set off from the rest of the sentence by commas. For example:

- Our minivan**, which has stickers from every state we've visited,** seems like part of the family.

If you read this sentence out loud, you can hear that the words *which has stickers from every state we've visited* interrupt the flow of thought.

Here are some other examples of sentences with interrupters:

- Liza**, who was wearing a new dress,** yelled at the waiter who spilled wine on her.

- The waiter**, however,** was not very apologetic.

- The restaurant manager**, afraid that Liza might cause a scene,** rushed to help.

More about Interrupters

A word group that identifies another word in the sentence is not an interrupter. It is needed for the full meaning of the sentence and should not be set off with commas.* For instance, consider the boldfaced words in the following sentences:

- The man **who came to the party with Joy** says he was kidnapped by aliens.

- Harvey**, who came to the party with Joy,** says he was kidnapped by aliens.

*Grammar books sometimes refer to interrupters as "nonrestrictive elements" and essential descriptions as "restrictive elements."

In the first sentence, the boldfaced words are needed to identify the man. Without them, we would not know who said he was kidnapped by aliens. Such essential words are not interrupters and should not be set off with commas. In the second sentence, however, we know who said he was kidnapped by aliens even without the boldfaced words. (It was Harvey.) In that case, the boldfaced words are not essential to the main message of the sentence. So in the second sentence, *who came to the party with Joy* is an interrupter and should be set off by commas.

To find out whether a word group is an interrupter, try reading the sentence without it. The first sentence above would then read: "The man says he was kidnapped by aliens." This version makes us ask, "Which man?" The boldfaced words are essential to answer that question. If we read the second sentence without the boldfaced words, we would not be omitting essential information: "Harvey says he was kidnapped by aliens."

● Practice 1

Four of the following five sentences contain interrupters. Insert commas around the interrupting word groups. One sentence includes a word group that provides essential information and should not be enclosed by commas.

1. Penguins' wings, which are short and thick, are not designed for flight.

2. King Arthur, according to legend, will return some day to rule Britain.

3. Our basketball coach, it is rumored, is about to be fired.

4. The woman who sat in front of me at the concert was wearing strong perfume.

5. Grandfather likes to joke that his hometown, which has only one traffic light and two gas stations, could be missed if a traveler blinked.

● Practice 2

Write three sentences using the suggested interrupters. Add words both before and after the interrupting words. Then add the necessary commas.   *Answers will vary.*

1. Use the words *who is my best friend* in the middle of a sentence.

   Lisa, who is my best friend, always has time to listen to my problems.

   _____

2. Use the words *which is my favorite snack* in the middle of a sentence.

   Frozen yogurt, which is my favorite snack, is low in calories.

   _____

3. Use the words *wearing an all-white outfit* in the middle of a sentence.

   Dolores, wearing an all-white outfit, posed at the top of the stairs.

   _____

FOR WORDS OF DIRECT ADDRESS AND SHORT EXPRESSIONS

For words of direct address: Use commas to set off names or other words used to address directly the person or people being spoken to.

- You, Mr. Gimble, are the lucky winner of a ballpoint pen.
- Ladies and gentlemen, the sword-swallower is unable to perform tonight due to a bad sore throat.

For short expressions: Use commas to set off words such as *well, yes, no,* and *oh.*

- No, you cannot have a raise.
- Well, I thought I would at least ask.

IN DATES, ADDRESSES, AND LETTERS

Within a date: Place commas after the the day of the week (if used), the date, and the year.

- Friday, October 13, 2003, was the date of the wedding.
- On March 7, 1876, Alexander Graham Bell received a patent for the telephone.

In an address within a sentence: Place a comma after each part of the address except between the state and the ZIP code.

- Send your comments about *English Essentials: What Everyone Needs to Know about Grammar, Punctuation, and Usage* to Townsend Press, 1038 Industrial Drive, West Berlin, NJ 08091-9164.

In informal letters: Place a comma after the opening and closing.

- Dear Grandma,   ● With love,   ● Fondly,

    Note In business letters, a colon is used after the opening, but a comma is still used after the closing.

- Dear Mr. Cramer: ● Dear Homeowner: ● Yours truly,

● Practice 3

Insert commas where needed **a)** to set off words of direct address and short expressions and **b)** in dates and addresses.

1. Why are you studying so late, Kimberly?

2. Well, look who's coming in our direction.

3. My sister lives at 2 Dog Lane, Canine, SC 09999.

4. It's about time that you woke up, sleepy head, and got out of bed.

5. San Franciscans were surprised on the morning of April 18, 1906, by a major earthquake.

● Practice 4

Complete each sentence as indicated, inserting commas where needed.

1. ___(Answers will vary.)_____ is my home address.
   (Fill in your address.)

2. ___(Answers will vary.)_____ is the date that I was born.
   (Fill in your complete date of birth.)

3. Dear ___Susan,_____

   Meet me at the fountain in the mall tomorrow.

                    Sincerely,
   _____

                    Marco

   (Complete the heading of the above letter with the word *Susan*, and add as a closing the word *Sincerely*.)

Another use of the comma is to set off direct quotations from the rest of a sentence, as explained in "Quotation Marks" on pages 127–136.

Name _____ Section _____ Date _____

Score: (Number right) _____ x 10 = _____ %

More about Commas: TEST 1

On the lines provided, write the word or words in each sentence that need to be followed by a comma. Include each missing comma as well.

1. In my opinion Jesse you owe Jeff an apology.

opinion, Jesse, _____

2. Poison ivy which grows almost everywhere in North America is not welcome anywhere.

ivy, . . . America, _____

3. The first battle of the American Civil War occurred on April 12 1861 in South Carolina.

12, 1861, _____

4. Hey get away from our car!

Hey, _____

5. Oh I'm afraid this isn't what I ordered.

Oh, _____

6. It is important fellow union members to stick together during this strike.

important, . . . members, _____

7. You can write to the President at The White House 1900 Pennsylvania Avenue Washington DC 20500.

House, 1900 Pennsylvania Avenue, Washington, DC _____

8. The fact is Your Honor that the wrong man is on trial.

is, . . . Honor, _____

9. The sick child a blanket draped over his shoulders slumped in his chair.

child, . . . shoulders, _____

10. The models looking bored and unfriendly strolled down the runway.

models, . . . unfriendly, _____

Name _____   Section _____ Date _____

Score: (Number right) _____ x 10 = _____%

More about Commas: TEST 2

In each space, write the letter of the **one** comma rule that applies to the sentence. Then insert one or more commas where they belong in the sentence.

> **a** Around interrupting words
> **b** To set off words of direct address and short expressions
> **c** In dates, addresses, and letters

_____b_____ **1.** I'm sorry, sir, but the diner is now closing.

_____b_____ **2.** This coffee shop, my friends, is a non-smoking area.

_____c_____ **3.** I'm already planning my fiftieth birthday party for Friday, March 6, 2035, at Disney World.

_____b_____ **4.** No, you may not have a third piece of chocolate cake.

_____a_____ **5.** The campers, unused to the silence of the forest, found it hard to sleep.

_____c_____ **6.** Eric jokingly gave his address as 25 Main Street, Elmhurst, Illinois, North America, Planet Earth.

_____c_____ **7.** Our final exam will be given on Wednesday, June 2.

_____b_____ **8.** Yes, I have dated both Louise and her sister.

_____a_____ **9.** Diamonds, the most expensive jewels on Earth, are closely related to lumps of coal.

_____c_____ **10.** Many visitors take the tour of the NBC Studios at 3000 Alameda Avenue, Burbank, California.

More about Apostrophes

REVIEW OF THE APOSTROPHE IN POSSESSIVES

To show that something belongs to someone, we could say, for example, the stereo owned by Rita. But it's much simpler to say:

- *Rita's stereo*

To make most nouns possessive, add an apostrophe plus an *s*. To help you decide which word to make possessive, ask yourself the following:

1 What is owned?

2 Who is the owner?

Then put the apostrophe plus an *s* after the name of the owner. **Here's an example:**

What is owned? *The stereo*

Who is the owner? *Rita*

When an apostrophe plus an *s* is added to the name of the owner, the result is the possessive form of the word: *Rita's*. That word is then followed by what is owned: *Rita's stereo*.

Here is another example:

- the waiting room belonging to the doctor

Again, ask yourself, "What is owned?" The answer is *waiting room*. Then ask, "Who is the owner?" The answer is *the doctor*. So add an apostrophe plus *s* after the name of the owner and add what is owned: *the doctor's waiting room*. The apostrophe plus *s* shows that the waiting room belongs to the doctor.

Here is a third example:

- the hopes of everyone

Again, ask yourself, "What is owned?" The answer is *hopes*. Then ask, "Who is the owner?" The answer is *everyone*. So add an apostrophe plus *s* after the name of the owner and add what is owned: *everyone's hopes*. The apostrophe plus *s* shows that the hopes belong to everyone.

● Practice 1

Rewrite the items below as possessives with an apostrophe plus *s*. In the first column, write the name of the owner. In the second column, write the possessive form plus what is owned. One is done for you as an example.

	Who is the owner?	*Possessive form plus what is owned*
1. the bike belonging to Randy	Randy	Randy's bike
2. the purr of the cat	cat	cat's purr
3. the temper of our neighbor	neighbor	neighbor's temper
4. the ending of the story	story	story's ending
5. the mummy belonging to the museum	museum	museum's mummy

● Practice 2

Underline the word in each sentence that needs an apostrophe plus *s*. That word is the owner. Then write the word correctly, along with what is owned, in the space provided. The first one is done for you as an example.

1. I tracked mud on my <u>mother</u> white rug.   *mother's white rug*
2. <u>Vietnam</u> climate is hot and damp.   *Vietnam's climate*
3. A <u>gorilla</u> diet is mainly vegetarian.   *gorilla's diet*
4. The <u>photographer</u> camera was stolen.   *photographer's camera*
5. The <u>bride</u> wedding dress was knee-high.   *bride's wedding dress*

● Practice 3

Write three sentences that include words ending in an apostrophe plus *s*.

1. _____ *Answers will vary.* _____

_____

2. _____

_____

3. _____

_____

Showing Possession with Singular and Plural Nouns That End in *s*

An apostrophe plus *s* is used to show possession even with a singular noun that already ends in *s*:

- Gus**'s** computer (the computer belonging to Gus)
- The boss**'s** secretary (the secretary belonging to the boss)

However, an apostrophe alone is used to show possession with a plural noun that ends in *s*:

- the contestant**s'** answers (the answers of a number of contestants)
- the three lawyer**s'** office (the office belonging to three lawyers)

● Practice 4

Underline the word that needs an apostrophe in each sentence below. Then write that word, adding the ' or the '*s*, in the space provided.

bass's	1. Adam carefully removed the fishhook from the <u>bass</u> mouth.
lions'	2. The <u>lions</u> keeper has worked with them from birth.
Otis's	3. <u>Otis</u> story about being kidnapped by a flying saucer is hard to believe.
twins'	4. The <u>twins</u> mother was a twin herself.
Olsons'	5. The <u>Olsons</u> home has a secret passageway.

WHEN *NOT* TO USE AN APOSTROPHE

Do *NOT* Use an Apostrophe in Plurals and with Verbs

People sometimes confuse possessive and plural forms of nouns. Remember that a plural is formed simply by adding an *s* to a noun; no apostrophe is used. Look at the sentence below to see which words are plural and which word is possessive:

● Lola's necklace has pearls and diamond chips.

The words *pearls* and *chips* are plurals—there is more than one pearl, and there is more than one diamond chip. But *Lola's*, the word with the apostrophe plus *s*, is possessive. Lola owns the necklace.

Also, many verbs end with an *s*. Do not use an apostrophe in a verb.

● Jenny **plays** poker once a week.
● She often **wins**.

● Practice 5

In the spaces provided under each sentence, correctly write the one word that needs an apostrophe. Also, explain why the other word or words ending in *s* do not get apostrophes.

Example   The patients eyes opened slowly after surgery.

patients: patient's, meaning "belonging to the patient"

eyes: eyes, meaning "more than one eye"

1. In a new version of the fairy tale, the princes wife rescues him from fire-breathing dragons.

   princes: prince's, meaning "belonging to the prince"

   rescues: rescues—a verb

   dragons: dragons, meaning "more than one dragon"

2. The chocolates in the silver box are a gift from my mothers best friend.

   chocolates: chocolates, meaning "more than one chocolate"

   mothers: mother's, meaning "belonging to my mother"

3. It takes eight minutes for the suns light to reach Earth.

   takes: takes—a verb

   minutes: minutes, meaning "more than one minute"

   suns: sun's, meaning "belonging to the sun"

4. Sheer white curtains and fresh lilacs added to the rooms simple charm.

   curtains: curtains, meaning "more than one curtain"

   lilacs: lilacs, meaning "more than one lilac"

   rooms: room's, meaning "belonging to the room"

5. Studies show that a rooms color affects our moods.

Studies:	Studies, meaning "more than one study"
rooms:	room's, meaning "belonging to the room"
affects:	affects—a verb
moods:	moods, meaning "more than one mood"

Do *NOT* Use an Apostrophe with Possessive Pronouns

Do not use an apostrophe in the possessive pronouns *his, hers, its, yours, ours, theirs,* and *whose.*

- Those seats are **ours**.
- **His** car is purple.

People often confuse certain possessive pronouns with contractions. For instance, *its* is often confused with *it's*. The following sentence includes both words:

- **It's** sad that our old tree is losing **its** leaves.

The word *it's* is a contraction meaning *it is*. Contractions, of course, do have apostrophes. *Its* means *belonging to it*—the leaves belong to it (the tree). *Its* is a possessive pronoun and does not have an apostrophe.

Following are examples of other possessive pronouns and the contractions they are confused with.

- The Pratts rarely mow **their** lawn. **They're** not concerned about the looks of the neighborhood.

  Their means *belonging to them* (the lawn belongs to them). *They're* is a contraction that means *they are*.

- **You're** going to fall if you do not tie **your** shoelaces.

  You're is a contraction that means *you are*. *Your* means *belonging to you* (the shoelaces belong to you).

- **Who's** the person **whose** car is blocking ours?

  Who's is a contraction meaning *who is*. *Whose* means *belonging to whom* (the car belonging to whom).

● Practice 6

Underline the correct word within each pair of parentheses.

1. We arranged with two neighborhood boys to mow our lawn, but now (*they're/their*) father tells me (*they're/their*) going to camp for a month.

2. Darryl told his son, "If (*you're/your*) homework is not done by seven o'clock, (*you're/your*) not going to watch the movie."

3. (*Who's/Whose*) turn is it to wash the dishes, and (*who's/whose*) going to dry them?

4. (*It's/Its*) difficult, if not impossible, to get toothpaste back into (*it's/its*) tube.

5. The fruit salad on the table is (*hers'/hers*), and the freshly baked bread is (*ours'/ours*).

Name _____   Section _____   Date _____

Score: (Number right) _____ x 10 = _____ %

More about Apostrophes: TEST 1

Each of the sentences below contains **one** word that needs an apostrophe. Write the word, with its apostrophe, in the space provided.

1. Susans eyes were glassy with fatigue.

_____ Susan's _____

2. There is no bread, so well have crackers with our soup.

_____ we'll _____

3. Fixing drippy faucets is the landlords job.

_____ landlord's _____

4. I havent ever gone on a roller coaster, and I never will.

_____ haven't _____

5. Four tiny packages arrived in Saturdays mail.

_____ Saturday's _____

6. Leo knows his girlfriend is angry at him, but hes not sure why.

_____ he's _____

7. Many presents have been delivered to the brides home.

_____ bride's _____

8. The keyboards plastic cover protects the keys from crumbs and dust.

_____ keyboard's _____

9. There are about 100,000 hairs on the average persons head.

_____ person's _____

10. The soft moans in the classroom made it clear that students werent expecting the test.

_____ weren't _____

Name _____ Section _____ Date _____

Score: (Number right) _____ x 10 = _____%

More about Apostrophes: TEST 2

Each of the sentences below contains **one** word that needs an apostrophe. Write the word, with its apostrophe, in the space provided.

1. We didnt recognize our teacher at first without his beard.

    didn't

2. Both of Janes husbands were named Andrew.

    Jane's

3. Half-finished paintings filled the artists studio.

    artist's

4. Someone will be taking in our mail while were away on vacation.

    we're

5. Floridas neighbors are Alabama and Georgia.

    Florida's

6. The snowflakes glittered in the flashlights glare.

    flashlight's

7. The farmers may lose their entire wheat crop if it doesnt rain soon.

    doesn't

8. Someday Ill tell you about the day Uncle Harry was chased by some mad chickens.

    I'll

9. The two brothers relationship has remained strong through the years.

    brothers'

10. The film reviewers were careful not to give away the movies surprise ending.

    movie's

③⓪ More about Quotation Marks

REVIEW OF QUOTATIONS WITH SPLIT SENTENCES

In a direct quotation, one sentence may be split into two parts:

- "Add the eggs to the sauce," said the TV chef, "blending them together."

Note that the chef's exact words are set off by two sets of quotation marks. The words *said the TV chef* are not included in the quotation marks since they were not spoken by the chef.

The words *blending them together* begin with a small letter because they are a continuation of a sentence, not a new sentence. (The full sentence spoken by the instructor is "Add the eggs to the sauce, blending them together.")

Commas are used to set off the quoted parts from the rest of the sentence:

- "Add the eggs to the sauce," said the TV chef, "blending them together."
                            ^   ^

QUOTATIONS OF MORE THAN ONE SENTENCE

A direct quotation can be divided into separate sentences:

- "I really hate my job," Stan told his wife. "I think I'd better start looking for a new one."
  The words *Stan told his wife* are not part of the direct quotation.

At times, a direct quotation will be more than one sentence:

- Our minister always says, "It's every citizen's responsibility to vote. If you don't vote, you shouldn't complain."

Note that only one pair of quotation marks is used. Do not use quotation marks for each new sentence as long as the quotation is not interrupted.

● Practice 1

Insert quotation marks where needed in the following sentences.

1. "The wait for a table," said the restaurant hostess, "will be about forty minutes."
   ^   ^   ^   ^

2. "I don't mind if you borrow my new sweater," said my sister, "but I don't expect to find it rolled
   ^up in a ball under your bed."
             ^

3. The newspaper editor said to the new reporter, "I'm sorry to have to tell you this. I can't use the article that you spent two weeks writing." ^
                                                                                          ^

4. "Why don't you go to the video store," suggested Sara, "and pick up a movie for us to watch
   ^tonight."   ^   ^
           ^

5. "Our math teacher is unfair," complained James. "He assigns four hours of homework for each
   ^class. Does he think we have nothing else to do?"
                                ^   ^   ^
                                                  ^

QUOTATIONS WITH QUESTION MARKS AND EXCLAMATION POINTS

If a direct quotation is a question, place the question mark within the quotation marks:

● "Where are my red shoes?" asked Lana.

After a question mark, no comma is used to set off the direct quotation.

If the entire sentence is a question, place the question mark after the quotation marks:

● Did you say "Thank you"?

An exclamation point also goes within quotation marks unless it applies to the whole sentence.

● The kids shouted, "Let's go to the pool!"

INDIRECT QUOTATIONS

Often we express someone's spoken or written thoughts without repeating the exact words used. When we use an **indirect quotation**, we put the message into our own words. Indirect quotations do not require quotation marks.

The following example shows how the same material could be handled as either a direct or an indirect quotation.

Direct Quotation

● The baker said, **"I forgot** to put yeast in the dough."

The words *I forgot* tell us that the baker's exact words are being used—he's referring to himself. Since his exact words are being used, they must be put in quotation marks.

Indirect Quotation

● The baker said **that he had forgotten** to put yeast in the dough.

The sentence refers to the baker as *he*, so we know that the baker's exact words are not being quoted. Quotation marks are not used for indirect quotations. The word *that* often signals an indirect quotation.

Here are a few more examples of indirect quotations:

● The boss said that workers could have a day off on their birthdays.
● Mom told us not to answer the front door.
● The park rangers warned us to keep our windows closed.

● Practice 2

Rewrite each of the following indirect quotations as a direct quotation. The direct quotation will include the words that someone actually spoke.

Note that you will have to change some of the words as well as add capital letters, quotation marks, and any other punctuation needed. The first one is done for you as an example.

1. The child asked if the Milky Way candy bar was really full of milk.

The child asked, "Is the Milky Way candy bar really full of milk?"

2. My sister said that she would help me do the report if she could wear my new blouse.

My sister said, "I will help do the report if I can wear your new blouse."

3. The bookstore manager grumbled that he couldn't take back books with writing in them.

The bookstore manager grumbled, "I can't take back books with writing in them."

4. The teacher warned us a surprise quiz was coming soon.

The teacher warned us, "A surprise quiz is coming soon."

5. The officer asked me if I was lost.

The officer asked me, "Are you lost?"

QUOTATION MARKS FOR TITLES OF SHORT WORKS

Use quotation marks to set off the titles of short stories, newspaper or magazine articles, songs, poems, episodes of TV series, book chapters, and other parts of longer works.

- Our teacher assigned the short story "The Open Boat" by Stephen Crane.
- The familiar song "For He's a Jolly Good Fellow" is over two-hundred years old.
- The witty poet Ogden Nash wrote a poem titled "Never Mind the Overcoat, Button Up That Lip."

Note The titles of longer works, such as books, newspapers, magazines, plays, movies, TV series, and record albums, should be underlined when handwritten. When typed on a computer, such titles should appear in *italic type.*

- Our assignment was to read the chapter titled "The Traits of Happy People" in a book by David Meyers, The Pursuit of Happiness.
- "Three Words That Can Change Your Life" was the first article I turned to in the current issue of Reader's Digest.

● Practice 3

Insert quotation marks or underlines where needed in the sentences below.

1. The chapter titled "Extrasensory Perception" in the textbook Psychology Today says there is no evidence that ESP actually exists.

2. The article "Policing the Police" in Newsweek magazine is about good cops who go bad.

3. The beloved song "Over the Rainbow" was first heard in the movie The Wizard of Oz.

4. The editor of the Daily Tribune has received many letters supporting and opposing her editorial "Let's Ban Proms in Schools."

Name _____ Section _____ Date _____

Score: (Number right) _____ x 10 = _____ %

More about Quotation Marks: TEST 1

Add opening and closing quotation marks where needed. One sentence does not need quotation marks.

1. "Somebody has stuck gum all over my computer keyboard," Coco said angrily.

2. "One lucky caller wins a trip to Disneyland," the radio announcer promised.

3. "I bought a truck," Julie stated, "because I sit higher and feel safer."

4. "When you see me next," laughed the brunette, "I'll be a blonde."

5. The racecar driver said he wanted a quart of milk waiting for him at the finish line.

6. "More Children Alone" is the title of a recent article in the New York Times.

7. An hour after lunch, Rudy said, "I'm starving. I hope dinner will be ready soon."

8. The park ranger said, "Watch out for ticks."

9. "I need to move back home," said Wally to his parents.

10. The Monopoly card that I drew said, "Do not pass Go. Do not collect $200."

Name _____ Section _____ Date _____

Score: (Number right) _____ x 10 = _____ %

More about Quotation Marks: TEST 2

On the lines provided, rewrite the following sentences, adding quotation marks as needed. One sentence does not need quotation marks.

1. Our coach said to us, I received some wonderful news this morning.

Our coach said to us, "I received some wonderful news this morning."

2. What If a Comet Hits the Earth? is the title of a recent article in *Time* magazine.

"What If a Comet Hits the Earth?" is the title of a recent article in <u>Time</u> magazine.

3. Aren't you going to do the dishes? It's your turn, my brother reminded me.

"Aren't you going to do the dishes? It's your turn," my brother reminded me.

4. My friends asked me to meet them at the mall.

No quotation marks needed.

5. Abraham Lincoln said, When I do good, I feel good. When I do bad, I feel bad. And that's my religion.

Abraham Lincoln said, "When I do good, I feel good. When I do bad, I feel bad. And that's my

religion."

6. Sleet has made the roads very icy, the TV announcer warned. If you don't need to go out, stay home.

"Sleet has made the roads very icy," the TV announcer warned. "If you don't need to go

out, stay home."

7. A poem by Shel Silverstein begins with the words, I am writing these poems from inside a lion.

A poem by Shel Silverstein begins with the words, "I am writing these poems from inside a

lion."

8. This vacation was lots of fun, said the woman, but after all of this sightseeing, I'm going to need a vacation from my vacation.

"This vacation was lots of fun," said the woman, "but after all of this sightseeing, I'm

going to need a vacation from my vacation."

9. If you have finished complaining, my father said quietly, you may go clean your room now.

"If you have finished complaining," my father said quietly, "you may go clean your room now."

10. The handmade poster had a photograph of a cocker spaniel and the words, Curly has been missing since Sunday night. Please call us if you've seen him.

The handmade poster had a photograph of a cocker spaniel and the words, "Curly has been

missing since Sunday night. Please call us if you've seen him."

㉛ More about Homonyms

You have already reviewed a number of common homonyms (words that sound alike). This section describes some other homonyms as well as other confusing words.

OTHER HOMONYMS

buy   to purchase
by   (1) close to; (2) no later than; (3) through the action of

● **Buy** furniture from Sofas Inc. **by** the end of the year, and you won't have to pay until March.

    Spelling hint   I'd like to b**uy** something for **U**.

Fill in each blank with either *buy* or *by*.

1. Why must you _____buy_____ such expensive designer jeans?
2. The beautiful mural in the lobby was painted _____by_____ a student.
3. An old dog was sleeping on the front porch _____by_____ the screen door.
4. We have to turn in our research papers _____by_____ the end of the month.
5. My sister is hoping to _____buy_____ a home of her own this year.

passed   (the past tense of *pass*) (1) handed to; (2) went by; (3) completed successfully
past   (1) the time before the present; (2) by

● In the **past**, I have **passed** all my courses, but I may not pass them all this semester.

    Spelling hint   If you need a verb, use **passed**. The *-ed* at its end shows it is the past tense of the verb *pass*.

Fill in each blank with either *passed* or *past*.

1. Only five minutes have _____passed_____ since I last looked at the clock.
2. A bumblebee just flew _____past_____ my head.
3. Mick _____passed_____ his driver's test on the third try.
4. Unfortunately, one of the cars that Marylou _____passed_____ on the highway was a police car.
5. Life was not always as carefree in the _____past_____ as some people would like to believe.

principal   (1) main; (2) the person in charge of a school
principle   a guideline or rule

● Our **principal** believes in the **principle** of giving teachers a great deal of freedom.

    Spelling hint   Ideally, a school princi**pal** should be a **pal**.

Fill in each blank with either *principal* or *principle*.

1. My aunt is the ____principal____ owner of a beauty shop on Mill Avenue.

2. I try to live by the ____principle____ of treating others as I want to be treated.

3. Mr. Larson became ____principal____ of Coles High School after teaching there for years.

4. The ____principal____ reason the Butlers are moving to California is to be near their grandchildren.

5. Our basketball coach taught us to follow the ____principle____ of being gracious in defeat as well as in victory.

OTHER CONFUSING WORDS

Here are some words that are not homonyms but are still confusing words. In most cases they have similar sounds and are often misused and misspelled.

a   used before words that begin with a consonant sound

an   used before words that begin with a vowel or a silent *h* (as in *an hour*).

● Would you like **an** ice-cream cone or **a** shake?

Fill in each blank with either *a* or *an*.

1. ____An____ insect has six legs and a three-part body.

2. I left ____a____ note on the kitchen counter saying when I'd be back.

3. Is that ____an____ alligator you are petting in that photograph?

4. A hush fell over the circus audience when ____a____ tightrope walker fell.

5. Although she worked hard, Louise was shocked to receive such ____an____ honor as "Worker of the Year."

accept   (1) to receive; (2) to agree to take; (3) to believe in

except   (1) excluding or leaving out; (2) but

● All the employees **except** the part-timers were willing to **accept** the new contract.

Fill in each blank with either *accept* or *except*.

1. Mrs. Carlotti says she will ____accept____ an appointment to the school board.

2. My daughter likes all types of food ____except____ meat, fish, dairy products, and vegetables.

3. Whatever your decision is, I will ____accept____ it.

4. All of my relatives attended our family reunion ____except____ for an elderly aunt.

5. At the company dinner, Meredith will ____accept____ the award on behalf of her department.

advice   opinion meant to be helpful
advise   to give an opinion meant to be helpful
● Never take the **advice** of someone who **advises** you to act against your conscience.

Fill in each blank with either *advice* or *advise*.
1. "I _____ advise _____ you to replace your fan belt," the gas station attendant said.
2. Don't seek _____ advice _____ from anybody you don't admire.
3. Employment experts _____ advise _____ people to get training throughout their lives.
4. There's so much conflicting _____ advice _____ about diet that it's no wonder people are confused about what they should eat.
5. My son's kindergarten teacher said the best _____ advice _____ she could give parents is to read regularly to their children.

affect   to influence
effect   a result
● Divorce **affects** an entire family, and its **effects**—both good and bad—last for years.

Fill in each blank with either *affect* or *effect*.
1. Your actions _____ affect _____ those around you, whether you're aware of it or not.
2. The child spattered red paint on the paper and then stepped back to admire the _____ effect _____ .
3. According to psychologists, the color of the clothes we wear _____ affect _____ s our moods.
4. What will be the economic _____ effect _____ s if the factory closes?
5. The referees did not allow the obnoxious behavior of some fans to _____ affect _____ their decisions.

desert   (1) a verb meaning "to leave or abandon"; (2) a noun meaning "a dry region with little or no plant growth"
dessert   a sweet course eaten at the end of a meal
● The children were willing to **desert** the TV set only when **dessert** was served.

Fill in each blank with either *desert* or *dessert*.
1. For me, a real _____ dessert _____ must contain chocolate.
2. As a result of irrigation, this area is now farmland instead of _____ desert _____ .
3. What causes a parent to _____ desert _____ his or her children?
4. If I'm not very hungry, I skip the meal and eat _____ dessert _____ .
5. Certain medications can make your mouth feel as dry as a _____ desert _____ .

fewer   used for items that can be counted
less   used for general amounts

● As our congregation ages, our church is left with **fewer** members and **less** financial support.

Fill in each blank with either *fewer* or *less*.

1. By the 1920s, there were _____fewer_____ horses and more cars on the road.

2. When I get too little sleep, I have _____less_____ patience than usual.

3. Whose car had _____fewer_____ miles on it, yours or Carl's?

4. Two-percent milk has _____less_____ fat in it than whole milk.

5. Two-percent milk also contains _____fewer_____ calories.

loose   (1) not tight; (2) free; not confined
lose   (1) to misplace; (2) to not win; (3) to be deprived of something one has had

● If you don't fix that **loose** steering wheel, you could **lose** control of your car.

Fill in each blank with either *loose* or *lose*.

1. I _____lose_____ my keys at least once a week.

2. A _____loose_____ shutter was banging against the side of the house.

3. I always _____lose_____ when I play chess against my computer.

4. Clyde was warned that he would _____lose_____ his job if he were late to work one more time.

5. In our town, it's illegal to allow cats and dogs to run _____loose_____.

quiet   (1) silent; (2) relaxing and peaceful
quite   (1) truly; (2) very; (3) completely
quit   (1) to stop doing something; (2) to resign from one's job

● Giselle was **quiet** after saying she might want to **quit** her job but that she wasn't **quite** sure.

Fill in each blank with either *quiet*, *quite*, or *quit*.

1. The rain had frozen, and the roads were _____quite_____ slippery.

2. Let's spend a _____quiet_____ evening at home tonight.

3. The waitress began to take my dish, but I wasn't _____quite_____ finished.

4. My speech teacher told me to _____quit_____ saying the word *like* so much, but, like, what's wrong with that word?

5. We had enjoyed the glitter and noisy excitement of Las Vegas, but we were glad to be back home in our _____quiet_____ little town.

than a word used in comparisons
then (1) at that time; (2) next

● First Dad proved he was a better wrestler **than** I am; **then** he helped me improve.

Fill in each blank with either *than* or *then*.

1. I scrubbed the potatoes, and _____then_____ I poked fork holes in them.
2. Crossword puzzles are more difficult _____than_____ word searches.
3. My parents were born in the 1960s. There were no cell phones or websites _____then_____.
4. Every eligible voter should learn about the candidates and _____then_____ go and vote.
5. The tiny family-owned shop is always more crowded _____than_____ the huge supermarket.

use to make use of
used (to) accustomed to or in the habit of

● I am **used to** very spicy food, but when I cook for others, I **use** much less hot pepper.

    Spelling hint Do not forget to include the *d* with *used to*.

Fill in each blank with either *use* or *used*.

1. After spending six years in Alaska, I am _____used_____ to cold weather.
2. Should I _____use_____ a paste or liquid wax on the car?
3. After you get married, will you _____use_____ your husband's last name?
4. Since she is the youngest of four girls, Elaine is _____used_____ to wearing hand-me-downs.
5. Because you _____used_____ the cell phone all day, you should recharge the battery.

were the past tense of *are*
we're contraction of *we are*

● **We're** going to visit the town in Florida where my grandparents **were** born.

Fill in each blank with either *were* or *we're*.

1. Where _____were_____ you when I needed you?
2. _____We're_____ having a quiz on Friday.
3. Our relatives _____were_____ not surprised to hear of my brother's divorce.
4. I don't think _____we're_____ going to have to wait more than five minutes to get seated.
5. The Beatles _____were_____ once known as Long John and the Silver Beatles.

Name _____   Section _____   Date _____

Score: (Number right) _____ x 5 = _____%

More about Homonyms: TEST 1

In the space provided, write the word that correctly fits each sentence.

by, buy
use, used

1. At first the motion of the airplane bothered Randall, but _____*by*_____ the time the flight was over, he was _____*used*_____ to it.

advice, advise
except, accept

2. Even people who won't usually take _____*advice*_____ somehow _____*accept*_____ it from Rosalie.

principal, principle
quit, quite, quiet

3. The _____*principal*_____ of my old school _____*quit*_____ his job to stay home and take care of his grandchildren.

effects, affects
loose, lose

4. Despite the terrible _____*effects*_____ of the earthquake, people didn't _____*lose*_____ their sense of humor.

less, fewer
less, fewer

5. One benefit of watching _____*less*_____ TV is that you are exposed to _____*fewer*_____ commercials.

past, passed
quiet, quite, quit

6. When Eleanor learned that she had _____*passed*_____ her GED exam, she disturbed her usually _____*quiet*_____ house with a shout of joy.

we're, were
a, an

7. Tonight _____*we're*_____ going to see _____*an*_____ old movie called *The Three Faces of Eve.*

principal, principle
a, an

8. A basic _____*principle*_____ that _____*a*_____ student doctor learns in training is "First, do no harm."

lose, loose
then, than

9. In order to _____*lose*_____ weight, it's better to exercise and eat sensibly _____*than*_____ to starve yourself.

use, used
than, then

10. I am more _____*used*_____ to spending an evening watching TV _____*than*_____ reading or exercising.

Name _____ Section _____ Date _____

Score: (Number right) _____ x 5 = _____%

More about Homonyms: TEST 2

In the space provided, write the word that correctly fits each sentence.

were, we're   **1.** Tomorrow ____we're____ going to buy ____an____ afghan for Mom.
a, an

dessert, desert   **2.** Gina likes to hike into the ____desert____ because of the sense of
piece, peace   ____peace____ she feels there.

advice, advise   **3.** Some of the best ____advice____ I ever got was this: "When you
lose, loose   ____lose____ your temper, count to ten before you speak."

then, than   **4.** First we'll have salad, ____then____ a main course, and finally
desert, dessert   ____dessert____.

were, we're   **5.** Because ____we're____ going to be traveling in a hot climate, I
loose, lose   packed clothes that were ____loose____ and cool.

quite, quit, quiet   **6.** Some medications, unfortunately, have ____quite____ a few unpleasant
affects, effects   side ____effects____.

fewer, less   **7.** More than half of today's college students are female; far ____fewer____ women
passed, past   went to college in the ____past____.

quit, quiet, quiet   **8.** The boy was a poor sport who would ____quit____ the game early if
lose, loose   he saw he was going to ____lose____.

advise, advice   **9.** Even though the job doesn't pay much now, I strongly ____advise____
accept, except   you to ____accept____ it. It's a wonderful opportunity.

principal, principle   **10.** Until my graduation, I had never seen our ____principal____ wearing
than, then   anything other ____than____ a suit and tie.

32   More about Capital Letters

Other Rules for Capital Letters

You have already reviewed (on pages 147–156) the following uses of capital letters:

1   **The first word in a sentence or direct quotation**

2   **The word "I" and people's names**

3   **Names of specific places, institutions, and languages**

4   **Product names**

5   **Calendar items**

6   **Titles**

This chapter will consider other uses of capitals:

7   **Capitalize a word that is used as a substitute for the name of a family member. Also, capitalize words like *aunt, uncle,* and *cousin* when they are used as part of people's names.**

- My biggest fan at the dirt-bike competitions was **M**om.

- Go help **G**randfather carry those heavy bags.

- Phil is staying at **U**ncle **R**aymond's house for the holidays.

BUT Do not capitalize words such as *mom* or *grandfather* when they come after possessive words such as *my, her,* or *our.*

- My grandmother lives next door to my parents.

- Phil and his uncle are both recovered alcoholics.

8   **Capitalize the names of specific groups: races, religions, nationalities, companies, clubs, and other organizations.**

- Edward, who is **P**olish-**A**merican, sometimes cooks **C**hinese dishes for his **N**orthside **C**hess **C**lub meetings.

- Arlene, the local president of **M**others **A**gainst **D**runk **D**riving, is a part-time real estate agent for **C**entury 21.

9   **Capitalize the names of specific school courses.**

- This semester, Jody has **D**ance 101, **G**eneral **P**sychology, and **E**conomics 235.

BUT The names of general subject areas are not capitalized.

- This semester, Jody has a gym class, a psychology course, and a business course.

10 **Capitalize the names of specific periods and famous events in history.**

- During the **Middle Ages**, only the nobility and the clegy could read and write.
- The act of protest in which 342 tea chests were thrown into the ocean came to be known as the **Boston Tea Party**.

11 **Capitalize the opening and closing of a letter.**

Capitalize words in the salutation of a letter.

- **Dear Ms. Axelrod:**
- **Dear Sir or Madam:**

Capitalize only the first word of the closing of a letter.

- **Sincerely** yours,
- **Yours** truly,

12 **Capitalize common abbreviations made up of the first letters of the words they represent:**

- IBM
- ABC
- FBI
- AIDS
- UFO
- NASA
- NAACP

Name _____ Section _____ Date _____

Score: (Number right) _____ x 5 = _____%

More about Capital Letters: TEST 1

Underline the **two** words that need capitalizing in each sentence. Then write those words correctly in the spaces provided.

1. Dear <u>sir</u>: Please tell me who played the character <u>aunt</u> Bea on the old *Andy Griffith Show.*
   Sincerely yours,
   Clint Hart

   Sir _____   Aunt _____

2. In today's <u>history</u> 201 class, we learned about the founding of the <u>naacp</u>.

   History _____   NAACP _____

3. All World <u>war</u> II veterans are invited to this Friday's ceremony at the <u>vfw</u> hall.

   War _____   VFW _____

4. During the period known as the <u>dark</u> <u>ages</u>, the rate of literacy fell in Europe.

   Dark _____   Ages _____

5. My mother is Mexican and a <u>baptist</u>, while my dad is <u>italian</u> and a Catholic.

   Baptist _____   Italian _____

6. When <u>grandma</u> retired from Blooming <u>valley</u> Nursery, her employers gave her a dozen rose bushes.

   Grandma _____   Valley _____

7. Dear <u>aunt</u> Sally,
   Thank you so much for your generous birthday check. I can certainly put it to good use!
   <u>with</u> love,
   Rachel

   Aunt _____   With _____

8. Uncle Leonardo is active in the local <u>sons</u> of <u>italy</u> social club.

   Sons _____   Italy _____

9. In our offices at <u>townsend</u> Press, we have Internet service through <u>aol</u>.

   Townsend _____   AOL _____

10. The Art <u>league</u> of Middletown is sponsoring a show of paintings by the artist known as <u>grandma</u> Moses.

    League _____   Grandma _____

Name _____ Section _____ Date _____

Score: (Number right) _____ x 5 = _____%

More about Capital Letters: TEST 2

Underline the **two** words that need capitalizing in each sentence. Then write those words correctly in the spaces provided.

1. Our neighborhood has many <u>asian</u>-language newspapers and a <u>buddhist</u> temple.

   _____Asian_____   _____Buddhist_____

2. The event known as the <u>march</u> on <u>washington</u>, which took place August 26, 1963, brought together more than 250,000 people to demonstrate for civil rights.

   _____March_____   _____Washington_____

3. Rodrigo has <u>social issues</u> 101 at the same time that his brother has a history class.

   _____Social_____   _____Issues_____

4. To her surprise, <u>mom</u> still remembers every word of the <u>gettysburg</u> Address, which she memorized as a fifth-grader.

   _____Mom_____   _____Gettysburg_____

5. Because <u>uncle</u> Josh talked so little about what he did at work, we joked that he was really a spy for the <u>cia</u>.

   _____Uncle_____   _____CIA_____

6. As a project for her 4-<u>h</u> club, Melinda is raising a <u>vietnamese</u> potbellied pig.

   _____H_____   _____Vietnamese_____

7. Dear <u>sir</u>:
   Your microwave has been repaired and can be picked up at your convenience.
   <u>sincerely,</u>
   Rick's Repairs

   _____Sir_____   _____Sincerely_____

8. The <u>italian</u> <u>renaissance</u>, which took place from 1420 to 1600, is known as a time of great artistic accomplishment.

   _____Italian_____   _____Renaissance_____

9. Because yesterday was a <u>jewish</u> holiday, our <u>chemistry</u> 101 class did not meet.

   _____Jewish_____   _____Chemistry_____

10. The <u>great depression</u> began in 1929 on Black Tuesday, the day the stock market crashed.

    _____Great_____   _____Depression_____

PART THREE: Proofreading

PART THREE: PROOFREADING

PREVIEW

Part Three describes how to proofread and includes ten practice tests:

33   Proofreading   295

34   Ten Proofreading Tests   303

33 Proofreading

Basics about Proofreading

An important step in becoming a good writer is learning to proofread. When you proofread, you check the next-to-final draft of a paper for grammar, punctuation, and other mistakes. Such mistakes are ones you did not find and fix in earlier drafts of a paper because you were working on content.

All too often, students skip the key step of proofreading in their rush to hand in a paper. As a result, their writing may contain careless errors that leave a bad impression and result in a lower grade. This chapter explains how to proofread effectively and suggests a sequence to follow when proofreading. The chapter also provides a series of practices to improve your proofreading skills.

HOW TO PROOFREAD

1 Proofreading is a special kind of reading that should not be rushed. Don't try to proofread a paper minutes before it is due. If you do, you are likely to see what you intended to write, not what is actually on the page. Instead, do one of the following:

● Read your writing out loud.

● Alternatively, do the reading "aloud" in your head, perhaps moving your lips as you read.

In either case, listen for spots that do not read smoothly and clearly. You will probably be able to hear where your sentences should begin and end. You will then be more likely to find any fragments and run-ons that are present. Other spots that do not read smoothly may reveal other grammar or punctuation errors. Take the time needed to check such spots closely.

2 Read through your paper several times, looking for different types of errors in each reading. Here is a good sequence to follow:

● Look for sentence fragments, run-ons, and comma splices.

● Look for verb mistakes.

● Look for capital letter and punctuation mistakes.

● Look for missing words or missing -s endings.

● Look for spelling mistakes, including errors in homonyms.

This chapter will give you practice in proofreading for the above mistakes. In addition, as you proofread your work, you should watch for problems with pronoun and modifier use, word choice, and parallelism.

SENTENCE FRAGMENTS, RUN-ONS, AND COMMA SPLICES

Sentence Fragments

When proofreading for sentence fragments, remember to look for the following:

- Dependent-word fragments
- Fragments without subjects
- Fragments without a subject and a verb (-*ing* and *to* fragments, example fragments)

In general, correct a fragment by doing one of the following:

1 Connect the fragment to the sentence that comes before or after it.

2 Create a completely new sentence by adding a subject and/or a verb.

To further refresh your memory about fragments, turn to pages 67–86.

Run-On Sentences and Comma Splices

When proofreading for run-on sentences and comma splices, keep the following definitions in mind:

- A **run-on sentence** results when one complete thought is immediately followed by another, with nothing between them.

- A **comma splice** is made up of two complete thoughts that are incorrectly joined by only a comma.

To correct run-on sentences and comma splices, do one of the following:

1 Use a period and a capital letter to create separate sentences.

2 Use a comma plus a joining word (such as *and, but,* or *so*) to connect the two complete thoughts into one compound sentence.

3 Use a dependent word (see page 97) to make one of the complete thoughts dependent upon the other one.

4 Use a semicolon to connect the two complete thoughts.

To further refresh your memory about run-on sentences and comma splices, turn to pages 87–106 and 261–264.

● Practice 1

Read each of the following short passages either aloud or to yourself. Each passage contains a sentence fragment, a run-on, or a comma splice. Find and underline the error. Then correct it in the space provided.   *Answers may vary.*

1. That bookcase is too heavy on top it could fall over. Take some of the big books off the highest shelf and put them on the bottom one.

   That bookcase is too heavy on top, so it could fall over.

2. The detective asked everyone to gather in the library. He announced that he had solved the mystery. And would soon reveal the name of the murderer. Suddenly the lights went out.

   He announced that he had solved the mystery and would soon reveal the name of the murderer.

3. That rocking chair is very old. It belonged to my great-grandfather, he brought it to the United States from Norway. I like to think about all the people who have sat in it over the years.

   It belonged to my great-grandfather; he brought it to the United States from Norway.

4. Before you leave the house. Please close all the windows in case it rains. I don't want the carpet to get soaked.

   Before you leave the house, please close all the windows in case it rains.

5. Midori is from Taiwan, she uses the English name Shirley, which is easier for her American friends to say. Everyone in her family has both a Chinese and an English name.

   Midori is from Taiwan. She uses the English name Shirley, which is easier for her American friends to say.

6. My aunt took a trip on a boat off the coast of California. She wanted to see whales. Whales are always sighted there. At a certain time of the year.

   Whales are always sighted there at a certain time of the year.

7. For vacation this year, we are going to rent a cabin. It is on a lake in the mountains we can swim, fish, and sunbathe there. Everyone in the family is looking forward to that week.

   Because it is on a lake in the mountains, we can swim, fish, and sunbathe there.

8. Rosalie went to the beauty parlor on Friday. <u>To get her long hair trimmed just a little.</u> However, she changed her mind and had it cut very short.

   <u>Rosalie went to the beauty parlor on Friday to get her long hair trimmed just a little.</u>

   _____

9. The Webbs put a white carpet in their living room. Now they feel that was a foolish choice. <u>Every bit of dirt or spilled food shows on the white surface. And is nearly impossible to get rid of.</u>

   <u>Every bit of dirt or spilled food shows on the white surface and is nearly impossible</u>

   <u>to get rid of.</u>

10. <u>That waiter is quick and hard-working, he is not friendly with customers.</u> For that reason he doesn't get very good tips. His boss tells him to smile and be more pleasant, but he doesn't seem to listen.

    <u>That waiter is quick and hard-working, but he is not friendly with customers.</u>

    _____

COMMON VERB MISTAKES

When proofreading, look for the following common verb mistakes:

- The wrong past or past participle forms of irregular verbs (pages 37–46)
- Lack of subject-verb agreement (pages 47–56; 235–241)
- Needless shifts of verb tense (pages 253–254)

● Practice 2

Read each of the following sentences either aloud or to yourself. Each contains a verb mistake. Find and cross out the error. Then correct it in the space provided.

swam	**1.**	The girls ~~swimmed~~ all the way to the raft.
wear	**2.**	The rock climbers ~~wears~~ safety ropes in case they fall.
did	**3.**	Because my brother studied hard, he ~~does~~ very well on the exam.
grew	**4.**	The strange-looking puppy ~~growed~~ up to be a beautiful dog.
is	**5.**	Neither of our cars ~~are~~ working right now.
answered	**6.**	The phone rang twenty times before someone ~~answers~~ it.
are	**7.**	The public swimming pools in the city ~~is~~ not open yet.
slept	**8.**	Somehow, I ~~sleeped~~ through last night's loud thunderstorm.
is	**9.**	There ~~are~~ poison ivy growing all over that empty lot.
claims	**10.**	Gerald tells everybody it's his birthday and then ~~claimed~~ he doesn't want presents.

CAPITAL LETTER AND PUNCTUATION MISTAKES

When proofreading, be sure the following begin with **capital letters**:

- The first word in a sentence or direct quotation
- The word *I* and people's names
- Family names
- Names of specific places and languages
- Names of specific groups
- Names of days of the week, months, and holidays (but not the seasons)
- Brand names
- Titles
- Names of specific school courses
- Names of historical periods and well-known events
- Opening and closing of a letter

When proofreading, look for **commas** in the following places:

- Between items in a series
- After introductory material
- Around words that interrupt the flow of a sentence
- Between complete thoughts connected by a joining word
- Before and/or after words of direct address and short expressions
- In dates, addresses and letters

When proofreading, be sure **apostrophes** are used in the following:

- Contractions
- Possessives (but not in plurals or verbs)

When proofreading, look for quotation marks around direct quotations. Eliminate any quotation marks around indirect quotations.

Finally, remember to also watch for problems with colons, semicolons, hyphens, dashes, and parentheses.

To further refresh your memory, turn to "Capital Letters," pages 147–156; "The Comma," pages 107–116; "The Apostrophe," pages 117–126; "Quotation Marks," pages 127–136; and "Punctuation Marks," pages 171–177.

● Practice 3

Read each of the following sentences either aloud or to yourself. Each sentence contains an error in capitalization, an error in comma or apostrophe use, or two missing quotation marks. Find the mistake, and correct it in the space provided.

_____sauce,_____ **1.** I loaded up my low-fat frozen yogurt with fudge sauce peanuts, cherries, and whipped cream.

_____Bob's_____ **2.** Bobs uncle is an actor in a soap opera.

_____yelled,_____ **3.** The deli clerk yelled "Who's next?"

Chicago	**4.** Our flight to chicago was delayed two hours because of mechanical problems.
"Please . . . Tom,"	**5.** Please call me Tom, our business instructor said.
summer	**6.** I dread the Summer because I get hay fever so badly.
doesn't	**7.** A person doesnt have to be great at a sport to be a great coach.
character,	**8.** Although he's only a cartoon character Mickey Mouse is loved by millions.
watermelons	**9.** The fresh watermelon's in the supermarket look delicious.
question," . . . June. "I	**10.** "I'd like to ask you a question, Marvin told June. I hope you don't think it's too personal."

MISSING -S ENDINGS AND MISSING WORDS

Since you know what you meant when you wrote something, it is easy for you not to notice when a word ending or even a whole word is missing. The following two sections will give you practice in proofreading for such omissions.

Missing -s Endings

When you proofread, remember the following about noun and verb endings:

- The plural form of most nouns ends in *s* (for example, two *cups* of coffee).
- Present tense verbs for the singular third-person subjects end with an *s*.

To further refresh your memory about the present tense, turn to pages 243–244.

● Practice 4

Read each of the following sentences either aloud or to yourself. In each case an -*s* ending is needed on one of the nouns or verbs in the sentence. Find and cross out the error. Then correct it in the space provided, being sure to add the *s* to the word.

telephones	**1.** All of the pay ~~telephone~~ are being used.
looks	**2.** You should check your front left tire because it ~~look~~ a little flat.
jokes	**3.** My uncle is always telling terrible ~~joke~~.
barns	**4.** Most ~~barn~~ are painted a dark red color.
makes	**5.** Ella ~~make~~ new friends quite easily.
speaks	**6.** Luis got his job because he ~~speak~~ Spanish and English equally well.
closes	**7.** The drugstore ~~close~~ at nine o'clock, but the other mall stores stay open till ten.
grows	**8.** The grass always ~~grow~~ faster whenever we have a heavy summer rain.
cans	**9.** There are two ~~can~~ of soda hidden on the shelf of the refrigerator.
freckles	**10.** Many red-haired people have ~~freckle~~ on their skin and also get sunburned quickly.

Missing Words

When you proofread, look for places where you may have omitted such short words as *a, of, the,* or *to.*

● Practice 5

Read each of the following sentences either aloud or to yourself. In each sentence, one of the following little words has been omitted:

a	and	by	of	the	to	with

Add a caret (∧) at the spot where the word is missing. Then write the missing word in the space provided.

Example _____of_____ My new pair ∧ jeans is too tight.

_____of_____ **1.** Several pieces ∧ this puzzle are missing.

_____to_____ **2.** When she went to the grocery store, Louise forgot ∧ buy bread.

_____of_____ **3.** Some ∧ the programs on TV are too violent for children.

_____with_____ **4.** That orange shirt looks great ∧ the black pants.

_____a_____ **5.** I didn't think I had a chance of winning ∧ prize in the contest.

_____and_____ **6.** Paul plays both the piano ∧ the bass guitar.

_____the_____ **7.** Sandra became tired climbing up ∧ steep hill.

_____by_____ **8.** Everyone was surprised ∧ the school principal's announcement.

_____with_____ **9.** Do you drink your coffee ∧ cream or just sugar?

_____to_____ **10.** It's hard ∧ pay attention to a boring speaker.

HOMONYM MISTAKES

When proofreading, pay special attention to the spelling of words that are easily confused with other words.

To refresh your memory of the homonyms listed in this book, turn to pages 137–146 and 282–288.

● Practice 6

Read each of the following sentences either aloud or to yourself. Each sentence contains a mistake in a commonly confused word. Find and cross out the error. Then correct it in the space provided.

_____too_____ **1.** We left the beach early because there were ~~to~~ many flies.

_____your_____ **2.** It's ~~you're~~ own fault that you missed the deadline.

_____whose_____ **3.** No one knows ~~who's~~ sweatshirt this is.

_____you're_____ **4.** If ~~your~~ hungry, fix yourself something to eat.

_____its_____ **5.** I can't get close enough to the stray dog to read the tag on ~~it's~~ collar.

_____they're_____ **6.** My cousins have promised that ~~their~~ coming here soon for a visit.

_____two_____   **7.** I can think of ~~too~~ practical reasons for staying in school: to improve your skills and to prepare for a better job.

_____their_____   **8.** These greeting cards have pictures on ~~they're~~ covers, but there's no message inside.

_____it's_____   **9.** Although ~~its~~ tempting to keep the money, you should return it to the man whose name appears in the wallet.

_____passed_____   **10.** As we waited in the emergency room to hear whether our sick friend would be all right, time ~~past~~ slowly.

A Note on Making Corrections in Your Papers

You can add minor corrections to the final draft of a paper and still hand it in. Just make the corrections neatly. Add missing punctuation marks right in the text, exactly where they belong. Draw a straight line through any words or punctuation you wish to eliminate or correct. Add new material by inserting a caret (∧) at the point where the addition should be. Then write the new word or words above the line at that point. Here's an example of a sentence that was corrected during proofreading:

-    Some Hondas are made in ~~japan~~ Japan, but others are made ∧in this country.

Retype or recopy a paper if you discover a number of errors.

● Practice 7

Here are five sentences, each of which contains **two** of the types of errors covered in this chapter. Correct the errors by crossing out or adding words or punctuation marks, as in the example above.

Corrections in sentence 2 may vary.

1. Helena is taking two ~~english course~~ English courses in school this semester.

2. I feel sorry for ~~Donnas dog, it~~ Donna's dog. It lost a leg in a car accident.

3. Rusty cans, plastic bags, and scraps of wood washed up on ∧the deserted beach.

4. My mother ~~take~~ takes night classes at college, ~~wear~~ where she is learning to use a computer.

5. When the power came back ~~on. All~~ on, all the digital clocks in the house began to blink, ∧and the refrigerator motor started to hum.

34 Ten Proofreading Tests

Name _____ Section _____ Date _____

Score: (Number right) _____ x 20 = _____ %

Proofreading: TEST 1

Read the following passage either aloud or to yourself, looking for the following **five** mistakes:

Corrections may vary.

    1 fragment
    1 apostrophe mistake
    1 missing word
    1 missing comma
    1 verb mistake

Correct the mistakes, crossing out or adding words or punctuation marks as needed.

¹Can you tell the difference between an alligator and a crocodile? ²In order to do so, you'd probably need to see the two animals side by side. ³An ~~alligators~~ *alligator's* snout is shorter and broader than that of a crocodile. ⁴When an alligator's mouth is ~~shut.~~ ~~⁵You~~ *shut, you* can see only the top teeth protruding outside the mouth. ⁶But with ⌄*a* crocodile, you can see several of its bottom teeth as well as its top teeth. ⁷The most important difference, however, is in behavior rather than looks. ⁸Although alligators are dangerous,they ~~does~~ *do* not often attack people. ⁹But crocodiles are definitely aggressive toward humans.

Name _____ Section _____ Date _____

Score: (Number right) _____ x 20 = _____%

Proofreading: TEST 2

Read the following passage either aloud or to yourself, looking for the following **five** mistakes:

Corrections may vary.

    1 comma splice
    2 verb mistakes
    1 missing word
    1 homonym mistake

Correct the mistakes, crossing out or adding words or punctuation marks as needed.

¹My aunt is the thriftiest person I have ever known. ²She will do just about anything to save a penny. ³For example, she never throws away old socks;/she uses them as dust rags. ⁴Instead of using a sandwich bag once and disposing of it, she ~~wash~~ *washes* and re-uses it.

⁵When she receives a gift, she carefully unwraps it without tearing the wrapping paper. ⁶She'll use that paper to wrap *the* ^ next gift she gives. ⁷Her old milk cartons become bird feeders. ⁸Her tin cans become flowerpots. ⁹Plastic bags from the grocery store ~~becomes~~ *become* liners for her wastebaskets. ¹⁰When her family's blue jeans are too worn out to ~~where~~ *wear*, she recycles them into cozy quilts for the beds. ¹¹She really is a model of thriftiness.

Name _____ Section _____ Date _____

Score: (Number right) _____ x 20 = _____ %

Proofreading: TEST 3

Read the following passage either aloud or to yourself, looking for the following **five** mistakes:

Corrections may vary.

2 fragments
1 comma splice
1 missing quotation mark
1 homonym mistake

Correct the mistakes, crossing out or adding words or punctuation marks as needed.

¹When I was twelve, my family moved to a new town. ²Our new house was in a large development. ³On my first day there, I went for a walk. ⁴As I left, my mother told me, "Don't get lost." ⁵I rolled my eyes at her silly warning and walked for a

time hoping

long ~~time. ⁶Hoping~~ to meet some of the kids who lived near us. ⁷Finally, I got tired

hungry and

and ~~hungry. ⁸And~~ turned to go back home. ⁹That's when I realized how much alike all

knew

the houses looked. ¹⁰I realized, too, that I didn't know my new address. ¹¹All I ~~new~~ was that the street was named after a tree. ¹²I began looking at street signs and read, "Plum Lane," "Poplar Street," "Elm Court," and "Maple Avenue." ¹³They were all named after trees. ¹⁴I walked around the development for more than two hours, too

help. Then

embarrassed to ask for ~~help, then~~ I spotted my family's car parked outside our house.

Name _____ Section _____ Date _____

Score: (Number right) _____ x 20 = _____%

Proofreading: TEST 4

Read the following passage either aloud or to yourself, looking for the following **five** mistakes:

Corrections may vary.

1 fragment
1 comma splice
1 missing capital letter
1 missing apostrophe
1 verb mistake

Correct the mistakes, crossing out or adding words or punctuation marks as needed.

¹When I was nineteen, I lived in Costa Rica for a few months. ²This beautiful country is filled with fruits and flowers growing everywhere. ³The country is also blessed with rain forests, mountains, and inactive volcanoes. ⁴One of my favorite memories ~~are~~ *is* of a time I stayed overnight on the beach with some friends. ⁵At about midnight, we decided to stand waist-deep in the warm ocean water. ⁶A gentle rain began to fall, *and* we could see lightning flashing in the clouds many miles away. ⁷Suddenly, we all gasped in amazement. ⁸Lines of flickering green light were dancing across the tops of the ~~waves. ⁹As~~ *waves as* they rolled toward us. ¹⁰We learned later that the light was caused by tiny glowing animals which live on the ocean's surface. ¹¹That night was a magical time for us.

Name _____ Section _____ Date _____

Score: (Number right) _____ x 20 = _____ %

Proofreading: TEST 5

Read the following passage either aloud or to yourself, looking for the following **five** mistakes:

Corrections may vary.

1 **fragment**
1 **run-on sentence**
1 **missing comma**
1 **missing apostrophe**
1 **verb mistake**

Correct the mistakes, crossing out or adding words or punctuation marks as needed.

                                                                    Zoo, it
¹When a group of rare white lions arrived at the Philadelphia ~~Zoo. ²It~~ was an

                                                            America. They
exciting event. ³The lions were the only ones of their kind in North ~~America they~~

soon became the zoo's most popular exhibit. ⁴The lions are native to southern

Africa. ⁵They are so rare because of a problem caused by their unusual color. ⁶Most

lions, with their golden-brown color, can sneak through grass and trees without

                                                            makes
being detected. ⁷But the moonlight shining on the white lions' coats ~~make~~ it

                            It's
difficult for them to hunt at night. ⁸~~Its~~ too easy for other animals to see them.

⁹Therefore, most white lions in the wild starve to death. ¹⁰Although all the white

lions in Philadelphia are female, the zoo is hoping to get a white male soon and raise
                          ^

a family of white lion cubs.

Name _____ Section _____ Date _____

Score: (Number right) _____ x 20 = _____ %

Proofreading: TEST 6

Read the following passage either aloud or to yourself, looking for the following **five** mistakes:

Corrections may vary.

1 run-on sentence
1 missing -*s* ending
1 capital letter mistake
1 missing quotation mark
1 verb mistake

Correct the mistakes, crossing out or adding words or punctuation marks as needed.

[1]Elaine and Don were on a long drive. [2]They stopped at a convenience store to buy something to drink. [3]While Elaine picked up cans of ~~p~~ P epsi and fruit juice, Don browsed through the snacks. [4]He decided that it would be fun to try something new and unusual, so he bought pickled hard-boiled eggs, a bag of pork rinds, and a tasty-looking sausage. [5]Back in the car, Elaine ~~nibbles~~ nibbled on a pickled egg. [6]"Hey, I like this," she said. [7] " What are you going to try first?" [8]But Don didn't answer her question ∧. He ~~He~~ just made choking sound s as he hurriedly opened a can and gulped down some soda. [9]"Don't eat that sausage!" he finally gasped. [10]Elaine picked up the sausage package and read the label. [11]"Fire-Eater's Favorite Chili Sausage," she said. [12]"Maybe you should have read the label first."

Name _____ Section _____ Date _____

Score: (Number right) _____ x 10 = _____ %

Proofreading: TEST 7

Read the following passage either aloud or to yourself, looking for the following **ten** mistakes:

Corrections may vary.

2 fragments
2 comma splices
2 missing apostrophes
1 missing comma
1 missing word
1 homonym mistake
1 verb mistake

Correct the mistakes, crossing out or adding words or punctuation marks as needed.

¹On TV, people who sleepwalk generally act like ~~zombies, they~~ [zombies; they] stagger along with their arms held stiffly in front of them. ²In fact (as you know if you've ever seen one), most sleepwalkers walk around quite normally. ³They may even perform routine ~~tasks. ⁴Such~~ [tasks such] as getting dressed or brushing their teeth. ⁵Sometimes they talk, although ~~there~~ [their] conversation may not make a lot of sense. ⁶Sleepwalking is a fairly common ~~behavior. ⁷Especially~~ [behavior, especially] among children. ⁸It occurs during periods of very deep sleep. ⁹In most cases, a person sleepwalks just a few ~~times, then~~ [times. Then] the sleepwalking stops forever. ¹⁰If sleepwalking becomes a frequent problem[,] the sleepwalker may need a doctor['s] help. ¹¹What should you do if you see someone sleepwalking? ¹²Leading the sleepwalker back [to] bed is usually all that is necessary. ¹³But if the sleepwalker ~~be~~ [is] in danger of injury, gently wake him or her up.

Name _____   Section _____ Date _____

Score: (Number right) _____ x 10 = _____%

Proofreading: TEST 8

Read the following passage either aloud or to yourself, looking for the following **ten** mistakes:

Corrections may vary.

1 missing capital letter
2 verb mistakes
2 missing apostrophes
2 homonym mistakes
2 comma splices
1 missing comma

Correct the mistakes, crossing out or adding words or punctuation marks as needed.

[1]George Orwell's famous novel *Animal Farm* is an example of an allegory. [2]In an allegory, characters and events act as symbols of other things. [3]In the book, the horses, sheep, pigs, cows, and other animals of Manor Farm ~~rebels~~ *rebel* against their drunken owner, ~~m~~*M*r. Jones. [4]With the pigs taking the lead, the animals drive all humans away from the ~~farm, they~~ *farm, and they* take control of it themselves. [5]They intend to turn the farm into a sort of paradise, where all the animals will work hard and live together in ~~piece~~ *peace* and equality. [6]But soon the pigs begin taking advantage of the situation. [7]They work less than the other animals and ~~changed~~ *change* the society's rules for ~~they're~~ *their* benefit. [8]By the time the book ends, the pigs are almost identical to human beings. [9]You can enjoy *Animal Farm* simply as a ~~story, you~~ *story, or you* can also read it as a warning against how a well-intentioned revolution can go wrong.

Name _____ Section _____ Date _____

Score: (Number right) _____ x 10 = _____%

Proofreading: TEST 9

Read the following passage either aloud or to yourself, looking for the following **ten** mistakes:

Corrections may vary.

2 fragments
1 run-on sentence
1 comma splice
2 missing commas
1 missing apostrophe
1 capital letter mistake
2 verb mistakes

Correct the mistakes, crossing out or adding words or punctuation marks as needed.

¹The city of Seattle, Washington, is known for its beauty. ²It has a cool, pleasant climate and is surrounded by spectacular mountain ranges. ³Seattle is home to the University of Washington, professional theater companies, an opera company, and several museums. ⁴That's the good news. ⁵On the other hand, the region around Seattle is also known for its enormous slugs. ⁶While there are slugs in other parts of the United States, they don't compare to the Seattle variety. ⁷Seattle slugs average four to five inches in length, and they come in a rainbow assortment of colors, including green with yellow spots. ⁸~~Including~~ ⁹When a pack of slugs moves into a Seattle garden, it ¹⁰~~It~~ can clean out a lettuce crop overnight.

¹¹The residents of the Seattle region have ~~thinked~~ thought up some creative ways to deal with the giant slugs. ¹²Most of that creativity is devoted to finding ways to kill them. ¹³The most effective method, they say, is to sprinkle the slugs with salt because the salted slugs dissolve on the spot. ¹⁴Another popular method is to fill a pie tin with half an inch of beer. ¹⁵The slugs crawl in, drink the beer, pass out, and drown.

¹⁶But others say you can learn to live with, and even love, the slimy slugs. ¹⁷Residents of the nearby town of Elma, Washington, ~~has~~ have an annual slug festival. ¹⁸They dress the slugs up in little costumes and have slug races. ¹⁹There are even rumors of slug cookbooks available in and around ~~Seattle, they~~ Seattle. They are for people who *really* love the creepy crawlers.

Name _____ Section _____ Date _____

Score: (Number right) _____ x 10 = _____%

Proofreading: TEST 10

Read the following passage either aloud or to yourself, looking for the following **ten** mistakes:

Corrections may vary.

1 fragment
1 run-on
1 missing capital
3 missing commas
2 missing apostrophes
1 verb mistake
1 homonym mistake

Correct the mistakes, crossing out or adding words or punctuation marks as needed.

¹One of the most amazing things about the Internet is the way it makes a ~~hole~~ *whole*

world of facts available to you. ²Have you ever wondered,for instance,what that little

bump of flesh just in front of your ear canal is called? ³Go to the Internet and type in

the name "Google," which is a good search engine. ⁴In the Google search field, type

"What is the bump in front of the ear called?" ⁵In less than a second, you've learned

that little bump is called the "tragus." ⁶And by the way, the pale half-moon at the base

of your fingernail is the "lunula." ⁷You ~~dont~~ *don't* even have to search for weird, interesting

facts. ⁸Just go to one of the hundreds of trivia sites online and read the items collected

there. ⁹Thanks to such sites, I now know that Murphy's Oil Soap is what most

zookeepers use to wash their elephants. ¹⁰Believe it or not, the people of Des Moines,

Iowa, ~~eats~~ *eat* more Jell-O than the people of any other city. ¹¹Another interesting fact

is that more films have been made about ḏracula *(D)* than about any other fictional

character. ¹²Getting weird facts off the Internet can be habit-~~forming you~~ *forming. You* may find it

very hard to stop with just one…or two…or ten. ¹³Before you know it,you have spent

an hour at the ~~computer.~~ *computer and* ~~¹⁴And~~ completely forgotten what you wanted to look up in

the first place.

PART FOUR Related Matters

PART FOUR
Related Matters

PREVIEW

Part Four includes three chapters that will further strengthen your English skills:

35   Spelling Improvement   315

36   Parts of Speech   325

37   Dictionary Use   337

35 Spelling Improvement

This chapter explains the following ways to improve your spelling:

1   Use the dictionary and other spelling aids

2   Keep a personal spelling list

3   Learn commonly confused words

4   Learn some helpful spelling rules

    a   *I* before *E* rule

    b   Silent *E* rule

    c   *Y* rule

    d   Doubling rule

    e   Rules for adding *-es* to nouns and verbs that end in *s, sh, ch,* or *x*

    f   Rules for adding *-es* to nouns and verbs ending in a consonant plus *y*

USE THE DICTIONARY AND OTHER SPELLING AIDS

The single most important way to improve your spelling is to get into the habit of checking words in a dictionary. But you may at times have trouble locating a given word. "If I can't spell a word," you might ask, "how can I find it in the dictionary?" The answer is that you have to guess what the letters might be.

Here are some hints to help you make informed guesses.

HINT 1

If you're not sure about the vowels in a word, you will have to experiment. Vowels often sound the same. So try an *i* in place of an *a*, an *e* in place of an *i*, and so on.

HINT 2

Consonants are sometimes doubled in a word. If you can't find your word with single consonants, try doubling them.

HINT 3

In the box on the following page are groups of letters or letter combinations that often sound alike. If your word isn't spelled with one of the letters in a pair or group shown in the box on the following page, it might be spelled with another in the same pair or group. For example, if it isn't spelled with a *k*, it may be spelled with a *c*.

Vowels				
ai / ay	au / aw	ee / ea	ou / ow	oo / u

Consonants

c / k   c / s   f / ph   g / j   sch / sc / sk   s / z

Combinations

re / ri   able / ible   ent / ant   er / or   tion / sion

● Practice 1

Use your dictionary and the above hints to find the correct spelling of the following words.

1. divelop — develop
2. diferent — different
3. sertain — certain
4. chearful — cheerful
5. sergery — surgery
6. skedule — schedule
7. fony — phony
8. comfortible — comfortable
9. mayer — mayor
10. paiment — payment
11. aukward — awkward
12. photografy — photography
13. asemble — assemble
14. seazon — season
15. dependant — dependent
16. terrable — terrible
17. dezign — design
18. rilease — release
19. funcsion — function
20. awthor — author

In addition to a dictionary, take advantage of a spelling checker on your computer. Also, pocket-size electronic spelling checkers are widely available.

KEEP A PERSONAL SPELLING LIST

In a special place, write down every word you misspell. Include its correct spelling, underline the difficult part of the word, and add any hints you can use to remember how to spell it. If spelling is a particular problem for you, you might even want to start a spelling notebook that has a separate page for each letter of the alphabet.

Here's one format you might use:

How I spelled it	Correct spelling	Hints
recieve	rec<u>ei</u>ve	I before E except after C
seperate	sep<u>a</u>rate	There's A RAT in sepARATe
alot	<u>a l</u>ot	Two words (like "a little")
alright	<u>all r</u>ight	Two words (like "all wrong")

Study your list regularly, and refer to it whenever you write and proofread a paper.

LEARN COMMONLY CONFUSED WORDS

Many spelling errors result from words that sound alike or almost alike but that are spelled differently, such as *break* and *brake*, *wear* and *where*, or *right* and *write*. To avoid such errors, study carefully the list of words on pages 137–140 and 282–286.

LEARN SOME HELPFUL SPELLING RULES

Even poor spellers can improve by following a few spelling rules.
Following are **SIX** rules that apply to many words.

RULE #1
I before E rule

I before E except after C
Or when sounded like *A*, as in *neighbor* and *weigh*.

	I before E	*Except after C*	*Or when sounded like A*
Examples	belief, chief field	receive, ceiling	vein, eight

Exceptions to the above rule include: either, leisure, foreign, science, society

● Practice 2

A. Complete each word with either *ie* or *ei*.

1. dec_ei_ve   **6.** pr_ie_st

2. bel_ie_ve   **7.** cash_ie_r

3. br_ie_f   **8.** w_ei_gh

4. fr_ei_ght   **9.** p_ie_ce

5. c_ei_ling   **10.** r_ei_ndeer

B. In each sentence, fill in the blank with either ***ie*** or ***ei***.

11. I rec_ei_ved some interesting junk mail today.

12. Many of the people in my n_ei_ghborhood are retired.

13. Norma never gave up her bel_ie_f in her husband's innocence.

14. What do you like to do in your l_ei_sure time?

15. There's a lot of traffic now, so don't ignore this y_ie_ld sign.

16. The r_ei_gn of Queen Victoria of Great Britain lasted over sixty years.

17. My parents are working hard to ach_ie_ve their retirement goals.

18. I have never traveled to any for_ei_gn countries.

19. My _ei_ghty-year-old grandfather still does a daily twenty pushups.

20. A th_ie_f broke into Parker's Bakery last night and stole all the dough.

RULE #2
Silent *E* rule

If a word ends in a silent (unpronounced) *e*, drop the *e* before adding an ending that starts with a vowel. Keep the *e* when adding an ending that begins with a consonant.

	Drop the e with endings that start with a vowel	*Keep the e with endings that start with a consonant*
Examples	like + ed = liked	love + ly = lovely
	confuse + ing = confusing	shame + ful = shameful
	fame + ous = famous	hope + less = hopeless
	guide + ance = guidance	manage + ment = management

Exceptions include: noticeable, argument, judgment, truly

● Practice 3

A. Write out each word shown.

1. abuse + ing = _____abusing_____
2. hope + ed = _____hoped_____
3. have + ing = _____having_____
4. desire + able = _____desirable_____
5. ridicule + ous = _____ridiculous_____
6. sincere + ity = _____sincerity_____

B. Write out each word shown.

7. sincere + ly = _____sincerely_____
8. peace + ful = _____peaceful_____
9. advance + ment = _____advancement_____
10. noise + less = _____noiseless_____
11. large + ness = _____largeness_____
12. grace + ful = _____graceful_____
13. bare + ly = _____barely_____

C. Write out each word shown.

14. write + ing = _____writing_____
15. care + ful = _____careful_____
16. safe + ly = _____safely_____
17. hire + ed = _____hired_____
18. serve + ing = _____serving_____
19. notice + able = _____noticeable_____
20. excite + ment = _____excitement_____

RULE #3
Y rule

Change the final *y* of a word to *i* when both of the following are present:

a the last two letters of the word are a consonant plus *y*. (Keep a *y* that follows a vowel.)

b the ending being added begins with a vowel or is **-ful**, **-ly**, or **-ness**.

Exception   Keep the *y* if the ending being added is **-ing**.

	Change the y to i	*Keep the y*
Examples	happy + ness = happiness	destroy + s = destroys
	lucky + ly = luckily	display + ed = displayed
	beauty + ful = beautiful	gray + ed = grayed
	try + ed = tried	try + ing = trying
	carry + er = carrier	carry + ing = carrying

● Practice 4

A. Write out each word shown.

1. rely + ed   =   _relied_
2. holy + ness   =   _holiness_
3. play + ful   =   _playful_
4. cry + ing   =   _crying_
5. cry + ed   =   _cried_
6. plenty + ful   =   _plentiful_
7. lazy + ness   =   _laziness_
8. fly + ing   =   _flying_
9. angry + ly   =   _angrily_
10. betray + ed   =   _betrayed_

B. Write out each word shown.

11. stay + ing =	_staying_	stay + ed =	_stayed_
12. busy + est =	_busiest_	busy + ly =	_busily_
13. silly + er =	_sillier_	silly + ness =	_silliness_
14. employ + ed =	_employed_	employ + er =	_employer_
15. bury + ing =	_burying_	bury + ed =	_buried_
16. dry + ing =	_drying_	dry + ed =	_dried_
17. happy + ly =	_happily_	happy + er =	_happier_
18. funny + er =	_funnier_	funny + est =	_funniest_
19. satisfy + ing =	_satisfying_	satisfy + ed =	_satisfied_
20. annoy + ed =	_annoyed_	annoy + ance =	_annoyance_

RULE #4
Doubling rule

Double the final consonant of a word before adding an ending when all three of the following are present:

a the last three letters of the word are a consonant, a vowel, and a consonant (CVC).

b the word is only one syllable (for example, *stop*) or is accented on the last syllable (for example, *begin*).

c The ending being added begins with a vowel.

	One-syllable words that end in CVC	*Words accented on the last syllable that end in CVC*
Examples	stop + ed = stopped	begin + ing = beginning
	flat + er = flatter	control + er = controller
	red + est = reddest	occur + ence = occurrence

● Practice 5

A. First note whether each one-syllable word ends in the CVC pattern or with another pattern (VVC, VCC, etc.), and write the pattern in the first column. Then add to each word the endings shown.

	Word	Pattern of Last Three Letters	-ed	-ing
Examples	trip	CVC	tripped	tripping
	growl	VCC	growled	growling
1.	jog	CVC	jogged	jogging
2.	learn	VCC	learned	learning
3.	slam	CVC	slammed	slamming
4.	wrap	CVC	wrapped	wrapping
5.	rain	VVC	rained	raining
6.	dot	CVC	dotted	dotting
7.	flood	VVC	flooded	flooding
8.	beg	CVC	begged	begging
9.	clip	CVC	clipped	clipping
10.	burn	VCC	burned	burning

B. First note whether each two-syllable word ends in the CVC pattern or with another pattern (VVC, VCC, etc.), and write the pattern in the first column. Then add to each word the endings shown. *If a word ends in CVC, remember to check to see if the final syllable is stressed or not.*

	Word	Pattern of Last Three Letters	-ed	-ing
Examples	admit	CVC	admitted	admitting
	recall	VCC	recalled	recalling
11.	expel	CVC	expelled	expelling
12.	perform	VCC	performed	performing
13.	enter	CVC	entered	entering
14.	omit	CVC	omitted	omitting
15.	murder	CVC	murdered	murdering
16.	prefer	CVC	preferred	preferring
17.	occur	CVC	occurred	occurring
18.	explain	VVC	explained	explaining
19.	submit	CVC	submitted	submitting
20.	reason	CVC	reasoned	reasoning

RULE #5

Rules for adding *-es* to nouns and verbs that end in *s, sh, ch,* or *x*

Most plurals are formed by adding *-s* to the singular noun, but in some cases *-es* is added. For nouns that end in *s, sh, ch,* or *x,* form the plural by adding *-es.*

Examples   kiss + es = kisses   coach + es = coaches
           wish + es = wishes   tax + es = taxes

Most third-person singular verbs end in *-s* (he runs, she sings, it grows). But for verbs that end in *s, sh, ch,* or *x,* form the third-person singular with *-es.*

Examples   miss + es = misses   catch + es = catches
           wash + es = washes   mix + es = mixes

● Practice 6

Add -s or -es as needed to each of the following words.

1. bush   <u>bushes</u>
2. mix   <u>mixes</u>
3. pitch   <u>pitches</u>
4. glass   <u>glasses</u>
5. carpet   <u>carpets</u>
6. crash   <u>crashes</u>
7. box   <u>boxes</u>
8. watch   <u>watches</u>
9. shine   <u>shines</u>
10. business   <u>businesses</u>

RULE #6
Rules for adding -es to nouns and verbs that end in a consonant plus y

For nouns that end in a consonant plus *y*, form the plural by changing the *y* to *i* and adding *-es*.

Examples   fly + es = fl**ies**   lady + es = lad**ies**

           canary + es = canar**ies**

For verbs that end in a consonant plus *y*, form the third-person singular by changing the *y* to *i* and adding *-es*.

Examples   pity + es =pit**ies**   marry + es = marr**ies**

           bully + es = bull**ies**

● Practice 7

Add -s or -es as needed to each of the following words. Where appropriate, change a final *y* to *i* before adding -es.

1. army   <u>armies</u>
2. try   <u>tries</u>
3. tray   <u>trays</u>
4. hurry   <u>hurries</u>
5. attorney   <u>attorneys</u>
6. variety   <u>varieties</u>
7. chimney   <u>chimneys</u>
8. baby   <u>babies</u>
9. journey   <u>journeys</u>
10. sympathy   <u>sympathies</u>

● Final Practice 1

Use the spelling rules in the chapter to write out the words indicated.

A. Complete each word with either *ie* or *ei*.

1. gr_ie_f   3. n_ei_ghbor   5. rel_ie_ve
2. dec_ei_ve   4. fr_ie_nd

B. Use the *silent e* rule to write out each word shown.

6. time + ed = _timed_   9. fame + ous = _famous_
7. time + ly = _timely_   10. change + ing = _changing_
8. hope + ful = _hopeful_

C. Use the *Y* rule to write out each word shown.

11. fry + ed = _fried_   14. duty + ful = _dutiful_
12. easy + ly = _easily_   15. lonely + ness = _loneliness_
13. stay + ed = _stayed_

D. Use the *doubling* rule to write out each word shown.

16. drop + ing = _dropping_   19. jump + er = _jumper_
17. pad + ing = _padding_   20. sad + est = _saddest_
18. prefer + ed = _preferred_

E. Add *-s* or *-es* as needed to each of the following words. Where appropriate, change a final *y* to *i* before adding *-es*.

21. box _boxes_   24. valley _valleys_
22. enemy _enemies_   25. porch _porches_
23. country _countries_

● **Final Practice 2**

Use the spelling rules in the chapter to write out the words indicated.

A. Complete each word with either *ie* or *ei*.

1. conc_ei_ve   3. sobr_ie_ty   5. ch_ie_f
2. f_ie_ld   4. v_ei_n

B. Use the *silent e* rule to write out each word shown.

6. come + ing = _____coming_____   9. accurate + ly = _____accurately_____
7. care + less = _____careless_____   10. choose + ing = _____choosing_____
8. desire + able = _____desirable_____

C. Use the *Y* rule to write out each word shown.

11. reply + ed = _____replied_____   14. glory + ous = _____glorious_____
12. pray + ing = _____praying_____   15. study + ed = _____studied_____
13. carry + ed = _____carried_____

D. Use the *doubling* rule to write out each word shown.

16. bark + ing = _____barking_____   19. mop + ed = _____mopped_____
17. rob + er = _____robber_____   20. refer + ing = _____referring_____
18. commit + ed = _____committed_____

E. Add *-s* or *-es* as needed to each of the following words. Where appropriate, change a final *y* to *i* before adding *-es*.

21. city _____cities_____   24. dress _____dresses_____
22. branch _____branches_____ 25. puppy _____puppies_____
23. subway _____subways_____

36 Parts of Speech

Words—the building blocks of sentences—can be divided into eight parts of speech. **Parts of speech** are classifications of words according to their meaning and use in a sentence.

This chapter will explain the eight parts of speech:

nouns	prepositions	conjunctions
pronouns	adjectives	interjections
verbs	adverbs	

NOUNS

A **noun** is a word that is used to name something: a person, a place, an object, or an idea. Here are some examples of nouns:

woman	city	pancake	freedom
Alice Walker	street	diamond	possibility
Steve Martin	Chicago	Corvette	mystery

Most nouns begin with a lowercase letter and are known as **common nouns**. These nouns name general things. Some nouns, however, begin with a capital letter. They are called **proper nouns**. While a common noun refers to a person or thing in general, a proper noun names someone or something specific. For example, *woman* is a common noun—it doesn't name a particular woman. On the other hand, Alice Walker is a proper noun because it names a specific woman.

● Practice 1

Insert any appropriate noun into each of the following blanks.   *Answers will vary.*

1. The shoplifter stole a(n) _____jacket_____ from the department store.

2. _____Randall_____ threw the football to me.

3. Tiny messages were scrawled on the _____paper_____.

4. A(n) _____baseball_____ crashed through the window.

5. Give the _____job_____ to Ellen.

325

Singular and Plural Nouns

Singular nouns name one person, place, object, or idea. **Plural nouns** refer to two or more persons, places, objects, or ideas. Most singular nouns can be made plural with the addition of an *s*.

Some nouns, like box, have irregular plurals. You can check the plural of nouns you think may be irregular by looking up the singular form in a dictionary.

Singular	Plural
goat	goats
alley	alleys
friend	friends
truth	truths
box	boxes

For more information on nouns, see "Subjects and Verbs," pages 27.

● Practice 2

Underline the three nouns in each sentence. Some are singular, and some are plural.

1. Two <u>bats</u> swooped over the <u>heads</u> of the frightened <u>children</u>.

2. The <u>artist</u> has purple <u>paint</u> on her <u>sleeve</u>.

3. The lost <u>dog</u> has <u>fleas</u> and a broken <u>leg</u>.

4. <u>Gwen</u> does her <u>homework</u> in green <u>ink</u>.

5. Some <u>farmers</u> plant <u>seeds</u> by <u>moonlight</u>.

PRONOUNS

A **pronoun** is a word that stands for a noun. Pronouns eliminate the need for constant repetition. Look at the following sentences:

- The phone rang, and Bill answered the phone.
- Lisa met Lisa's friends in the record store at the mall. Lisa meets Lisa's friends there every Saturday.
- The waiter rushed over to the new customers. The new customers asked the waiter for menus and coffee.

Now look at how much clearer and smoother the sentences sound with pronouns.

- The phone rang, and Bill answered **it**.
  The pronoun *it* is used to replace the word *phone*.
- Lisa met **her** friends in the mall record store. **She** meets **them** there every Saturday.
  The pronoun *her* is used to replace the word *Lisa*. The pronoun *she* replaces *Lisa*. The pronoun *them* replaces the words *Lisa's friends*.

- The waiter rushed over to the new customers. **They** asked **him** for menus and coffee.

  The pronoun *they* is used to replace the words *the new customers*. The pronoun *him* replaces the words *the waiter*.

Following is a list of commonly used pronouns known as **personal pronouns**:

I	you	he	she	it	we	they
me	your	him	her	its	us	them
my	yours	his	hers		our	their

● Practice 3

Fill in each blank with the appropriate personal pronoun.

1. Andrew feeds his pet lizard every day before school. _____He_____ also gives _____it_____ flies in the afternoon.

2. The female reporter interviewed the striking workers. _____They_____ told _____her_____ about their demand for higher wages and longer breaks.

3. Students should save all returned tests. _____They_____ should also keep _____their_____ review sheets.

4. The pilot announced that we would fly through some air pockets. _____He (or She)_____ said that we should be past _____them_____ soon.

5. Randy returned the calculator to Sheila last Friday. But Sheila insists _____she_____ never got _____it_____ back.

There are a number of types of pronouns. For convenient reference, they are described briefly in the box below.

Types of Pronouns

Personal pronouns can act in a sentence as subjects, objects, or possessives.

Singular   I, me, my, mine, you, your, yours, he, him, his, she, her, hers, it, its

Plural   we, us, our, ours, you, your, yours, they, them, their, theirs

Relative pronouns refer to someone or something already mentioned in the sentence.

who, whose, whom, which, that

Interrogative pronouns are used to ask questions.

who, whose, whom, which, what

Demonstrative pronouns are used to point out particular persons or things.

this, that, these, those

NOTE Do not use *them* (as in *them* shoes), *this here, that there, these here* or *those there* to point out.

Reflexive pronouns are those that end in *-self* or *-selves*. A reflexive pronoun is used as the object of a verb (as in *Cary cut **herself***) or the object of a preposition (as in *Jack sent a birthday card to **himself***) when the subject of the verb is the same as the object.

Singular   myself, yourself, himself, herself, itself

Plural   ourselves, yourselves, themselves

Intensive pronouns have exactly the same forms as reflexive pronouns. The difference is in how they are used. Intensive pronouns are used to add emphasis. (*I **myself** will need to read the contract before I sign it.*)

Indefinite pronouns do not refer to a particular person or thing.

each, either, everyone, nothing, both, several, all, any, most, none

Reciprocal pronouns express shared actions or feelings.

each other, one another

For more information on pronouns, see "Pronoun Forms," pages 178–186, and "Pronoun Problems," pages 187–196.

VERBS

Every complete sentence must contain at least one verb. There are two types of verbs: **action verbs** and **linking verbs**.

Action Verbs

An **action verb** tells what is being done in a sentence. For example, look at the following sentences:

- Mr. Jensen **swatted** at the bee with his hand.
- Rainwater **poured** into the storm sewer.
- The children **chanted** the words to the song.

In these sentences, the verbs are *swatted, poured,* and *chanted.* These words are all action verbs; they tell what is happening in each sentence.

For more about action verbs, see "Subjects and Verbs," pages 27 and 228.

● Practice 4

Insert an appropriate word into each blank. That word will be an action verb; it will tell what is happening in the sentence.   *Answers will vary.*

1. The surgeon _____cut_____ through the first layer of skin.

2. The animals in the cage _____sleep_____ all day.

3. An elderly woman on the street _____asked_____ me for directions.

4. A man in the restaurant _____called_____ to the waitress.

5. Our instructor _____graded_____ our papers over the weekend.

Linking Verbs

Some verbs are **linking verbs**. These verbs link (or join) a noun to something that is said about it. For example, look at the following sentence:

- The clouds **are** steel gray.

In this sentence, *are* is a linking verb. It joins the noun *clouds* to words that describe it: *steel gray.* Other common linking verbs include *am, appear, become, feel, is, look, seem, sound, was,* and *were.*

For more about linking verbs, see "Subjects and Verbs," page 27 and "More about Subjects and Verbs," pages 229–230.

● Practice 5

Into each slot, insert one of the following linking verbs: *am, feel, is, look, were*. Use each linking verb once.

1. The important papers _____were_____ in a desk drawer.

2. I _____am_____ anxious to get my test back.

3. The bananas _____look_____ ripe.

4. The grocery store _____is_____ open until 11 p.m.

5. Whenever I _____feel_____ angry, I go off by myself to calm down.

Helping Verbs

Sometimes the verb of a sentence consists of more than one word. In these cases, the main verb will be joined by one or more **helping verbs**. Look at the following sentence.

● The basketball team **will be leaving** for their game at six o'clock.
In this sentence, the main verb is *leaving*. The helping verbs are *will* and *be*.

Other helping verbs include *can, could, do, has, have, may, must, should,* and *would*.

For more information about helping verbs, see "Subjects and Verbs," pages 27–36; "More about Subjects and Verbs," pages 230–232; "More about Verbs," pages 242–250; and "Even More About Verbs," pages 254–255.

● Practice 6

Into each slot, insert one of the following helping verbs: *does, must, should, could,* and *has been*. Use each helping verb once.

1. You _____should_____ start writing your paper this weekend.

2. The victim _____could_____ describe her attacker in great detail.

3. You _____must_____ rinse the dishes before putting them into the dishwasher.

4. My neighbor _____has been_____ arrested for drunk driving.

5. The bus driver _____does_____ not make any extra stops.

PREPOSITIONS

A **preposition** is a word that connects a noun or a pronoun to another word in the sentence. For example, look at the following sentence:

● A man **in** the bus was snoring loudly.

    In is a preposition. It connects the noun *bus* to *man*.

Here is a list of common prepositions:

about	before	down	like	to
above	behind	during	of	toward
across	below	except	off	under
after	beneath	for	on	up
among	beside	from	over	with
around	between	in	since	without
at	by	into	through	

The noun or pronoun that a preposition connects to another word in the sentence is called the **object** of the preposition. A group of words that begins with a preposition and ends with its object is called a **prepositional phrase**. The words *in the bus*, for example, are a prepositional phrase.

Now read the following sentences and explanations.

● An ant was crawling **up the teacher's leg**.

    The noun *leg* is the object of the preposition *up*. *Up* connects *leg* with the word *crawling*. The prepositional phrase *up the teacher's leg* describes *crawling*. It tells just where the ant was crawling.

● The man **with the black mustache** left the restaurant quickly.

    The noun *mustache* is the object of the preposition *with*. The prepositional phrase *with the black mustache* describes the word *man*. It tells us exactly which man left the restaurant quickly.

● The plant **on the windowsill** was a present **from my mother**.

    The noun *windowsill* is the object of the preposition *on*. The prepositional phrase *on the windowsill* describes the word *plant*. It describes exactly which plant was a present.

    There is a second prepositional phrase in this sentence. The preposition is *from*, and its object is *mother*. The prepositional phrase *from my mother* explains *present*. It tells who gave the present.

For more about prepositions, see "Subjects and Verbs," page 29, "Subject-Verb Agreement," pages 47–56, and "More about Subjects and Verbs," page 226.

● **Practice 7**

Into each slot, insert one of the following prepositions: *of, by, with, in,* and *without.* Use each preposition once.

1. The letter from his girlfriend had been sprayed _____with_____ perfume.

2. The weedkiller quickly killed the dandelions _____in_____ our lawn.

3. _____Without_____ giving any notice, the tenant moved out of the expensive apartment.

4. Donald hungrily ate three scoops _____of_____ ice cream and an order of French fries.

5. The crates _____by_____ the back door contain glass bottles and old newspapers.

ADJECTIVES

An **adjective** is a word that describes a noun (the name of a person, place, or thing). Look at the following sentence.

● The dog lay down on a mat in front of the fireplace.

Now look at this sentence when adjectives have been inserted.

● The **shaggy** dog lay down on a **worn** mat in front of the fireplace.

The adjective *shaggy* describes the noun *dog;* the adjective *worn* describes the noun *mat.* Adjectives add spice to our writing. They also help us to identify particular people, places, or things.

Adjectives can be found in two places:

1 An adjective may come before the word it describes (a **damp** night, the **moldy** bread, a **striped** umbrella).

2 An adjective that describes the subject of a sentence may come after a linking verb. The linking verb may be a form of the verb *be* (he is **furious**, I am **exhausted**, they are **hungry**). Other linking verbs include *feel, look, sound, smell, taste, appear, seem,* and *become* (the soup tastes **salty**, your hands feel **dry**, the dog seems **lost**).

Note The words *a, an,* and *the* (called **articles**) are generally classified as adjectives.

For more information on adjectives, see "Adjectives and Adverbs," pages 197 and 200–203.

● Practice 8

Write any appropriate adjective in each slot.   *Answers will vary.*

1. The _____large_____ pizza was eaten greedily by the _____hungry_____ teenagers.

2. Melissa gave away the sofa because it was _____old_____ and _____worn_____.

3. Although the alley is _____dark_____ and _____lonely_____, Karen often takes it as a shortcut home.

4. The restaurant throws away lettuce that is _____wilted_____ and tomatoes that are _____overripe_____.

5. When I woke up in the morning, I had a(n) _____slight_____ fever and a(n) _____sore_____ throat.

ADVERBS

An **adverb** is a word that describes a verb, an adjective, or another adverb. Many adverbs end in the letters *ly*. Look at the following sentence:

- The canary sang in the pet-store window as the shoppers greeted each other.

Now look at this sentence after adverbs have been inserted.

- The canary sang **softly** in the pet-store window as the shoppers **loudly** greeted each other.

The adverbs add details to the sentence. They also allow the reader to contrast the singing of the canary to the noise the shoppers are making.

Look at the following sentences and the explanations of how adverbs are used in each case.

- The chef yelled **angrily** at the young waiter.
  The adverb *angrily* describes the verb *yelled*.

- My mother has an **extremely** busy schedule on Tuesdays.
  The adverb *extremely* describes the adjective *busy*.

- The sick man spoke **very** faintly to his loyal nurse.
  The adverb *very* describes the adverb *faintly*.

Some adverbs do not end in *-ly*. Examples include *very, often, never, always*, and *well*.

For more information on adverbs, see "Adjectives and Adverbs," pages 197–206, and "More about Subjects and Verbs," page 232.

● **Practice 9**   *Answers will vary.*

Write any appropriate adverb in each slot.

1. The water in the pot boiled _____ quickly _____ .

2. Carla _____ carefully _____ drove the car through _____ slowly _____ moving traffic.

3. The telephone operator spoke _____ softly _____ to the young child.

4. The game show contestant waved _____ happily _____ to his family in the audience.

5. Wes _____ rarely _____ studies, so it's no surprise that he did _____ very _____ poorly on his finals.

CONJUNCTIONS

Conjunctions are words that connect. There are two types of conjunctions, coordinating and subordinating.

Coordinating Conjunctions (Joining Words)

Coordinating conjunctions join two equal ideas. Look at the following sentence:

● Kevin **and** Steve interviewed for the job, **but** their friend Anne got it.

    In this sentence, the coordinating conjunction *and* connects the proper nouns *Kevin* and *Steve*. The coordinating conjunction *but* connects the first part of the sentence, *Kevin and Steve interviewed for the job*, to the second part, *their friend Anne got it*.

Following is a list of all the coordinating conjunctions. In this book, they are simply called **joining words**.

and	for	or	yet
but	nor	so	

For more on coordinating conjunctions, see information on joining words in "Sentence Types," pages 57–66, and "Run-Ons and Comma Splices," pages 87–96.

● Practice 10

Write a coordinating conjunction in each slot. Choose from the following: *and, but, so, or*, and *nor.* Use each conjunction once.

1. Either Jerome _____ or _____ Alex scored the winning touchdown.

2. I expected roses for my birthday, _____ but _____ I received a vase of plastic tulips from the discount store.

3. The cafeteria was serving liver and onions for lunch, _____ so _____ I bought a sandwich at the corner deli.

4. Marian brought a pack of playing cards _____ and _____ a pan of brownies to the company picnic.

5. Neither my sofa _____ nor _____ my armchair matches the rug in my living room.

Subordinating Conjunctions

When a **subordinating conjunction** is added to a word group, the words can no longer stand alone as an independent sentence. They are no longer a complete thought. For example, look at the following sentence:

● Karen fainted in class.

   The word group *Karen fainted in class* is a complete thought. It can stand alone as a sentence.

See what happens when a subordinating conjunction is added to a complete thought:

● **When** Karen fainted in class

Now the words cannot stand alone as a sentence. They are dependent on other words to complete the thought:

● **When** Karen fainted in class, we put her feet up on some books.

In this book, a word that begins a dependent word group is called a **dependent word**. Subordinating conjunctions are common dependent words.

Below are some subordinating conjunctions.

after	even if	unless	where
although	even though	until	wherever
as	if	when	whether
because	since	whenever	while
before	though		

Following are some more sentences with subordinating conjunctions:

- **After** she finished her last exam, Joanne said, "Now I can relax."
  After she finished her last exam is not a complete thought. It is dependent on the rest of the words to make up a complete sentence.

- Lamont listens to books on tape **while** he drives to work.
  While he drives to work cannot stand by itself as a sentence. It depends on the rest of the sentence to make up a complete thought.

- **Since** apples were on sale, we decided to make an apple pie for dessert.
  Since apples were on sale is not a complete sentence. It depends on *we decided to make an apple pie for dessert* to complete the thought.

For more information on subordinating conjunctions, see information on dependent words in "Sentence Types," pages 57–66; "Fragments I," pages 67–76; and "Run-Ons and Comma Splices II," pages 97–106.

● Practice 11

Write a logical subordinating conjunction in each slot. Choose from the following: *even though, because, until, when,* and *before.* Use each conjunction once.   *Answers may vary.*

1. The bank was closed down by federal regulators _____ because _____ it lost more money than it earned.

2. _____ When _____ Paula wants to look mysterious, she wears dark sunglasses and a scarf.

3. _____ Even though _____ the restaurant was closing in fifteen minutes, customers sipped their coffee slowly and continued to talk.

4. _____ Before _____ anyone else could answer it, Carl rushed to the phone and whispered, "It's me."

5. The waiter was instructed not to serve any food _____ until _____ the guests of honor arrived.

INTERJECTIONS

Interjections are words that can stand independently and are used to express emotion. Examples are *oh, wow, ouch,* and *oops.* These words are usually not found in formal writing:

- "**Hey!**" yelled Maggie. "That's my bike."   - **Oh,** we're late for class.

A FINAL NOTE

A word may function as more than one part of speech. For example, the word *dust* can be a verb or a noun, depending on its role in the sentence.

- I **dust** my bedroom once a month, whether it needs it or not. (verb)
- The top of my refrigerator is covered with an inch of **dust**. (noun)

37 Dictionary Use

OWNING A GOOD DICTIONARY

It is a good idea to own two dictionaries. The first dictionary should be a paperback that you can carry with you. Any of the following would be an excellent choice:

The American Heritage Dictionary, Paperback Edition
The Random House Dictionary, Paperback Edition
Webster's New World Dictionary, Paperback Edition

Your second dictionary should be a full-sized, hardcover edition which should be kept in the room where you study. All the above dictionaries come in hardbound versions, which contain a good deal more information than the paperback editions.

UNDERSTANDING DICTIONARY ENTRIES

Each word listed alphabetically in a dictionary is called an **entry word**. Here is a typical dictionary entry word:

> **thun·der** (thŭn′dər) *n.* **1.** The sound that follows lightning and is caused by rapidly expanding air in the path of the electrical discharge. **2.** A loud sound like thunder. —*v.* **1.** To produce a sound resembling thunder. **2.** To express in a loud or threatening way. —**thun′der·ous** *adj.*

Spelling and Syllables

The dictionary first gives the correct spelling and syllable breakdown of a word. Dots separate the words into syllables. Each syllable is a separate sound, and each sound includes a vowel. In the entry shown above, *thunder* is divided into two syllables.

● Practice 1

Use your dictionary to separate the following words into syllables. Put a slash (/) between each syllable and the next. Then write the number of syllables in each word. The first one is done for you as an example.

1. g u a r / a n / t e e   __3__ syllables
2. m o l /e /c u l e   __3__ syllables
3. v o /c a b /u /l a r /y   __5__ syllables
4. c a u /l i /f l o w /e r   __4__ syllables

Pronunciation Symbols and Accent Marks

Most dictionary entry words are followed first by a pronunciation guide in parentheses, as in the entry for thunder:

thun·der (thŭn′dər)

The information in parentheses includes two kinds of symbols: *pronunciation symbols* and *accent marks*. Following is an explanation of each.

Pronunciation Symbols

The pronunciation symbols tell the sounds of consonants and vowels in a word. The sounds of the consonants are probably familiar to you, but you may find it helpful to review the vowel sounds. Vowels are the letters *a, e, i, o, u,* and sometimes *y*. To know how to pronounce the vowel sounds, use the **pronunciation key** in your dictionary. Such a key typically appears at the front of a dictionary or at the bottom of every other page of the dictionary. Here is a pronunciation key for the vowels and a few other sounds that often confuse dictionary users.

Pronunciation Guide

ă hat	ā say	â dare	ĕ ten	ē she	ĭ sit	ī tie, my
ŏ lot	ō go	ô all	oi oil	ŏŏ look	ōō cool	
th thin	*th* this	ŭ up	ûr fur	yōō use	ə ago, easily	

The key tells you, for instance, that the sound of ă (called "short a") is pronounced like the *a* in *hat*, the sound of ā (called "long a") is pronounced like the *ay* in *say*, and so on. All the vowels with a cup-shaped symbol above them are called **short vowels**. All the vowels with a horizontal line above them are called **long vowels**. Note that long vowels have the sound of their own name. For example, long *a* sounds like the name of the letter *a*.

To use the above key, first find the symbol of the sound you wish to pronounce. For example, suppose you want to pronounce the short *i* sound. Locate the short *i* in the key and note how the sound is pronounced in the short word *(sit)* that appears next to the short *i*. This tells you that the short *i* has the sound of the *i* in the word *sit*. The key also tells you, for instance, that the short *e* has the sound of the *e* in the word *ten*, that the short *o* has the sound of the *o* in the word *lot*, and so on.

Finally, note that the last pronunciation symbol in the key looks like an upside-down e: ə. This symbol is known as the **schwa**. As you can see by the words that follow it, the schwa has a very short sound that sounds much like "uh" (as in *ago*) or "ih" (as in *easily*).

● Practice 2

Refer to the pronunciation key to answer the questions about the following words. Circle the letter of each of your answers.

1. hic·cup (hĭk′ŭp)
   The *i* in *hiccup* sounds like the *i* in
   (**a.**) pit.   **b.** pie.

2. si·lent (sī′lənt)
   The *i* in *silent* sounds like the *i* in
   a. pit.   (**b.**) pie.

3. na·tive (nā′tĭv)
   The *a* in *native* sounds like the *a* in
   a. father.   (**b.**) pay.

4. lot·ter·y (lŏt′ə-rē)
   The *o* in *lottery* sounds like the *o* in
   (**a.**) pot.   **b.** for.

● Practice 3

Use your dictionary to find and write in the pronunciation symbols for the following words. Make sure you can pronounce each word. The first word has been done for you as an example.

1. reluctant   _____*rĭ-lŭk′tənt*_____

2. homicide   _____*hŏm′ĭ-sīd*_____

3. extravagant   _____*ĭk-străv′ə-gənt*_____

4. unanimous   _____*yōō-năn′ə-məs*_____

Accent Marks

Notice the mark in the pronunciation guide for *thunder* that is similar to an apostrophe:

   thun·der (thŭn′dər)

The dark mark (′) is a bold accent mark, and it shows which syllable has the stronger stress. That means the syllable it follows is pronounced a little louder than the others. Syllables without an accent mark are unstressed. Some syllables are in between, and they are marked with a lighter accent mark (′).

The word *recognize*, for example, is accented like this:

   rec·og·nize (rĕk′əg-nīz′)

Say *recognize* to yourself. Can you hear that the strongest accent is on *rec*, the first syllable? Can you hear that the last syllable, *nize*, is also accented but not as strongly? If not, say the word to yourself again until you hear the differences in accent sounds.

● **Practice 4**

Answer the questions following each of the words below.

1. **pep·per·mint**   (pĕp′ər-mĭnt′)
   a. How many syllables are in *peppermint*?   3
   b. Which syllable is most strongly accented?   first

2. **in·ter·me·di·ate**   (ĭn′tər-mē′dē-ĭt)
   a. How many syllables are in *intermediate*?   5
   b. Which syllable is most strongly accented?   third

3. **in·her·it**   (ĭn-hĕr′ĭt)
   a. How many syllables are in *inherit*?   3
   b. Which syllable is accented?   second

4. **con·tra·dic·tion**   (kŏn′trə-dĭk′shən)
   a. How many syllables are in *contradiction*?   4
   b. Which syllable is most strongly accented?   third

Parts of Speech

Every word in the dictionary is either a noun, a verb, an adjective, or another part of speech. In dictionary entries, the parts of speech are shown by abbreviations in italics. In the entry for *thunder*, for example, the abbreviations *n.* and *v.* tell us that thunder can be both a noun and a verb.

When a word is more than one part of speech, the dictionary gives the definitions for each part of speech separately. In the above entry for thunder, the abbreviation telling us that thunder is a noun comes right after the pronunciation symbols; the two noun definitions follow. When the noun meanings end, the abbreviation *v.* tells us that the verb definitions will follow.

Parts of speech are abbreviated in order to save space. Following are common abbreviations for parts of speech.

n.—noun	*v.*—verb
pron.—pronoun	*conj.*—conjunction
adj.—adjective	*prep.*—preposition
adv.—adverb	*interj.*—interjection

Irregular Verb Forms and Irregular Spellings

After the part of speech, special information is given in entries for irregular verbs, for adjectives with irregularly spelled forms, and for irregularly spelled plurals.

For **irregular verbs**, the dictionary gives the past tense, the past participle, and the present participle. For example, the entry for *blow* shows that *blew* is the past tense, *blown* is the past participle, and *blowing* is the present participle.

> **blow** (blō) *v.* **blew** (bloo), **blown** (blōn), **blowing.**

For **adjectives with irregularly spelled forms**, the comparative (used when comparing two things) and the superlative (used when comparing three or more things) are shown after the part of speech. The entry for *skinny*, for instance, shows that the comparative form of that adjective is *skinnier* and the superlative form is *skinniest*.

> **skin·ny** (skĭn'ē) *adj.* **-ni·er, -ni·est.**

Irregular plural spellings are also included in this spot in an entry. For example, after the part of speech, the entry for *party* tells us that this word's plural ends in *-ies*.

> **par·ty** (pär'tē) *n., pl.* **-ties.**

Definitions

Words often have more than one meaning. When they do, their definitions may be numbered in the dictionary. You can tell which definition of a word fits a given sentence by the meaning of the sentence. For example, the following are dictionary definitions for the verb form of *surprise*:

1 To take unawares.

2 To attack suddenly and unexpectedly.

3 To astonish or amaze with the unexpected.

Which of these definitions best fits the sentence below?

> The soldiers *surprised* the enemy troops, who had bedded down for the night.
>
> The answer is definition 2: The soldiers *suddenly attacked* the enemy troops.

● **Practice 5**

A. Use your dictionary to answer the questions below about *obstinate*.

1. Which syllable in *obstinate* is most strongly accented? _first_

2. How many syllables are in the word *obstinate*? _3_

3. How many *schwa* sounds are in the word *obstinate*? _1_

4. Does the first syllable in *obstinate* have a long or short *o* sound? _short_

5. Which definition of *obstinate* applies in the following sentence? (Write out the full definition from your dictionary.)

   Felicia stayed home all week with an *obstinate* case of the flu.

   Definition: _difficult to alleviate or cure_

B. Use your dictionary to answer the questions below about *solitary*.

6. How many syllables are in the word *solitary*? _4_

7. Which syllable in *solitary* is most strongly accented? _first_

8. Does the first syllable in *solitary* have a long or short *o* sound? _short_

9. Which definition of *solitary* applies in the following sentence? (Write out the full definition from your dictionary.)

   The box of cookies was bought yesterday, and today there's only a *solitary* cookie remaining.

   Definition: _single; sole_

10. Which definition of *solitary* applies in the following sentence? (Write out the full definition from your dictionary.)

    Some people like to study in groups, but Sarita prefers *solitary* study.

    Definition: _happening or done alone_

Index

A, an, 283
Abbreviations, 222
    capital letters in, 290
Accent marks, 338–340
Accept, except, 283
Action verbs, 228–229, 329
    with adverbs, 199
Active voice, 254–256
Addresses, commas in, 267
Adjectives, 197–206. 332–333
    in comparisons, 200–202
    irregularly spelled in dictionary, 341
Adverbs, 197–206, 333–334
    in comparisons, 200–202
    using with action verbs, 199
Advice, advise, 284
Affect, effect, 284
Agreement:
    between pronoun and word replaced, 187–191
    between subject and verb, 47–56
    compound subjects, 47–48
And as joining word, 87, 334
Anecdote, in essay introduction, 6
Antecedent,
    pronoun agreement with, 187–188
    unclear reference, 192–193
Apostrophe, 117–126, 271–276
    in contractions, 117
    in possessives, 117
    incorrect use with plurals and verbs, 273
    incorrect use with possessive pronouns, 274
Assignments, writing, 16–23

Bad, badly, 197, 203
Basic goals in writing, 3
Basic forms of verb, 37, 242
Be, forms of, 30, 38, 229, 231
Brake, break, 138
Broad to narrow, in essay introduction, 7
But as joining word, 87,.334
Buy, by, 282

Capital letters, 147–156, 289–292
    in brand product names, 147
    in calendar items, 147
    in common abbreviations, 290
    in names of family members, 289
    in first word of sentence or direct quotation, 147
    in "I" and people's names, 147
    in names of specific periods and famous events, 290

Capital letters—*Cont.*
    in names of specific groups, 289
    in names of specific places, institutions, and languages, 147
    in names of specific school courses, 289
    in opening and closing of letters, 290
    in titles, 147
Central point, of an essay, 5–6
Clichés, 215
Collective nouns, 191
Colon, 172
Comma, 107–116, 265–270
    after introductory material, 107
    around interrupters, 265–266
    between complete thoughts connected by *and, but,* and *so,* 107
    between items in a series, 107
    in addresses, 267
    in dates, 267
    in letters, 267
    in numbers, 221
    with direct quotations, 127
    with short expressions, 267
    with words of direct address, 267
Comma splices, 87–106
Comparisons:
    with pronouns, 182
    using adjectives and adverbs, 200–202
Complex sentence, 57–66, 335
Compound sentence, 57–66, 87, 334
Compound subjects, 47, 226
Concluding paragraph, of an essay, 7
Confusing words, 283–286
Conjunctions, 57–66, 334–336
    coordinating, 334–335
    subordinating, 335–336
Consistent verb tense, 253–254
Contractions, apostrophe in, 117

Dangling modifiers, 207–213
Dash, 174–175
Dates, commas with, 220
Demonstrative pronouns, 328
Dependent–word fragments, 67–76
Desert, dessert, 284
Dictionary use, 337–342
    accent marks, 339–340
    definitions, 341–342
    entry word, 337
    irregular spellings, 341

Dictionary use—*Cont.*
    irregular verb forms, 341
    parts of speech, 340
    pronunciation symbols, 338
    spelling and syllables, 337
Direct address, words of, commas with, 267
Do, forms of, 30, 38, 231

Editing, as part of writing process, 14
Effect, affect, 284
Essay, 5–7
    versus a paragraph, 5
    paragraphs in:
        concluding, 7
        introductory, 6
        supporting, 7
    sample, 5
    thesis statement in, 5
    transitional sentences in, 7
    writing, 5–15
Example fragments, 77–86
Except, accept, 283
Exclamation point, 171–172
    with quotation marks, 127

Fewer, less, 285
First draft, as part of writing process, 12–13
For as joining word, 334
Fragments, sentence, 67–106
    common types of:
        dependent word, 67–76
        without a subject, 77–86
        example fragments, 77–86
        –ing and *to* fragments, 77–86
Freewriting, as prewriting technique, 9–10

Goals in writing, 3, 8
Good, well, 197, 202–203
Google, 15

Have, forms of, 30, 38, 231
Hear, here, 138
Helping verbs, 27, 37, 230–231, 330
Hole, whole, 138
Homonyms, 137–146, 283–288
Hyphen, 173–174

Indefinite pronouns, 189–190, 238, 328
Indenting first line of paper, 170
Indirect quotations, 278–279
Infinitive, 27
–ing and *to* fragments, 77–86
Interjections, 336
Interrogative pronouns, 183–184, 328
Interrupters, commas with, 265–266
Introductory material, commas with, 107

Irregular verbs, 37–46
    forms of three problem verbs, 38
    in dictionary, 341
    list of, 37
Items in a series, comma with, 107
Introductory paragraph, in an essay, 6–7
Its, it's, 137

Joining word, comma and, 87, 334

Knew, new, 140
Know, no, 138

Less, fewer, 285
Letters, capitals and commas in, 267, 290
Linking verbs, 27, 229–230, 329–330
Listing order, in organizing details, 8
List making, as prewriting technique, 9, 11
Loose, lose, 285
–ly words (adverbs), 197–206, 333–334

Main idea, 4
Main verbs, 230–231
Margins, 170
Misplaced modifiers, 207–213
Modals, 231
Modifiers, 207
    certain single words, 209
    dangling, 207–213
    misplaced, 207–213

New, knew, 140
No, know, 138
Nonrestrictive elements, 265
Nonstandard and standard verbs, 257–258
Nouns, 27, 325–326
    collective, 191
Numbers, guidelines to writing, 220–221

Object pronouns, 179
Opposite, in essay introduction, 7
Organizing supporting material, as goal in writing, 8
    listing order, 8
    time order, 8
Outlining, scratch, as part of writing process, 12

Papers:
    editing, 14
        and proofreading, 295–312
    making corrections in, 302
    outlining, 12
    prewriting, 9–11
    preparing, 169–170
    proofreading, 14, 295–312
    revising, 13–14
    writing, 9–14

Paragraph:
    versus essay, 5
    in essay:
        concluding, 7
        introductory, 5–6
        supporting, 7
    point and support in, 3–4
    sample, 4
    topic sentence in, 4
    writing, 4–15
Parallelism, 157–166
Parentheses, 175
Parts of speech, 325–336
Passed, past, 282
Passive voice, 254–256
Past participle, 37, 242
    in the dictionary, 341
Past tense form, 242, 244–243
    in the dictionary, 341
Peace, piece, 140
Period, 171
    with quotation marks, 127
Person, pronoun shifts in, 191–192
Personal pronouns, 178–186, 327–328
Plain, plane, 140
Plurals:
    incorrect use of apostrophe with, 273
    irregular spellings, in dictionary, 341
    of nouns, 326
    of subjects, 227, 236, 326
Point and support in writing, 3–6
Possessive pronouns, 179–180
    no apostrophe with, 180, 274
Prepositional phrases,
    between subject and verb, 47, 226, 235
Prepositions, 226–227, 331–332
Present participle, 242
Prewriting, as part of writing process, 9–11
Principal, principle, 282–283
Process, writing, 9–14
Pronouns, 178–196, 326–328
    agreement in gender, 189
    agreement with collective nouns, 191
    forms, 178–186
        subjects, objects and possessives, 178–181
            in comparisons, 182–183
            who and *whom*, 183–184
            with *and* and *or*, 181–182
    problems with, 187–196
    shifts in number, 187–188
    shifts in person, 191–192
    types, 328
        demonstrative, 328
        indefinite, 189–190, 238, 328
            plural, 238
            singular, 189, 238

Pronouns—*Cont.*
    types—*Cont.*
        indefinite—*Cont.*
            singular or plural, 238
        intensive, 328
        interrogative, 184, 328
        personal, 178–181, 327–328
            possessives, no apostrophe for, 274
        reciprocal, 328
        reflexive, 328
        relative, 239, 328
        unclear reference, 192–193
Pronunciation symbols, 338–340
Proofreading, 14, 295–312
    making corrections in papers, 302
Punctuation marks, 171–177
    apostrophe, 171–176, 271–276
    colon, 172
    comma, 107–116, 265–270
    dash, 174
    exclamation point, 171
        with quotation marks, 127
    hyphen, 173
    parentheses, 175
    period, 171
        with quotation marks, 127
    question mark, 171
        with quotation marks, 127
    quotation marks, 127–136, 277–281
    semicolon, 173, 261–264

Questions, asking, in essay introduction, 6
Questioning, as prewriting technique, 9–11
Question mark, 171
    with quotation marks, 127
Quiet, quite, quit, 285
Quotation marks, 127–136, 277–281
    for direct quotations, 127–136
    for quotations of more than one sentence, 277
    for quotations with split sentences, 277
    for titles of short works, 279
Quotations, indirect, 278–279

Regular verbs, 37, 243
    principal parts of, 242–243
Relative pronouns, 183–184, 239, 328
Restrictive elements, 265
Revising, as part of writing process, 13–14
Right, write, 138
Run–ons and comma splices, 87–106
    methods of correcting:
        use a comma and joining word, 87–96
        use a dependent word, 97–116
        use a period and a capital letter, 87–96
        use a semicolon, 261–264
        with a transitional word, 262–264

Scratch outline, as part of writing process, 12
Semicolon, 173, 261–262
    to join two complete thoughts, 261–262
    to separate items in a series when the items
        themselves contain commas, 173
Sentence types, 57–66
    complex sentence, 57
    compound sentence, 57
    simple sentence, 57
Series of items:
    commas with, 107
    semicolon with, 173
Short expressions, commas with, 267
Signal words, 8
Simple sentence, 57
Slang, 214–215
So as joining word, , 87, 334
Specific details, in writing, 4–5
Spelling, 315–324
    hints for finding in dictionary, 315–316
    homonyms and other confusing words, 137–146,
        283–286
    in dictionary entry, 337
    rules, 317–324
Standard and nonstandard verbs, 257–258
Subject(s):
    and verb, 27
    agreement with verbs, 47–56
    and prepositional phrases, 29, 226, 235
    collective noun, 191
    compound, 47, 236–237
    finding, 27
    relative pronoun, 239
    singular and plural, 227, 236
Subject pronouns, 178
Support in writing, 3–6

Tenses, verb, 242–254, 259–260
Than, then, 286
Their, there, they're, 137
Thesis statement, of an essay, 6
Threw, through, 140
Time order, in organizing details, 8
Titles:
    capitalizing, 169
    punctuation of longer works, 279
    punctuation of short works, 279

To, too, two, 137
Topic sentence, 4
Transitions, 7–8
Transitional sentences, 7
Transitional words, 8, 262

Use, used (to), 286

Verbs,
    action, 228–229, 329
    active, 254
    agreement with subjects, 47–56
    and prepositional phrases, 29, 226, 235
    basic forms, 37, 242
    before subject, 235–236
    finding, 27
    helping verbs, 27, 37, 230–231, 330
    irregular verbs, 37–46
        forms of three problem verbs, 38
        in dictionary, 341
        list of, 37
    linking verbs, 27, 229–230, 329–330
    main verbs, 230–231
    nonstandard and standard, 257–258
    passive, 254
    principal parts, 242
    tenses, 242–254, 259–260

Wear, where, 140
Weather, whether, 140
Who, whom, 183–184
Whole, hole, 138
Whose, who's, 138
Word choice, 214–219
    Clichés, 215
    Slang, 214–215
    Wordiness, 216–217
Writing, 16–23
    assignments, 16–23
    essays, 5–7
    goals in, 3, 8
    paragraphs, 4
    process, 9–14
    steps in, 9–14

Your, you're, 137–138